Abydos

NEW ASPECTS OF ANTIQUITY

General Editor: COLIN RENFREW

Consulting Editor for the Americas: JEREMY A. SABLOFF

DAVID O' CONNOR

Abydos

Egypt's First Pharaohs and the Cult of Osiris

With 113 illustrations, 11 in colour

Thames & Hudson

To Gülbün

David O'Connor is a leading authority on Abydos and has been involved
in research there for over 40 years. During his career he has excavated at
many sites in Nubia, as well as in Egypt at the great 'palace-city' of pharaoh
Amenhotep III at Malkata, but Abydos has long been his main interest.
A professor and curator at the University of Pennsylvania for many years,
O'Connor has also been a professor at the Institute of Fine Arts, New York
University since 1995. His interests cover the entirety of Egyptian culture
and he has authored or co-edited publications on Egyptian history and
kingship; pharaohs Thutmose III, Amenhotep III and Ramesses III;
ancient Nubia; and Egypt in Africa.

*On the cover: (front) A fecundity figure depicted in the temple of Seti I; arranged in
long rows, such figures represent the abundance bestowed on Egypt by the gods. Photo
akg - images / François Guénet; (back) pottery deposited for ritual purposes in front
of the entrance to King Peribsen's enclosure; Khasekhemwy's enclosure is in the
background. Photo Sandro Vannini.*

*Frontispiece: Bronze figure of Osiris, represented as the ruler of the dead; he wears
the Atef crown and holds a crook and flail, the insignia of kingship. Late Period.*

First published in the United Kingdom in 2009 by Thames & Hudson Ltd,
181A High Holborn, London WC1V 7QX

First paperback edition 2011

Copyright © 2009 and 2011 Thames & Hudson Ltd, London

British Library Cataloguing-in-Publication Data
A catalogue record for this book is available from the British Library

ISBN 978-0-500-28900-6

Printed and bound in China by Toppan Leefung Printing Limited

To find out about all our publications, please visit **www.thamesandhudson.com**.
There you can subscribe to our e-newsletter, browse or download our current catalogue,
and buy any titles that are in print.

CONTENTS

General Editor's foreword   7

Preface   9

Introduction   15
ABYDOS: MYSTERY AND REVELATION 15 ORGANIZING THE ABYDOS
STORY 17 DISCOVERY AND REDISCOVERY 19

PART I   Abydos and Osiris   22

1   The Discovery of Abydos   22
AN INVISIBLE ARCHAEOLOGY 23 EXCAVATING HORDES AND
EXPLODING CANS 26

2   Osiris – Eternal Lord Who Presides in Abydos   30
OSIRIS AND ABYDOS 31 OSIRIS AND HIS MEANINGS 35

3   The Temple of Seti I   42
'THE HOUSE THAT YOU LOVE' 43 A VISIT TO THE SETI TEMPLE 45
THE VISUAL WORLD OF THE SETI TEMPLE 52

PART II   Life Cycle of a Sacred Landscape   62

4   The Rediscovery of Abydos   62
GENESIS 63 EXPANDING HORIZONS 64

5   The Evolution of a Sacred Landscape   70
ABYDOS AND ITS LANDSCAPE 71 ARCHAEOLOGY AND THE ABYDOS
LANDSCAPE 74

6   The Expanding Landscape of the Middle Kingdom   86
ROYAL AND PRIVATE CULT IN MIDDLE KINGDOM ABYDOS 87
THE SENWOSRET III COMPLEX 96 THE SOCIETAL DIMENSIONS OF
THE ABYDOS LANDSCAPE 100

7   The Landscape Completed: Abydos in the New Kingdom   104
THE LAST ROYAL PYRAMID 105 THE CORE LANDSCAPE AND ITS ROYAL
MONUMENTS 110 THE 'TERRACES OF THE GREAT GOD' IN THE
NEW KINGDOM 114

8   The Climax of the Osiris Cult   120
TURBULENT TIMES 121 'THIRTY PINTS OF WINE . . . DAILY TO THE ALTAR
OF KHENTAMENTIU' 124 THE DESERT HINTERLAND 130

PART III Origins of the Abydos Landscape   136

9 **The Royal Tombs of Abydos**   136
   BIG FISH EAT LITTLE FISH 137 THE TOMBS IN CONTEXT 139
   PROTO-KINGS AT ABYDOS 141 EGYPT'S EARLIEST WRITING 143
   THE 1ST DYNASTY, 'THE KINGS OF THINIS' 147 THE 2ND DYNASTY AT
   UMM EL QA'AB 155

10 **The Mysterious Enclosures of Abydos**   158
    DISCOVERING THE ENCLOSURES 159 EXCAVATING THE ENCLOSURES 162
    THE ARCHAEOLOGY OF THE ENCLOSURES 168 THE ENCLOSURES AND THE
    ABYDOS LANDSCAPE 174 THE FUNCTIONS OF THE ABYDOS ENCLOSURES 177

11 **Boat Graves and Pyramid Origins**   182
    SAILING THROUGH ETERNITY 183 THE ABYDOS BOAT GRAVES 185
    MOUND AND PYRAMID 195 PRIMEVAL HILL OR CELESTIAL STAIRWAY? 198
    CONCLUSION 200

12 **Abydos: Summing-up**   201
    SACRED LANDSCAPES AND LOCAL DYNAMICS 202 ABYDOS AND EGYPT 204

    Visiting Abydos   207

    Chronology   208

    Notes to the Text   209

    Sources of Illustrations   209

    Select Bibliography   210

    Index   215

GENERAL EDITOR'S FOREWORD

When we think of ancient Egypt, it is often questions concerning the origins of this great civilization that remain the most fascinating and puzzling. By the time the first pyramids were built at Saqqara and then at Giza in the 3rd Dynasty, the monumentality and imposing style of Egyptian art and architecture seem already well established. But what is known of the preceding period? In recent years it is from the site of Abydos in Upper Egypt that much new evidence has been emerging about this time, casting light not only on the 1st and 2nd Dynasties of Egypt, but also upon their predecessors at the very end of the predynastic period. Here, it is clear, were located the first royal tombs, and from recent researches at Abydos come new insights into the origins of kingship in Egypt, and the formation there of early state organization. Moreover, we now have the earliest indications of writing in Egypt, which rival in antiquity those of Early Dynastic or Late Predynastic Mesopotamia.

In this fresh and original account of Abydos David O'Connor starts with the feature for which Abydos has been known in more recent times, the great temple erected by the New Kingdom pharaoh Seti I, father of Ramesses the Great. This remains one of the great monuments of the period and the most conspicuous on the site.

Abydos was most famous in the heyday of Egyptian civilization, in the Middle and New Kingdoms, for the temple of the god Osiris, brother of Isis and father of Horus. Here probably from as early as 2000 BC there took place the annual procession from the temple to the supposed tomb of the god, a structure that modern scholarship now recognizes as the re-used tomb of the First Dynasty pharaoh Djer. In the procession was re-enacted the murder of the god by his brother Seth, his dismemberment, his reconstitution by his faithful wife (and sister) Isis, and, through her divine skills, his posthumous conception of his divine successor Horus. David O'Connor discusses the great complex of Abydos at that time using the helpful concept of a sacred landscape, a terrain largely dedicated to the dead and dominated by the divine presence of Osiris, ruler of the netherworld, 'Eternal Lord Who Presides over Abydos'. We obtain an unusually clear picture of the rituals surrounding the death of the pharaoh at the height of Egyptian power and influence in the early years of the New Kingdom.

David O'Connor has been associated with research and excavation at Abydos since 1967, and is thus in an excellent position to summarize its complex history. He has himself been involved in the excavations of the early town and the study of the interesting and very early mud enclosures that represent some of the largest surviving monuments from Old Kingdom times, and has been able to clarify their likely function. Perhaps the most remarkable feature of the site is the survival of extensive remains of the tombs of the rulers of the 1st and 2nd Dynasties (including the tomb of Narmer, the legendary first pharaoh of a united Egypt), and of their predecessors. The whole cemetery area including these early burials is known in Arabic as the Umm el Qaʿab, the 'Mother of Pots', and constitutes one of the most interesting and informative cemeteries in the world of archaeology. O'Connor reviews the evidence of these early royal tombs: it is now clear that only during the 2nd Dynasty did Saqqara become the official burial place of the pharaohs. He reviews also the work of Günter Dreyer, of the German Archaeological Institute in Cairo, who has revealed the importance of the site in the late predynastic period, when what were in effect royal tombs were constructed, prior to what later chroniclers regarded as the officially recorded 1st Dynasty. The cemetery in question also includes the now famous Tomb U-j, with its series of inscribed labels that carry the evidence for writing in Egypt back to around 3300 BC, so allowing scholars to question the previously accepted theory that knowledge of writing came first to Egypt from Mesopotamia.

O'Connor is also able to give us a first-hand account of his discovery of the remarkable series of boat burials at Abydos, where no fewer than 14 full-scale predynastic wooden boats, all dating from before 3000 BC, have been found in remarkably well-preserved condition. This fleet – for they were buried together – now ranks as the earliest surviving assemblage of boats in the world. When excavation has proceeded further they will tell us much not only of the early history of river travel on the Nile, but also of the social organization inevitably required to effect these labour-intensive burials. Such a substantial input of labour here and in the massive enclosures of the same period anticipates in some ways the massive investment of labour which went into the construction of the first pyramids, only a few centuries later, when the practice of royal burial had left Abydos and been transferred to Saqqara.

Work continues at Abydos. One marvels at the seemingly inexhaustible resources of the site and at the scale and duration of the cult of Osiris. But for me what is most fascinating is the insight which we obtain into this burial ground of proto-kings and early kings at the crucial period when the Egyptian state was first emerging and the civilization of the pharaohs was taking shape.

Colin Renfrew

PREFACE

This book fills a major gap in the history of the centres of ancient Egyptian civilization. As the burial place of Egypt's earliest historical kings, and subsequently as the major cult centre, literally over millennia, for the god Osiris, ruler of the dead, Abydos' place in Egyptian history is of extraordinary significance. Yet Abydos has rarely been the subject of monographic or extended treatment and no major overview of the site and its history has been published over the last 30 years. Precisely during these three decades, however, many important archaeological discoveries have been made at Abydos, many of them within the context of a comprehensive, long-term approach to the site initiated by an expedition sponsored by the University of Pennsylvania Museum, the Peabody Museum of Natural History at Yale University and the Institute of Fine Arts of New York University.

This initiative has led to other institutional involvement, projects sponsored specifically by the University of Pennsylvania Museum (now the Penn Museum) alone; by the University of Michigan; and for a period, by the Institute of Egyptian Art and Archaeology of the Memphis State University, Tennessee, succeeded by the Oriental Institute of the University of Chicago. Contemporaneously with these activities, Peter Kuhlmann undertook a study of the important temple of Ramesses II at Abydos for the German Archaeological Institute, Cairo, while Werner Kaiser and Günter Dreyer initiated a long-running excavation of Abydos' early royal cemetery and its predecessors; additionally the Department of Anthropology of the University of Pittsburgh is sponsoring new excavations at the important prehistoric site of Mahasna, in the vicinity of Abydos, directed by David Anderson.

The results of the ongoing work are important, multifaceted and sometimes spectacular, opening up major new perspectives on Abydos and its significance, and leading us to reassess the already rich array of data recovered by earlier generations of archaeologists extending back into the 1860s. At the same time, archaeologists currently active at Abydos have brought into play methodologies and approaches based on what are called processual and post-processual archaeology, but always firmly related to the increasingly abundant material evidence recovered. As a result, Abydos is contributing in major ways to our understanding of ancient Egyptian culture as a whole, insofar as a multiplicity of issues are concerned – royal ideology and its origins and their earliest monumental manifestations; the socio-economic significance of mortuary data; the nature of urbanism and city planning at different periods of Egyptian history; cult practices involving temples, major festivals and a great variety of ancillary ritual structures; the impact of larger historical processes upon the history and archaeology of Abydos; and the ways in which activities at Abydos drew upon its past (sometimes, its very remote past) to re-affirm, yet also subtly modulate, major continuities in Egyptian cultural ideology and practice.

This book is an overview of the many new discoveries made about Abydos and my own personal interpretation of their significance, in terms of both the local and regional dynamics that shaped the actual and the conceptual landscape of Abydos over the millennia, as well as the complex relationships between Abydos on the one hand, and Egyptian history and culture in general on the other. Through this I will be introducing many readers to a younger generation of Egyptologists and others (most already well known in the discipline) to whom much of our new information and ideas are due. Their work is well covered in the succeeding chapters, so here in the Preface I wish to focus on more general acknowledgments, recognizing those individuals and institutions without whom the discoveries and ideas discussed below would never have taken place.

The Pennsylvania-Yale-Institute of Fine Arts, New York University Expedition to Abydos is co-directed by myself and Professor William Kelly Simpson of Yale University, who must be placed foremost in any acknowledgments. Without Professor Kelly Simpson, the Abydos Expedition would have been a very different, and a much attenuated affair; in fact, this expedition's very existence was a product of earlier achievements on his part, for it was the result of a collaborative Pennsylvania-Yale project involved in the archaeological salvage of Nubia during the 1960s, a project initiated and directed by Professor Kelly Simpson. He not only carried out work of great importance in Nubia, but also secured a most substantial grant of United States government funds which left a significant balance to be expended on subsequent work in Egypt proper. Indeed, it funded our operations at Abydos from 1967 to 1981, and also supported an epigraphic project directed by Professor Kelly Simpson at Giza as well.

Professor Kelly Simpson was not only very supportive of a project at Abydos, but brought valuable experience and maturity to our co-direction, which initiated some 35 years of collegial collaboration in the exploration of this fascinating site. Kelly Simpson himself has contributed in many ways to our better understanding of Abydos and its region. Apart from his participation in the expedition's fieldwork at Abydos itself, his publications over a long career have illuminated many aspects of Abydos, from the times of the earliest dynasties well into the New Kingdom and beyond. These contributions will be noted more specifically below, at the appropriate points, but include no less than six monographs. Four deal with Middle Kingdom papyri recovered from a tomb at Nag el-Deir, near Thinis, the capital of the nome or province in which Abydos lay. The documents are administrative in content, and open up fascinating windows upon the governance and economy of the province and its relationships with central royal power, a nexus of relationships of which Abydos itself was an important part. The other two monographs bear directly upon Abydos. The more recent (1995) covers a wealth of most informative inscribed material recovered by the expedition, ranging from the Old Kingdom to the Third Intermediate Period, i.e. from the 24th through the 8th centuries BC. The other (1974a) is one of the landmark publications in Egyptology, highly original in its observations and a seminal study which has stimulated much further research by others. Focused on unique ritual practices of Middle Kingdom Egyptians (20th–18th centuries BC) at Abydos, Kelly Simpson's study combines philology and archaeology to reconstruct groups of inscribed stelae and other artifacts reflecting complex societal and ritual relationships.

Equally important has been the extraordinarily generous Egyptian policy towards our, as to all other non-Egyptian, research projects in that country. Egypt has a long tradition of not only caring for and exploring its unique cultural heritage, but also of encouraging the participation of non-Egyptian institutions, scholars and others in this process, today even more so than in the past. The generosity and vision of Egypt in these regards is expressed specifically through the Ministry of Culture and the Supreme Council of Antiquities (formerly known as the Egyptian Antiquities Organization), the Secretary General of which reports to the Minister. The Supreme Council issues the permits for each project's work and provides an exceptionally cordial and collaborative context in which to carry that work out. After more than 35 years of excavating at Abydos, it would be impossible for me and my colleagues to recognize individually every Egyptian official, scholar and other who has facilitated our activities, but perhaps a few of the more recent can stand for the whole.

The current Minister of Culture, Dr Farouk Hosni, has provided leadership to the maintenance and further development of Egypt's rich culture for many years, and we are all appreciative of the positive relationships he has fostered between Egypt and the outside world. Naturally, researchers at Abydos have benefited from the positive attitudes of a whole series of Director Generals of the Antiquities Organization, and more recently of Secretary Generals of the Supreme Council. To list them all here is not practical, but one would wish to especially acknowledge the present Secretary General, Dr Zahi Hawass, and his immediate predecessor, Dr Gaballa Ali Gaballa. Dr Gaballa is one of the most distinguished philologists and historians of ancient Egypt, whose unfailing thoughtfulness and consideration were always a great boon to excavators and epigraphers working in Egypt.

Egyptology, and especially scholars working in Egypt today, are especially indebted to Dr Hawass, who is himself an internationally renowned archaeologist and has made many major discoveries throughout his career, discoveries described with his characteristic vivacity and thoroughness in his recent autobiography *Secrets From the Sand* (2003a). Dr Hawass has also proved to be an exceptionally dynamic Secretary General, whose international fame projects a most positive image of the care Egypt has dedicated to its ancient cultural heritage. He also provides leadership and inspiration to the many members and employees of the Supreme Council of Antiquities, and to the large number of Egyptian and non-Egyptian scholars active in fieldwork in Egypt.

While upholding the traditional Egyptian openness to professional scholars from all over the world, Dr Hawass is also involving all of us in his vision for a set of priorities focused on the conservation and management of Egypt's archaeological sites, and encouraging of the excavation of especially vulnerable sites, particularly in the Egyptian Delta. The challenges faced by the Ministry of Culture and the Supreme Council of Antiquities are very great, and include the serious deterioration of major temples at Luxor, Abydos and elsewhere, but under the leadership of Dr Hawass, and with much financial aid from the Egyptian government and international sources, these problems are being energetically addressed and important results achieved. At Abydos itself all the current archaeological projects include significant conservation and restoration elements, such as our own project's stabilization of one of the earliest standing monuments to survive anywhere in Egypt (the royal mortuary enclosure of King Khasekhemwy, *c.* 2700 BC); and all plan future initiatives along these lines. Moreover, we all look forward to collaborating closely with Dr Hawass' plan for a comprehensive programme of site management, visitor accessibility and protection at Abydos (such as he has set in motion at other sites in Egypt), and thus expressing our appreciation for the exceptional research opportunities provided to us over many years.

While I cannot list all the other senior officials who have made our and others' work at Abydos possible over more than 30 years, I must record our great good fortune in having started the Pennsylvania-Yale Expedition (later joined by the Institute of Fine Arts, New York University) under the aegis of the then Director-General, the late Dr Gamal Mokhtar. Dr Mokhtar was one of the most effective leaders of the Antiquities Service I have ever encountered in Egypt: a highly qualified scholar, he also combined authority and wisdom to a degree I have rarely seen, and was an inspiration, as well as a mentor, to many younger Egyptian Egyptologists both in the Antiquities Department and in academia. These included many of the able officials responsible for Abydos at a regional level, who were and are based in Sohag, the governorate capital; Balliana near Abydos; and Abydos itself. These men and women have been absolutely essential for the success of our work, not least in providing the same cordiality and supportiveness that we experienced in Cairo as well. They are too numerous to enumerate individually for the most part, but I do wish to acknowledge especially two officials with whom we had excellent working relationships for many years. Dr Yahia el Masry was Director-General of Antiquities for the Sohag governorate and Mr Ahmed el Khattib was Chief Inspector at Balliana. Both have since moved on to other appointments. In addition, we have in recent years also benefited from the generosity of the authorities in providing all of our and other projects at Abydos with a 24-hour police presence through the entire course of every season.

Insofar as our Expedition's work in Egypt is concerned, I must also acknowledge the very significant role of the American Research Center in Egypt (currently directed by Dr Gerry D. Scott III) in facilitating our activities, as it does for so many other projects sponsored by United States institutions. The Center's presence and its many services have made our work much easier, while its excellent and carefully fostered relationships with the Egyptian authorities have contributed greatly to the success of American scholarly endeavours in general. Given the Abydos Expedition's long relationship with the Center (since 1967), it is impossible to single out most of the individual directors and other officers who have been so helpful to us, but I am sure they will all appreciate that two individuals of exceptionally long standing need to be specifically acknowledged.

Mme Amira el-Khattab is currently the Deputy Director for Research and Government Relations of the Center, and has long been of key importance in facilitating the work of scholars and projects in sometimes very challenging circumstances. Mme Amira on the one hand maintains the most courteous and effective relations with the officials of the Supreme Council of Antiquities, by whom she is highly respected; and, on the other hand, is an invaluable advisor to innumerable projects, handling their complex needs with great efficiency, dispatch and – most important of all! – good humour. Also extremely important is the Egyptian Antiquities Project, set up in 1993 within the American Research Center in Egypt in order to implement a major grant from the United States Agency for International Development in Egypt for the study and conservation of significant monuments, art works and manuscript resources from pharaonic, Graeco-Roman, Coptic and Islamic times. The success of the Egyptian Antiquities Project in all of these areas (which includes substantial support to relevant activities of the Pennsylvania-Yale-Institute of Fine Arts, New York University Expedition to Abydos) owes much to its long-time Director, the late Dr Robert ('Chip') K. Vincent, Jr and his outstanding staff, with whom I and my associates have enjoyed an excellent working relationship for a number of years.

In the United States, not only institutions but also key individuals need to be acknowledged. Through the good offices of Professor Kelly Simpson, Yale University in particular has been especially supportive of the Expedition's publication programme, while the University of Pennsylvania Museum is a long-time financial supporter as well as the provider of essential office space and facilities. Froelich Rainey, the Museum's charismatic Director when the Expedition was initiated, was unfailingly and enthusiastically supportive, and that support has been generously continued by his successors, most notably Dr Jeremy Sabloff, the Director from 1994 to 2004, and his distinguished predecessor, Dr Robert Dyson.

In particular, special note should be made of the role of Dr David Silverman in fostering a continuing close and cordial relationship between the Abydos Expedition and the Egyptian Section of the University of Pennsylvania Museum. Dr Silverman, my colleague for many years, succeeded me as head of that section, and is currently both Eckley B. Coxe, Jr Professor in Egyptology and

Curator-in-Charge of the Egyptian Section. We owe much to him, and to Dr Sabloff, for the facilities provided for the Expedition at the University of Pennsylvania Museum; and also for the collaborative environment they have fostered. Dr Silverman includes amongst his many scholarly accomplishments a deep knowledge of Middle Kingdom Abydos, having not only studied many of the commemorative stelae produced at Abydos during that time, but also himself directed a project at Abydos under the aegis of the Expedition, undertaking the epigraphic recording of a significant but badly damaged temple built for King Ramesses II, which he will publish in due course. Finally, it should be noted that Mr Bruce Mainwaring, a major supporter of the University of Pennsylvania Museum and Chairman Emeritus of its Board of Overseers, provided a generous grant making possible the first fully detailed topographical and archaeological map of Abydos as a whole.

Chronologically last in entering into a relationship with the Expedition, but now its most generous supporter, is the Institute of Fine Arts of New York University, where I now serve as Lila Acheson Wallace Professor in Egyptian Art and Archaeology. The initiative here was taken by the Institute's former Director, Dr James McCredie, under whose aegis the Institute had already undertaken major projects at Samothrace in Greece (directed by Dr McCredie) and Aphrodisias in Turkey, as well as sponsoring the late Dr Donald Hansen's excavations in Iraq, Yemen and Syria. Moreover, in earlier years my distinguished predecessor at the Institute of Fine Arts, the late Professor Bernard Bothmer, had already initiated important field projects at Mendes, in which Dr Hansen was deeply involved, and Memphis. The Abydos Expedition has been added to this distinguished roster, and it has been a pleasure for myself, for the Associate Director of our Early Dynastic Project, Dr Matthew Adams, and for our other Expedition members to operate in as supportive an atmosphere as that of the Institute of Fine Arts, as fostered by Dr McCredie and by his successor as Director, Dr Mariët Westermann, also a source of unfailing support. Of course, any success we may have achieved at Abydos is ultimately dependent on a much larger group of people than those mentioned so far. These include the many young men and women from United States and other institutions who have participated so enthusiastically as site supervisors, conservators and in many other roles; our outstanding Egyptian work force, superbly led in succession by three extremely able *reises* or foremen: Hofni Ibrahim Salama, Mohammed Ali Abdelrahim Mahfouz and Ibrahim Mohammed Ali; and last but definitely not least, an efficient domestic staff, initially organized by Carol Rauch and Bastawi el-Laisy Ali, and now managed by Ahmed Ragab Ahmed. It is also a pleasure to note the positive relations we have always enjoyed with the people of Abydos today, the inhabitants of the villages along its flank, who have generously tolerated and indeed facilitated the seasonal infestation of their landscape by arcane researchers such as ourselves.

In the preparation of this book I should like to note the essential assistance provided by Dr J. J. Shirley and Dr Laurel Bestock.

INTRODUCTION

Abydos: Mystery and Revelation

Abydos is one of the most fascinating sites in Egypt. For millennia, Abydos was the cult centre for Egypt's perhaps most popular god, Osiris, who ruled the netherworld and guaranteed every deceased Egyptian eternal existence. Even more than most Egyptian cults, that of Osiris highlighted both mystery and revelation in ways that found complex ritual and symbolic expression. As a result there developed over Abydos' vast landscape not only an extraordinary array of royal, elite and lower-order temples, chapels and tombs, but also towns that serviced their cults and endowments and the needs of innumerable pilgrims. Much about Abydos seems unique in Egyptian culture, but in other ways its archaeology illuminates broader patterns of ritual, urban and economic activity valid for all Egypt.

Archaeologists and the public have experienced Abydos in ways different from those of the ancient Egyptians. Since the 1860s one extraordinary discovery has followed another at Abydos, each a further surprising revelation about the historical and cultural richness of the site. First, the vast, lavishly decorated temple of Seti I (c. 1290–1279 BC) was fully unearthed, and proved to be by far the best-preserved Bronze Age temple in Egypt. Later, and completely unexpectedly, the tombs of Egypt's earliest historic kings (c. 2950–2650 BC) were discovered there. Initially so mysterious that their original excavator did not at first realize what they were, the contents of these tombs were to become the chief source for understanding Egypt's earliest civilization, the product of a long series of prehistoric developments. In addition to these finds, over time an incredible array of later royal monuments has been revealed at Abydos, as well as unique evidence about elite and lower-order ritual and mortuary practices.

Recently, new discoveries about Abydos have followed each other even more rapidly than in the past. The graves of kings much earlier than the 1st and 2nd Dynasties have been located, as have those of their immediate predecessors; a fleet of boats – the earliest surviving built boats in the world – has been discovered buried far out in the desert; and a wealth of new information about Abydos in historic times revealed. Yet each discovery raises new questions and issues, and indicates that further mysteries remain to be explored and resolved. Abydos will continue to intrigue archaeologists, Egyptologists and lay enthusiasts for many generations to come.

Nevertheless, we can certainly appreciate what Abydos meant to ancient Egyptians for much of its history. The cult of Osiris, which over time created at Abydos a uniquely distinctive landscape combining natural topography and built forms in complex and ever-changing ways, was an especially strange one. In myth, Osiris was the only Egyptian deity who experienced violent death – murdered in fact by his own brother, the aggressive Seth – and then achieved regeneration, returning to life as ruler of the dead. At one level, Osiris' myth provided the model for rituals ensuring all Egyptians could survive after death; at another, it structured the system of royal succession in Egypt, for Osiris, once ruler of the living, was eventually succeeded as such by his legitimate heir, his posthumously conceived son Horus.

Because of the especially mysterious and even horrifying aspects of his myth, many of the Abydos rituals for Osiris were esoteric in content and carried out in secluded areas. Yet at the same time dramatic revelation was involved, for Osiris' story was also exposed to a large audience made up of all social classes. Every year a procession, bearing images of Osiris and associated deities, traversed some 2 km (c. 1 mile) of open desert between Osiris' temple at the edge of the floodplain and his supposed tomb deep in the desert, and then returned to the temple. During the procession the attack of Sethian enemies was beaten off, and the triumphant revival of Osiris was ritually enacted, probably generating much emotion amongst those who witnessed these events.

Whether the establishment of Osiris' cult at Abydos in c. 2000 BC, or perhaps earlier, has any connection to the earlier royal tombs on the site is one of the enigmas of Abydos waiting to be solved. One of these tombs was identified as that of Osiris, and became a focus of royal and popular cult; but what the Egyptians actually knew about the original royal owner of this and nearby tombs – which seem so revelatory to us – is as yet uncertain.

The archaeology of Abydos is challenging, and the story of how earlier and more recent archaeologists have met this challenge and deduced so much about the site's history and meaning is an especially intriguing one. Well over 3,000 years ago, the problems that would face future archaeologists were becoming evident. Pharaoh Ramesses II (c. 1279–1213 BC), preparing to complete the temple of his father Seti I at Abydos, was recorded as having found Abydos' already numerous royal monuments falling into ruin. Many indeed had been left unfinished and were becoming 'mere rubbish'.

Now, millennia later, we realize that despite much useful textual information, most of the history, complexity and meanings of Abydos are conveyed by its archaeology. In this regard, Abydos delights archaeologists, as over the generations they display their skills in the recovery, interpretation and imaginative but sound reconstruction of often challenging archaeological remains. At Abydos some richly decorated temples, those of Seti I and Ramesses II, have survived virtually or substantially intact. Others, however, are largely gone, razed in antiquity so that their constituent materials could be reused. Such now-missing temples have to be reconstructed, in the imagination, by reference to plans still visible as scratched lines on surviving temple floors and from fragments of columns, lintels and cornices, as well as hundreds, even thousands, of still-decorated flakes surviving from the reliefs and texts once covering the temple's walls. Moreover, several massive mud-brick enclosures of various dates survive and are readily accessible to archaeological study. Others, however, were razed to a few centimetres above ground level and can be found only via sub-surface magnetic survey and excavation. More generally, tombs, chapels and even houses at Abydos can be relatively well preserved, but most often they prove severely denuded, and require the most painstaking excavation in order to gain insight into the ritual practices, social structure and symbolic meanings they represent.

Fortunately, all these challenges are meat and drink to the archaeologist. Like others at Abydos, I have found that weeks or months of long, hot, windy days in the field have not lessened the intense enjoyment as fascinating materials are periodically revealed. These remains illuminate every level of the ancient Egyptian experience. At one extreme, an entire fleet of buried vessels emerges; at the other, the remains of a cemetery of newborns, delivered to the protection of Osiris 'lord of births', is exposed. Overall, the flow of data is almost overwhelming, yet at the same time stimulating and absorbing.

Organizing the Abydos Story

This book is the first comprehensive monographic treatment of Abydos attempted for many years. Good overviews of Abydos have been provided by Herman Kees (1961), Barry Kemp (1975a) and others, and in 1968 Eberhard Otto published a major comparative study of Abydos and Thebes, *Egyptian Art and the Cults of Osiris and Amun*. My purposes here, however, are different. I review the discoveries of earlier generations of archaeologists and take a fresh look at their importance. But above all I introduce the reader to the many extraordinary and exciting new discoveries about Abydos made over the past three decades or so. Much of this new material has not yet been published in detail, but my treatment of it brings out something of its great significance and interest.

An obvious way to tell the story of Abydos is simply from beginning to end, from the earliest ancient activity at the site to the latest. However, while such an approach is natural and helpful for some Egyptian sites, it would be a misleading one in the case of Abydos. A sequential narrative about Abydos would inevitably convey the impression that we understand more about the cultural and social dynamics shaping its history than we actually do. In reality, the situation is complicated. Excavation, until recently, has been sporadic, uncoordinated and widely scattered. As a result, much about the dynamics underlying the development of Abydos remains mysterious.

For example, on the west bank at Thebes an almost continuous series of New Kingdom royal mortuary temples provides a narrative backbone for any discussion of the region's archaeology. However, at Abydos royal temples similar in function to the Theban ones are less common. King Senwosret III built the first; almost 300 years later, King Ahmose had the second constructed; and finally, over 200 years further on, the temples of Seti I and Ramesses II were built. Other royal temples will certainly be discovered at Abydos, but the extant ones do not provide an adequate structure for a narrative history of the site.

Therefore, I have divided my presentation into the discussion of several different, if interrelated topics, instead of following a simple narrative sequence. This approach is similar to that an archaeologist might take to the study and excavation of a site, for it moves from the existing surface features and known history of Abydos into a kind of conceptual stratigraphy running *back* to the earliest period of Abydos' history. My approach is truer to the problems Abydos presents to its interpreters, and also highlights the fact that only intensified and expanded excavations in many parts of Abydos will lead to a fuller and more coherent understanding of its development over time.

Thus, Part I focuses on Abydos as the visitor sees it today, visually dominated by the temple of Seti I, and explores the cult of Osiris that was so central to the site's history. It also outlines the known archaeology of Abydos, as defined by its earlier excavators over a period extending from the 1850s into the 1930s.

Part II takes the reader further back in time. Here, the discussion interweaves old and new discoveries to outline the development of Abydos from the Old Kingdom into the early centuries AD. The central theme is the ways in which the various manifestations of the cult of Osiris over this long span of time stimulated the expansion, then contraction, of a sacred landscape, which is one of the most striking to survive in Egypt. At Abydos natural features (floodplain, low desert, and high desert plateau), built forms, ritual practices and symbolic meanings are integrated into an extraordinary whole. At the same time, the more mundane aspects of ancient Egypt are also well represented. Along Abydos' flanks towns and villages developed, in part to service the constructional and ritual needs of Abydos, in part to administer the economic resources of its many cults and in part to exploit the opportunities created by Abydos' popularity as a national cult centre.

Part III moves to the earliest known archaeology of Abydos (other than the Palaeolithic period), which is perhaps also its most fascinating. At this time Abydos housed the tombs and the mortuary cult installations (the enclosures discussed in Chapter 10) of all the kings of the 1st Dynasty, and of the last two of the 2nd Dynasty. In addition, even earlier rulers were buried near the site of the later royal tombs. During the last two decades, exciting discoveries have been made about all these early remains, and these are comprehensively described for the first time in Part III.

In the 1st and 2nd Dynasties the central concerns at Abydos were the royal tombs and mortuary monuments, and their tutelary deity, the god Khentamentiu. Presumably the latter had a temple on or near the site occupied by its Old Kingdom successor, although no textual reference to this assumed earlier temple survives. However, while the Old Kingdom rulers supported the then temple of Khentamentiu, no trace has survived of any interest on their part in the cults of the early kings buried at Abydos. Yet the last of these kings was entombed only some 75 years earlier than Snefru, founder of the 4th Dynasty!

It is sometimes argued that an indirect proof of awareness of the early royal cults is indicated by the respect shown to the royal mortuary cult enclosures located due west in the desert not far from the Old Kingdom temple of Khentamentiu. The Old Kingdom cemeteries of Abydos avoided the area occupied by these enclosures (only one of which, however, might have still been visible) and instead lay northwest of the Khentamentiu temple and its town, or southwest in the 'Middle Cemetery'. Both areas, however, were convenient and accessible, and it is possible that these factors rather than respect for the early royal enclosures led to their use as cemeteries.

Later, in the Middle Kingdom, the royal tombs of the 1st and 2nd Dynasties – set deep in the desert – were unquestionably of interest to the Egyptians. Early in their history, these tombs had been plundered, sometimes burnt, and became filled with debris and sand. Günter Dreyer, however, has shown that most, maybe all, were excavated out in the Middle Kingdom, and their structures sometimes renovated. On the objects removed from these tombs, literate Egyptians could have read the names of their royal owners. However, one of these tombs was in fact identified as that of Osiris, rather than its original owner, King Djer of the 1st Dynasty. Were the other tombs also thought of as belonging to deities or primeval beings, and the inscribed objects in them simply early royal gifts?

In the New Kingdom and later, the early royal tomb regarded as that of Osiris continued to be used for ritual purposes, but again little specific awareness of the early kings once buried at Abydos is evident. In the temple of Seti I a comprehensive king list is displayed, and is sometimes cited by scholars as reflecting such awareness, but this is doubtful. The names provided in the list for 1st and 2nd Dynasty kings are sometimes close to the Early Dynastic original, but more often bear little or no relationship to it. Thus, a 'corrupt', secondary source was utilized, not original early monuments or items bearing 1st and 2nd Dynasty royal names. Moreover, such king lists are not peculiar to Abydos. Similar ones occur at Karnak (under Thutmose III) and Saqqara (in the tomb of an official of Ramesses II), while a famous example on papyrus – the 'Turin Canon of Kings', in the time of Ramesses II – probably came from Thebes.

Discovery and Rediscovery

As well as moving backwards in time, this book is also organized around the interrelated themes of discovery and rediscovery. The discovery – the first extensive delineation of Abydos' archaeology – was due to the many archaeologists working there between 1858 and the late 1930s. In addition, epigraphic work on the temple of Seti I persisted up to 1959. Although variable in quality (some work was excellent, some less so) and uneven in publication, this earlier phase of exploration created an invaluable database. It greatly expanded our knowledge of Abydos and has been instrumental in guiding the strategies of more recent excavators.

Substantial archaeological activity recommenced at Abydos in 1967, and continues today. This second phase of exploration is one of rediscovery, in several senses. After the long gap (over 30 years) in excavation, its resumption and increasing expansion has been something of a reawakening of our awareness of Abydos' importance and the need to explore its remains further. Moreover, rediscovery is further involved in that many monuments and areas of Abydos already partially excavated in the past have now started to yield an often amazing amount of important new information.

In the 1860s excavations at Abydos were conducted by the French archaeologist Auguste Mariette and his deputies, but thereafter nearly all the early archaeologists and epigraphers were British. Their work is often referred to in this book, and they have been discussed more fully by Barry Kemp (1982) and T. G. H. James (1982). The more recent excavations have often been sponsored by the combined expedition to Abydos of the University Museum of Archaeology & Anthropology, University of Pennsylvania; the Peabody Museum, Yale University; and the Institute of Fine Arts, New York University. The co-directors of this expedition are William Kelly Simpson (Yale) and David O'Connor. Various other institutions are also involved, some working in association with the combined expedition, some independently. All have benefited from sponsorship by the American Research Center in Egypt, based in Cairo. Equally important have been new excavations at the site of the early royal tombs (Umm el Qaʻab), initiated by Werner Kaiser and Günter Dreyer and continued by the latter, under the aegis of the German Archaeological Institute, Cairo.

It is important to note that Egyptian scholars and the Egyptian government have, throughout the history of excavation at Abydos, also made important contributions to our knowledge of the site, and indeed to its very survival. For example, the wide-ranging excavations of Auguste Mariette, and his epigraphic work on the temple of Seti I, were carried out on behalf of the then Egyptian government. Indeed, Mariette ultimately became the first director of the Egyptian Antiquities Service. Subsequently, Egyptian Egyptologists conducted a number of excavations at Abydos, many taking the form of 'salvage archaeology', intended to test land wanted for development or to follow up on accidental discoveries. Some projects were more ambitious, in particular the clearance of a very large block of magazines (by E. B. Ghazouli) next to the Seti I temple. In all, articles and reports generated by these Egyptian-sponsored operations are an important source of information about Abydos.

Equally important, at Abydos as throughout Egypt, the Egyptian authorities have maintained and protected this vast site and ensured its temples remain accessible to the scholar and the visitor, and its archaeology to the excavator. Egypt was the second country in the world (after Greece) to set up a government organization charged specifically with the management of monuments, sites and museums, and backed up by powerful legislation. Now, in a continuation of this forward-thinking attitude, one finds in every governorate a network of directors, inspectors, engineers, guards and others responsible for regional archaeology and museums, and implementing the policies set by the headquarters of the Supreme Council of Antiquities in Cairo.

Such oversight is vital for sites like Abydos. Thanks to the initiatives of Dr Zahi Hawass, a major highway was diverted from Abydos, and a protective wall is being built around the entire site. At another level, all projects operating at Abydos have benefited enormously from the support and collaboration provided by the regional officials. Particularly important has been the cordial collaboration between these officials, and our and other projects, in providing special protection to various parts of Abydos as, inevitably, the neighbouring villages grow in size. Currently, and through the generosity of Bruce Mainwaring, the Pennsylvania-Yale-Institute of Fine Arts, New York University Expedition is preparing a detailed topographical and archaeological map of the whole of Abydos, which will not only be a valuable scholarly resource, but an important aid to the Supreme Council of Antiquities in defining the full extent of Abydos' archaeology and ensuring its preservation in the future.

Excavation projects at Abydos have yet another Egyptian dimension, namely the Egyptian excavators and labourers who comprise their workforces. Working closely with project site supervisors, these workmen have been an essential part of any project's success. Our expedition in particular has enjoyed the services of an excellent local workforce throughout its activities at Abydos, but the core group of highly skilled excavators are natives of Quft (often called Coptos in Egyptological literature), a town some distance away to the southeast. The tradition of using 'Quftis' actually goes back to Flinders Petrie, and their techniques have changed surprisingly little over the years. Quftis and local labourers alike prefer to use a *touriya*, or hoe, for much of the excavating; wheelbarrows are not used and spoil is removed from the excavations by boys shouldering baskets or – a recent daring innovation – metal buckets. Nevertheless, the system is a surprisingly efficient and sensitive method of exploring Egyptian archaeological remains. Once, however, stratified remains, structures or burials are involved, the Quftis – working always under the close supervision of site supervisors – are superb at wielding trowel and brush, as well as more delicate instruments.

However, even the best workers are of little use without leadership, and we have been especially fortunate in engaging, in succession, the great abilities of three *reises*, or foremen. A *reis* is a key person on any archaeological project in Egypt. He represents the skilled workmen and their needs, oversees the entire workforce throughout each working day to ensure it operates efficiently and cheerfully, and contributes his own archaeological expertise to especially demanding situations. It is a great pleasure for me to acknowledge here the leadership provided to our workmen by Reis Hofni Ibrahim Salama; Reis Mohammed Ali Abdel Rahim Mahfouz; and our current foreman, Reis Ibrahim Mohammed Ali. The rediscovery of Abydos owes as much to them as to anyone else.

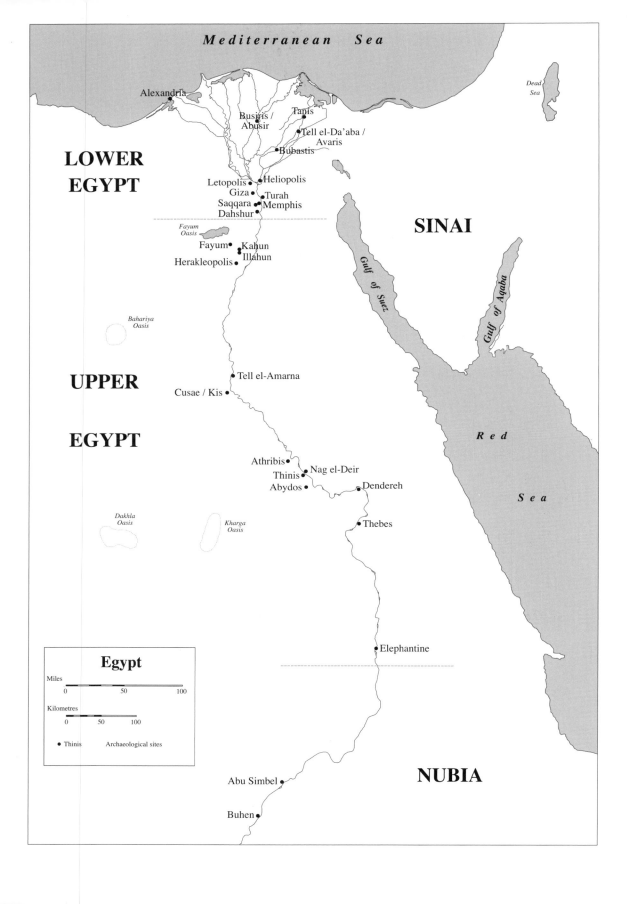

Mediterranean Sea

Dead
Sea

Alexandria

Busiris /
Abusir

Tanis

Tell el-Da'aba /
Avaris

Bubastis

**LOWER
EGYPT**

Letopolis

Heliopolis

SINAI

Giza

Turah

Saqqara

Memphis

Dahshur

*Fayum
Oasis*

Fayum

Kahun

Illahun

Herakleopolis

Gulf of Suez

Gulf of Aqaba

*Bahariya
Oasis*

UPPER

Tell el-Amarna

Cusae / Kis

EGYPT

Red

Athribis

Nag el-Deir

Thinis

Abydos

Dendereh

Sea

*Dakhla
Oasis*

*Kharga
Oasis*

Thebes

Elephantine

Egypt

Miles

0   50   100

Kilometres

0   50   100

● Thinis   Archaeological sites

NUBIA

Abu Simbel

Buhen

PART I   Abydos and Osiris

CHAPTER ONE

THE DISCOVERY OF ABYDOS

An Invisible Archaeology

Abydos, as the crow flies, is about 413 km (256 miles) south of Memphis, near modern Cairo, and 91 km (56 miles) northwest of Thebes. An enormous site, its known archaeological remains are scattered over some 8 sq. km (5 sq. miles) of the low desert adjoining the western floodplain of southern Egypt, and other remains may extend under the floodplain itself. Yet Abydos' archaeology is largely invisible to the visitors who scan its endless expanse of undulating hillocks of sand and excavational spoil.

For almost four millennia Abydos experienced a rich variety of activities. Substantial temples and even a pyramid were built, vast cemetery fields developed, and several towns and villages were established, expanded and eventually abandoned. Yet visible surviving remains are rare: two impressive stone-built temples, the larger seemingly half-sunk into the ground, and far to their northwest two massive mud-brick enclosures defining seemingly empty space.

In fact, these circumstances are typical of most major Egyptian sites. Memphis, Alexandria and many other central places are denuded and overbuilt by post-pharaonic and modern structures. They seem insignificant to visitors familiar with the vast sweep of the pyramid and mastaba fields radiating around Memphis from Giza to Dahshur, or the many-columned temples and beautifully painted rock-cut tombs of Thebes. Yet in their day, centres such as Memphis and Abydos comprised dense and extensive agglomerations of temples and towns, chapels and tombs, all locales for richly varied patterns of life and activity. Remote from ancient Egypt's two major centres of Memphis and Thebes, Abydos seems peripheral and backcountry in location. In reality, it was of great importance to pharaonic Egyptians and, unlike many other sites, it still preserves much of its original ambience.

Abydos extends over a wide expanse of low-lying desert that fills a deep embayment in the dramatically high cliffs typical of the Nile gorge in southern Egypt. Today, the site is not pristine. Ever-expanding rural villages stretch

1 *Map of Egypt showing the sites mentioned in the text.*

2 *View of Abydos. The cultivated plain is in the foreground, behind are the cliffs that dominate the site.*

almost continuously along its northeastern flank, the junction between the low desert and the cultivated floodplain, while towards the rear of the site massive electricity pylons and sprawling 'desert farms' intrude upon the terrain. Yet these visual distractions are overwhelmed and minimized by the grand scale of Abydos' boldly coloured and sharply defined topography.

Lush green fields and dense groves of trees extending for some 9 km (5.5 miles) southwest of the Nile abruptly yield to the tan-coloured low desert. Beyond the latter tower dark and rugged cliff faces are pierced here and there by arid valleys winding tortuously back through the plateau of the high desert. The impact of this landscape upon the viewer is very real, if hard to define. As it emerges from or fades into darkness at dawn and dusk, its colours and contours soften in the cool golden or blue light. But on a typical, intensely bright and windless day at noon the starkly modelled topography has a powerful effect: it both stimulates and overawes through the harsh contrast it presents to the diminutively scaled life of the floodplain extending before it. Moreover, ancient Egyptian sources reveal the landscape of Abydos had tremendous creative force for them as the home of the god Osiris; his myth roused deep feelings on the Egyptians' part, and offered the surest route to immortality after death.

Thanks to its rare but impressive surviving monuments, Abydos – called something like Abdju by ancient Egyptians – never disappeared completely from view. Especially conspicuous is the huge stone temple (occupying about 1 ha, or almost 2.5 acres) built for pharaoh Seti I early in the 13th century BC. Visitors have long marvelled at it. The geographer Strabo, for example, visited Seti's temple in 20 BC and called it 'a remarkable structure' with a 'subterranean fountain' reached via vaulted galleries. Today, however, the once-tall pylons and high-walled courts of the temple have largely disappeared, and its well-preserved, still-roofed rear portion seems sunk into the desert scarp, in part because of sand dunes and excavational spoil heaps on either side.

The rest of Abydos' visible archaeology is either less prominent or more enigmatic. Next to Seti's temple, but at first glance concealed from view behind modern village houses, is an impressive, relatively well-preserved temple of Seti's son, pharaoh Ramesses II (c. 1279–1213 BC). At about 0.27 ha (0.67 acres), it is noticeably smaller than his father's.

Far to the northwest, a massive mud-brick enclosure still stands 11 m (36 ft) high and defines a space as large as that of Seti's temple, but seemingly devoid of structures. An enigma to most visitors, the correct designation in Arabic for this enclosure is 'Shunet el Zebib' ('storehouse of grapes'), or, abbreviated, the

3 *Map of the monuments of Abydos.*

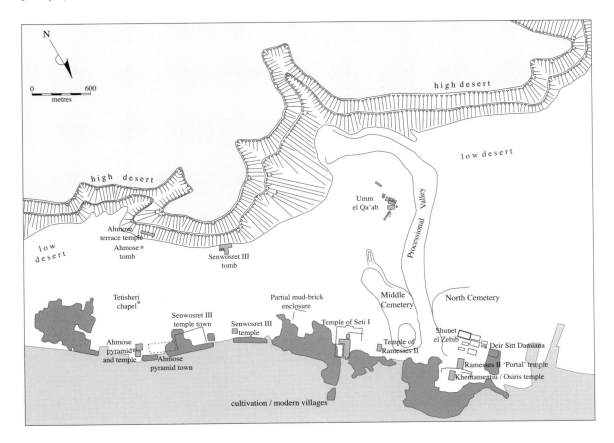

Shuneh. Earlier than the famous step pyramid of King Djoser (*c.* 2650 BC) at Saqqara, the Shuneh was built in *c.* 2660 BC and is by far the largest of those of Egypt's earliest monuments that still stand.

To the northeast of the Shuneh, about 350 m (1,148 ft) away, another set of massive mud-brick walls surrounds an area once occupied by the temple of Osiris, chief god of Abydos, and its associated town. Of the often rebuilt temple little remains to be seen, but Osiris, as ruler of the dead, was of extraordinary significance to all Egyptians. Indeed, his temple still functioned in the Greek geographer Strabo's day, and later.

The Osiris temple marks Abydos' northwestern extremity. At its other extremity, over 3 km (1.86 miles) to the southeast, is a prominent but rarely visited mound of sand and rubble, still rising 30 m (98 ft) above the desert surface. This was once a unique monument, virtually the last royal pyramid ever built in Egypt. Constructed for pharaoh Ahmose (*c.* 1539–1514 BC), it was originally 50 m (164 ft) high, and encased by a fine limestone coating. In size and height it can be compared to as famous a monument as the smallest, and much earlier, Giza pyramid of King Menkaure, which was about 66.5 m (218 ft) high.

With Abydos no longer a living entity, its few still-visible but largely enigmatic monuments hardly sufficed to tell its story. By the 19th century AD Abydos had long been a site awaiting discovery. From *c.* 3500 BC to the early centuries AD innumerable tombs, many temples and cult chapels and substantial towns and villages had spread across its expanse. However, even during ancient times (as well as later), structures were demolished so their materials could be reused: tombs were plundered and once-thriving towns fell into ruin. Over these extensive but often denuded remains there accumulated sand dunes, plunderers' spoil heaps, and sometimes villages that are still occupied, and indeed expanding, today. Nevertheless, so important a site could not be ignored once systematic archaeology began to develop in Egypt, and by the 1860s the dust clouds of large-scale excavations had begun to rise above Abydos.

Excavating Hordes and Exploding Cans

Between 1858 and 1926 many, mostly British, archaeologists worked at Abydos, but two in particular – because of their wide-ranging excavations – did most to articulate Abydos' hitherto invisible archaeology. In both methods and personalities, Auguste Mariette and Flinders Petrie were a study in contrasts.

Mariette, appointed in 1858 as the first head of Egypt's nascent Antiquities Organization, unleashed hordes of loosely supervised workmen onto Abydos from 1858 to 1861. Mariette recovered vast quantities of inscribed and artifactual materials, and published the first significant archaeological reports on Abydos, but specific contexts, let alone such niceties as stratigraphy, were mostly unrecorded.

Petrie, both on his own and later alongside younger colleagues, conducted and promoted much more focused and meticulous excavations in many parts of Abydos (1899–1903, 1921–22). Important structural complexes which had

4 *Professor and Mrs Flinders Petrie at Abydos in* 1900.

minimal surface archaeology, and were thus often overlooked by Mariette's workers, were identified from one end of Abydos to the other, and made known through rapid, if sometimes summary, publication.

Mariette died in 1881, a year after Petrie first visited Egypt, and they never interacted with each other. Both men were intensely dedicated researchers, with very different methods of working. Mariette liked to live in relative comfort at Saqqara, which was convenient for his administrative responsibilities, while he delegated excavations elsewhere to others. Petrie, however, was always on site, moving from one makeshift base camp to another, keeping a close eye on his assistants and developing a notorious reputation for austerity. Supposedly, at the end of each excavation season he buried the remaining canned goods at the camp. At the outset of the next season they were dug up and hurled against the nearest wall; those which did not explode were considered fit to eat! Despite these eccentricities Petrie inspired great respect throughout his career, as well as much – if sometimes bemused – affection.

The few extant monuments of Abydos had been mapped earlier, for example by Napoleon's *savants* (1798–99), Lepsius' scholarly Prussian expedition (1842–45) and others. But it was Mariette, Petrie and their colleagues and successors who demonstrated in detail how Abydos' archaeology had developed over time, diffusing outwards in ever-expanding radii towards the southeast from an initial centre at Abydos' northern corner.

Petrie located at the northern corner, near the site of what later became the Osiris temple, a substantial town extending through Dynasty 'o' and the 1st and 2nd Dynasties (c. 2950–2650 BC). The town's development was associated with an exceptionally important cemetery almost 2 km (1.24 miles) due south. Today called 'Umm el Qa'ab' – 'the Mother of Pots', because of its dense spreads of surface sherds – the cemetery lay close to the cliffs marking the edge of the high desert. Petrie, and his less able predecessor Emile-Clément Amélineau, showed that many kings of the 1st and 2nd Dynasties were buried here, as were their predecessors.

Equally importantly, Petrie and his associates demonstrated that several large brick enclosures (one of them the Shunet el Zebib, mentioned above) also dated from the 1st and 2nd Dynasties, as did two vast rectangular layouts of subsidiary graves nearby. The enclosures were due north of the royal tombs, but quite far away, since they stood on the low desert close to the early town.

Kings were no longer buried at Abydos after c. 2650 BC, but the town continued to be important through the Old Kingdom (c. 2650–2130 BC) when its focus was a temple of Khentamentiu, a local deity attested since the 1st Dynasty. At this time, Abydos experienced its first major expansion to the southeast, in the form of the Middle Cemetery, adjacent to the town. Mariette and others revealed that its many graves included those of high-ranking Old Kingdom officials, perhaps because Abydos had become a sub-capital as headquarters of an important royal official, 'the Overseer of Southern Egypt'.

Amongst those buried here was an official called Weni, whose tomb chapel yielded a famous autobiographical text. Besides much else, Weni described a confidential inquiry he had conducted into a 'secret charge ... against Queen Weret-Yamtes', a wife of King Pepi I (6th Dynasty). Direct reference to such a sensitive event is otherwise unknown amongst the surviving annals of the Egyptian elite. Recently, in a spectacular discovery, Janet Richards relocated Weni's tomb, which had been lost to sight since Mariette's day (see Chapter 5).

By c. 2000 BC Osiris, ruler of the dead and popular with king and commoner alike, was established at Abydos. Important new developments were stimulated around the old central core, at the northern corner, as was a major axial expansion to the southeast.

In the north, Senwosret I (c. 1919–1875 BC) of the 12th Dynasty built a new temple dedicated to Osiris-Khentamentiu, a combination of the older and the newer deity. Throughout the 12th and 13th Dynasties (c. 1938–1630 BC) kings lavished attention on this temple, while some of them built royal 'ka-chapels' in its vicinity. The ka was the life-force of an individual, and could receive cult both before and after death. Southwest of the town the area around the early enclosures had been kept free of graves. Now, during the Middle Kingdom, it filled in with a vast cemetery (the 'North Cemetery') of intermingled elite and lower-order graves.

A major expansion to the southeast was due to King Senwosret III (*c.* 1836–1818 BC), who built for himself a cenotaph, or dummy mortuary complex, 2.3 km (1.4 miles) southeast of the Osiris temple. At the floodplain edge was a 'valley temple', while at the cliff foot 1 km (0.62 miles) to the southwest the largest royal tomb of the Middle Kingdom was cut. Most scholars believe Senwosret was not buried here, but rather under his pyramid at Dahshur, but a few suggest otherwise. The New Kingdom (*c.* 1539–1075 BC) was characterized by a further expansion to the southeast, as well as major developments along the axis running from there to the Osiris temple.

Furthest southeast was pharaoh Ahmose's pyramid, mentioned above. It loomed over a valley temple at the floodplain edge, while far to the southwest, near a 'terrace temple' at the cliff's foot, was a gigantic subterranean tomb. Some believe Ahmose was buried here, others that his real tomb was at Thebes.

Other large 18th Dynasty (*c.* 1539–1292 BC) monuments have not been located, although clearly a number of smaller royal chapels of this date were built near the Osiris temple. Half way between that temple and Ahmose's pyramid is an exposed corner of an otherwise unexcavated, but seemingly very large mud-brick enclosure. It might indicate the precincts of a large temple similar in scale, for example, to others built elsewhere by the 18th Dynasty pharaoh Amenhotep III (*c.* 1390–1353 BC); but it could also be part of an extensive enclosed town attached to the Seti temple. If so, the latter was not only the largest monument at Abydos, but would have generated a new urban centre as well. Such a shift in the settlement pattern is further suggested by the relative rarity of New Kingdom burials in the North and Middle cemeteries, adjacent to the older, north corner town.

Nevertheless, here the Osiris temple continued to receive substantial royal attention throughout the New Kingdom, as abundant textual evidence shows, and the northwestern area in general seemingly became a renewed focus of attention later. For example, there is a profusion of graves datable to the Third Intermediate Period (*c.* 1075–656 BC), the Late Period (664–332 BC), and to Graeco-Roman times (332 BC–AD 641) in the North and Middle cemeteries. Moreover, surviving archaeology attests that the Osiris temple itself was rebuilt on an impressive scale in the reign of pharaoh Nectanebo I (381–362 BC) and continued to be a viable cult centre until Egypt's pagan temples were officially closed by the Christian emperor Theodosius I in AD 392. Notwithstanding, the temple of Seti I still included a cult place for the god Bes well into the 5th century AD.

In a sense, religious life at Abydos has never ceased. The Seti temple for a while incorporated a Christian church. Elsewhere, medieval Coptic anchorites carved cells into the brick walls of the Shunet el Zebib (already incredibly old in their time) while slightly further north a modern village houses a church, founded perhaps in the 6th century AD. Mosques and churches rise from the villages flanking Abydos today, and some adventurous foreign visitors genuinely believe they have access to the supernatural via Seti's still-imposing temple.

CHAPTER TWO

OSIRIS – ETERNAL LORD WHO PRESIDES IN ABYDOS

Osiris and Abydos

For almost three quarters of its 4,000-year-long history, Abydos and Osiris were inextricably linked. What happened earlier is told in the third part of this book, but from *c.* 2000 BC onwards most of Abydos' archaeology was generated by the beliefs and practices associated with the cult of Osiris.

Starting in *c.* 2450 BC, funerary inscriptions throughout Egypt refer to Osiris as lord of the Thinite province (in which Abydos was located) and, more rarely, of Abydos itself. More usually Khentamentiu is identified as lord (tutelary deity) of Abydos, but the two deities may already have been identified as two aspects of the same being. Osiris was also called lord of Djedu, or Busiris (today Abusir), a site in the east-central Delta – its archaeology is almost completely unknown.

At any rate, after *c.* 2000 BC the temple in northwest Abydos was identified as that of Osiris-Khentamentiu, i.e. 'Osiris, foremost of westerners, the blessed dead'. Here, Osiris was venerated much as any regionally important deity would have been, yet his significance extended much further. Osiris' importance and popularity throughout Egypt was rivalled only by that of the sun-god Re, or of his later New Kingdom manifestation, Amun-Re.

Osiris enjoyed great popularity for two reasons. Firstly, all deities underwent a form of death and regeneration, but not in the dramatic form Osiris experienced. Osiris died violently, either by accident or, according to another and eventually more popular tradition, by murder. Moreover, his corpse was fragmented or dismembered, a process analogous – in accelerated form – to the decay dead bodies experienced. Osiris' body was reassembled and mummified thanks to his wife-sister Isis and his other sister Nephthys. Ritually, the sisters rendered Osiris capable of generating new life, a process leading ultimately to his own regeneration. Thus, the story of Osiris provided Egyptians with an archetypal event that denied the finality and annihilation death seemed to bring. All, including even the other deities, were promised renewed life after death through ritual identification with Osiris.

The second reason for Osiris' popularity was that his regenerated form was as ruler of the netherworld or *Duat*, a mysterious realm set simultaneously in

5 *Osiris and Isis, depicted in the temple of Seti I. The god wears the Atef crown and is wrapped like a mummy. He holds an emblem of divinity and the crook and flail of kingship.*

6 *Limestone stela discovered by the PYIFA at the 'Portal' temple of Ramesses II. Perhaps dating to the 18th Dynasty, the upper portion of the stela shows the veneration of Osiris by the king's scribe Si-mut and his daughter, Wer-el. Unusually, his wife, the chantress of Amun, Biat, is shown below, seated next to 'her son Huy'.*

the night sky and below ground, a place all deceased Egyptians had to enter and traverse in order to experience renewal and regeneration after death. As ruler, Osiris controlled entry into the netherworld and guaranteed the safety and refreshment of all who dwelt in it.

Osiris, then, was a deity of both regional and national significance. Like other regional temples, Osiris' temple benefited from royal gifts, benefactions and rebuilding programmes, and had in its vicinity royal *ka*-chapels linking the mortuary cults of the specific kings to the temple and the offerings its deity received. However, other manifestations of royal interest in Abydos reflected Osiris' national significance. The building of large royal mortuary temples and tombs (at Abydos, cenotaphs or dummy tombs) attested at Abydos for Senwosret III, Ahmose, Seti I and perhaps Ramesses II, is paralleled only at major royal centres such as Thebes, or Memphis and its vicinity.

By the New Kingdom, regional as well as centrally located deities frequently made festival appearances during which their images were carried out of the temple and processed through the town or even further. This practice might go back to earlier times, as was certainly true in Osiris' case. At Abydos he enjoyed an impressive, annually performed processional festival throughout the Middle Kingdom, which attracted much national attention.

7 A view across the low desert to the site of the Early Dynastic royal tombs, close to the foot of the cliffs; one of these was later identified as the tomb of Osiris.

8 *Limestone stela or lintel (incomplete) discovered by the PYIFA at the 'Portal' temple of Ramesses II. Dating to the New Kingdom, it shows 'the Osiris Khay' and members of his family. Above they adore Amun of Thebes on the left, and Osiris of Abydos on the right (now gone). Below is depicted a ritual voyage to Thebes (left) and the return to Abydos (right; only the stern of the vessel survives).*

Royal officials were sent to participate in the festival on the king's behalf, and since stelae from Abydos often celebrate the relationship between the individual commemorated and the festival, it seems likely that Egyptians came from all over Egypt to witness and participate in it. Thus Osiris' temple was a place of national pilgrimage, although some people did not travel but commissioned others to set up stelae in Abydos on their behalf.

Also reflecting Abydos' national significance is the 'voyage' deceased individuals were often said to make to Abydos and Busiris, and which is sometimes depicted with seeming exactitude on tomb-chapel walls. In reality, the voyages might have been symbolic events, acted out during the funerary and burial ritual at the deceased's home town, but their symbolic value alone again points out Abydos' national importance. Like other regional centres, Abydos had large cemeteries, especially to the south and southwest of the town in its northern corner. The impressive size of these cemeteries in the Old and Middle Kingdoms, and after the New Kingdom, suggests either that Abydos itself had an unusually large population, or that it was a popular burial ground for the entire region. However, other cemeteries are known elsewhere in the Abydos region, for example at Nag el-Deir. Some of the people buried at Abydos actually came from quite far away, so its national significance may also have influenced the growth of the site's cemeteries, despite a general preference for burial near one's home town.

Osiris and his Meanings

What do we know about this popular deity from whom Abydos' archaeology derived many of its functions and meanings? Fortunately, Osiris' mythology has survived in extended narrative form, as well as in the scattered, non-narrative references that are the usual evidence used to reconstruct Egyptian mythology. This latter circumstance has led to the opinion, held by many, that the natures and relationships of Egyptian deities were conveyed not by mythological narratives but rather through noncontinuous forms of writing such as hymns and ritual texts.

The apparent absence of mythological narrative may not be real, however, and could be the result of accident rather than actual cultural practice. The rich mythology of Mesopotamia, for example, is documented almost entirely on durable clay tablets, whereas their Egyptian equivalents – papyrus documents – were more fragile and therefore less likely to survive. Only rarely, and especially in Osiris' case, was continuous mythological narrative inscribed on stone stelae or wall faces.

The longest and most famous version of Osiris' myth is provided by Plutarch and was written somewhere between AD 110 and 120. Its value is qualified in that it includes speculation about Osiris by the Greeks, along with much information derived from original Egyptian sources. Narrative treatments of the myth by native Egyptians are naturally less problematical in this regard. A long hymn inscribed on the funerary stela of the official Amenmose during the 18th Dynasty (c. 1539–1292 BC) is an especially important and relatively early example.[1] Like countless Egyptians since the Old Kingdom, Amenmose hoped that after death and burial he would share in the food offerings Osiris was regularly proffered by the Egyptian king, and would receive from Osiris the power of 'transformation'. This would permit Amenmose first to enter the netherworld, and then thereafter to experience endlessly repeated regenerations or 'rebirths', ensuring his personal immortality. Thus Amenmose prayed he would be 'supplied among the favoured ones before Wennefer [Osiris], receiving the offerings that go up on the altar of the great god, breathing the sweet north wind and drinking from the river's pools'. In Egyptian cosmological terms, air and water were conceived as conveyors of life to both the living and the dead.

The text of Amenmose's stela includes a celebratory hymn, preceding the prayers to Osiris. In the hymn Osiris is invoked in his 'many forms', specifically as found at a number of towns where he had temples, including Abydos and Busiris. Osiris is described as currently the awe-inspiring ruler of the dead 'to whom those in the netherworld kiss the ground'. Earlier however, the hymn states that Osiris had been a ruler on earth, over the living; as 'heir to the kingship of the Two Lands', i.e. Egypt, Osiris had succeeded his divine father Geb as ruler. Other New Kingdom sources actually identify a whole dynasty of gods as Egypt's earliest rulers – Ptah, Re, Shu, Geb, Osiris, Seth and Horus.

Amenmose's hymn goes on to describe how Osiris became transformed from ruler of the living to that of the dead. Osiris' death by murder is implied (direct

9 *In a scene in the temple of Seti I the murdered, dismembered but reassembled Osiris is shown lying on a bier. His consort, the goddess Isis, descends in the form of a kite onto his erect phallus, which has been defaced. As a result, Isis will give birth to Osiris' son Horus, who also stands at the foot of the bier, while his mother, Isis, stands at the head. In the atemporal divine world, deities can appear multiple times in the same scene.*

reference to the murder is usually avoided), while it is explicitly stated that, despite his mummified state, Osiris' wife Isis and sister Nephthys were able to restimulate his sexual potency. Isis is impregnated and gives birth to Osiris' son and heir, the god Horus, whom she raises 'in solitude, his abode unknown'. This secrecy was necessary to protect Horus from Osiris' brother Seth, identified in other sources as the murderer and usurper, who naturally sought to eliminate Horus as his potential rival.

In Amenmose's hymn Horus, once mature, is indeed recognized as Osiris' heir by the council composed of Egypt's senior deities. Thus, Horus is crowned as ruler of Egypt and the world while Osiris – fully revived by Horus' victory over Seth – assumes the kingship of the netherworld. Seth, the violent usurper, experienced humiliation and worse. The deities gave 'to Isis' son his foe [Seth], his attack [against Horus] collapsed, the disturber suffered hurt, his fate overtook the offender'.

10 *Limestone lintel (incomplete) discovered by the PYIFA at the 'Portal' temple of Ramesses II. Dating to the reign of Amenhotep III, the lintel depicts Osiris as ruler of the dead, enthroned in a shrine. 'Giving praise to Osiris, kissing the ground for the lord of the necropolis' is Karoya, who perhaps served on a royal ship, his mother and his wife.*

The coherent narrative on Amenmose's stela records all the essential components of Osiris' myth, which itself goes back to much earlier times. Although presented in non-continuous fashion, these components are all included in the collection of spells and incantations known as the 'Pyramid Texts' inscribed on the walls of royal burial chambers (and eventually elsewhere) since the reign of the Old Kingdom ruler Unas (5th Dynasty); and the Pyramid Texts in turn must have drawn upon even older sources.

The references to Osiris in the Pyramid Texts suggest to many scholars that his myth, as described above, was the coalescence of several originally independent 'constellations'. The term constellation refers to specific interactive relationships between deities; each constellation is a virtually independent verbal 'icon', representing a particular interrelationship of cosmological and other significance. Such constellations are, many scholars suggest, the Egyptian alternative to continuous mythological narratives, which did not develop until much later. However, it is possible that these icons were actually distilled out of already existing myths.

Some scholars suggest Osiris' myth may have been generated by the evolution of the rituals and mummification techniques applied to the bodies of early historical kings, but it seems more likely that it may have developed to provide hope for those facing death, and consolation to their surviving kin.

The constellations relevant to the secluded raising of Horus by Isis had their own emblematic power. These images of the divine magician Isis protecting a growing child god from all manner of natural and supernatural dangers were often invoked in spells, charms, amulets and medical recipes intended to protect or heal ordinary Egyptians. And yet a third component of Osiris' myth may

11 *King Seti I makes an offering to the goddess Isis who is in the form of a statue in a shrine. Relief in the temple of Seti I, Abydos.*

originally have been an independent entity. The conflict between Horus, Osiris' heir, and Osiris' murderer Seth provided on the divine level a guarantee that the processes of orderly and legitimate succession, which gave Egyptian kingship its stability, would always triumph, no matter how threatening the circumstances.

Thus, Osiris' myth may have combined several, originally independent components, but the fact that all are intermingled in the Pyramid Texts is a good indication they were forming into a coherent whole early in Egyptian history. Another important indication of the developing integrity of the myth is a yet further series of constellations found in the Pyramid Texts. These relate to the creation and functioning of the cosmos and in this connection link together the deities around whom Osiris' myth was constructed, namely, Osiris, Isis, Nephthys, Seth and Horus. Taken together, these constellations comprise what is called the 'Heliopolitan cosmogony', in which the sun-god (whose principal cult centre was Heliopolis, called Wenu by Egyptians) played a vital role. The constellations depict the repeated involvement of various forms of the sun-god in the creation, growth and maintenance of the cosmos; and simultaneously present these processes as taking on the form of a divine lineage, including Osiris, descended from the sun-god.

Atum, the primeval form of the sun-god, initiates cosmogony through his own self-formation, then 'gives birth' to his children, Shu and Tefnut. Together, this god and goddess represent or embody the void that provides a 'place' in otherwise endless and formless chaos, a place in which the cosmos can grow. Shu and Tefnut in turn give birth to Geb and Nut, the earth and the sky; and the structured cosmos thus formed is then occupied by all the beings – deities, humans, animals and plants – which Atum has conceptualized. They are vitalized or brought to life by the first actual sunrise, that of Re-Horakhty, the form the sun-god manifests during the daily cycle marked by sunrise and sunset.

Geb and Nut are the parents of the divine couples Osiris and Isis, and Nephthys and Seth. In the context of cosmogony and cosmic process, these latter deities overlap both life and death and the worlds of the living and the dead. Osiris is murdered and dies, yet revives and relives. Seth is the archetypal murderer, yet survives his crime, for which he is not executed. Osiris is integrated fully into the netherworld, yet is powerfully and vitally manifest in the world of the living as well. He is embodied in its life-endowed or life-giving features, such as the annual inundation and the vegetation it generates, and the moon and stars moving through the night sky. Seth, in the upper world of the living, is associated with turbulence and sterility, thunderstorm and desert. Yet he also functions as the aggressive form of cosmic order, repelling threatening chaotic force in both the upper and nether worlds.

The birth of Horus marks the closing of the cosmogonic circle and the initiation of endlessly recurrent, cyclically structured renewals of cosmos. Horus is simultaneously the last manifestation of the sun-god involved in the cosmogony, and – as Osiris' son – the conclusion of the divine lineage and the complete cosmos it represents. In origin Horus is the 'distant one' (*horu*), the sun itself, but his function now is to both rule the cosmos and to become embodied in the Egyptian kingship and its mortal incumbents. Thus, cosmic order and rulership is translated onto the human or terrestrial level.

The cosmos, now complete, depends upon eternal stability (*djet*), the everlastingness of its created components, and on eternal recurrence (*neheh*), the divinely inspired, repeated renewals of those components. Horus guarantees the cosmic processes will be orderly and protected from interruption. The sun-god daily sets and 'dies', yet regenerates via union with Osiris, a process repeated by all deities, as well as deceased Egyptians. Rising again, the sun-god revitalizes the cosmos and its inhabitants, a process endlessly repeated until the end of time and being.

For the Egyptians, then, Osiris was the focus of an extraordinary cluster of meanings and associations, but also, as many allusions make clear, he inspired strong emotional reactions. The components of his myth may relate to abstract issues such as the interpretation of death, the stability of the cosmos and the avoidance of evil; moreover, as James Allen notes, at one level the genealogical structure of the divine lineage through which cosmogony is expressed can be seen as 'no more than a means of expressing the interdependence and causality that the Egyptians saw among the various forces and elements of the natural world'.[2] Yet the human dimensions of these complex relationships are often evoked, as when Atum the creator says (in the Pyramid Texts) of his children, the cosmic forces Shu and Tefnut: 'I shall live with my twins, my fledglings with me in their midst ... it is on them I have come to rely, with their arms about me.'

This evocation in divine contexts of the human emotions, feelings, anxieties and even the humour experienced by the Egyptians themselves is especially prominent in the case of Osiris and deities associated closely with him. The emotional impact of his murder and subsequent tribulations upon Osiris himself is conveyed by a subtly powerful aversion to referring directly to these events, but the intense grief of Isis and Nephthys is often poignantly conveyed. Many stories developed about the adventures of Isis and Horus, hiding yet threatened in the marshes. These stories evoke Isis' fierce maternal love, and some are distinctly earthy in tone. At one point, for example, Isis urinates in a magically abundant fashion to extinguish a supernaturally generated fire that threatens Horus!

The conflict of Horus and Seth, a crucial element in Osiris' myth, was also provided with much human interest, especially but not uniquely evident in a famous and extraordinary literary work. This story, called by modern scholars 'The Contendings of Horus and Seth', was extant by c. 1150 BC, and has earlier antecedents.[3] Despite its humorous and even farcical features, the story's close adherence to the myth of Osiris and its essential meanings indicate a complex composition, operating at more than one level. The tale highlights episodes in the struggle between Horus, seeking to maintain legitimacy and the rulership, and Seth, trying to reclaim illegitimately the kingship already awarded to Horus. Via a variety of episodes Seth emerges as an aggressive buffoon, and Horus as a sophisticated trickster who is powerfully assisted by his resourceful and magical mother Isis. For example, Seth seeks homosexual dominance over Horus, only to be laughably 'inseminated' by Horus instead. In another event, the two gods compete against each other by rowing supposedly stone boats, but Horus cunningly uses a wooden boat disguised to look like stone while a bemused Seth rapidly sinks in his genuinely stone vessel.

Thus, Egyptian theologians explored the meaning of the cosmos through the myth of Osiris and other deities, while Egyptians in general were edified and solaced by prayers and hymns to Osiris, as well as instructed and entertained by tales such as the 'Contendings'. However, the ultimate importance of Osiris for king and commoner alike was that all, after death, hoped to be judged blameless before Osiris and hence worthy of entry into the netherworld. There, the royal and other dead sought identification with Osiris (indeed, deceased Egyptians were habitually referred to as 'the Osiris so-and-so'), and thus a guarantee of their own regeneration, the enjoyment of offerings, and continuing participation in the great cycle of solar renewal.

12 *Small limestone stela 16 cm (6.2 in) high recovered by the PYIFA from the 'Portal' temple of Ramesses II. Roughly shaped, the stela represents the non-elite veneration of Osiris; the scene, sketched in ink, shows 'the servitor Huy' making an offering to Osiris.*

The various meanings that Osiris had for the Egyptians find expression in his iconography, the ways in which he was represented in Egyptian art. Typically, whether shown standing or enthroned, Osiris is immobilized in wrappings, a reference to his permanently mummified state. His face, however, is fully visible and his hands are free so they can grasp the shepherd's crook and the farmer's flail. These regalia are emblematic of Egyptian kingship and refer to Osiris' roles as first terrestrial then netherworld ruler. In some representations Osiris' erect penis is also shown emerging from his wrappings as Isis, in the form of a bird, hovers over the recumbent god and is impregnated by him.

Osiris nearly always appears in fully human form, without the animal or bird head that many Egyptian deities display. He often wears a tall white crown flanked by two large feathers. This 'Atef' crown represents both southern and northern Egypt, its comprehensive character referring to both Osiris' earthly rule and his subsequent universality as king of all deceased deities, kings and humans.

In Egyptian art most deities have flesh-coloured or golden yellow skin. Osiris, however, is often shown as an eerie green, or even black. These colours may well have been interpreted by Egyptians as emblematic of the green vegetation and black earth produced by the inundation – both embodiments of Osiris – but perhaps their ultimate inspiration was the colour of dead bodies during the process of decay, and even of mummification. Osiris was the ultimate guarantor against the finality of such decay. Paradoxically, decay's physical manifestations thus became ennobled, and redolent of the potential for renewed life that Osiris represented.

Abydos, then, was one of the two principal cult centres (largely unknown Busiris being the other) for a god who was at the centre of a rich complexity of meanings, associations and myths. The rest of the first half of this book will focus on the degree to which we can reconstruct the patterns of activity that reflected this complexity specifically at Abydos, in terms of both ritual and larger, associated patterns of societal activity.

13 *View of the pillared façade of the Seti temple.*

CHAPTER THREE

THE TEMPLE OF SETI I

'The House that You Love'

The temple of Seti I (*c.* 1290–1279 BC) is a spectacular example of the royal interest in Abydos generated by Osiris' presence there, but it also has unusual human interest. Although like other pharaohs Seti had numerous temples built throughout Egypt, according to surviving texts his greatest affection was for his Abydos temple. It was set 'in the province which he loved, his heart's desire ever since he had been on earth, the sacred soil of Wennefer [Osiris]'.[1]

Seti's temple is best described as dedicated to Seti-as-Osiris, and as such was part of a larger and more complex picture. By Seti's time Osiris had many cult places throughout Egypt, each, however, usually subordinate in status and size to the temple of the chief deity of the town involved. Osiris' own primary temples were at Busiris and Abydos, where his temple lies about 1 km (0.62 miles) northwest of Seti's.

The exact form of Osiris' temple at Abydos before the Late Period (664–332 BC) is uncertain, but it was a focus of an annual festival of national significance. Throughout Egypt a festival of Osiris was celebrated during the annual inundation (July to September), but the version at Abydos was the most famous and had a close relationship with the topography and archaeology of the site. The other focus of Osiris' festival was one of the old royal tombs at Umm el Qa'ab, almost 2 km (1.2 miles) south of the Osiris temple. This tomb was now identified as that of Osiris, and the long shallow desert valley linking it to the temple was the route followed by the annual processional festival. The god's image was carried out of the temple and along the valley, the drama of Osiris' myth being ceremonially enacted en route. At Umm el Qa'ab the image of Osiris was ritually buried and regenerated, then carried back in triumph to his temple.

Naturally, the Osiris temple was of great interest to Egyptian royalty throughout the New Kingdom. For example, Ramesses III (*c.* 1187–1156 BC) built a stone-walled enclosure 'towering like a mountain' around 'the temple of Osiris and Horus son of Isis',[2] while Ramesses IV (*c.* 1156–1150 BC) thought his benefactions for the Osiris temple entitled him to a 134-year-long reign!

Seti's temple, for its part, was not intended to outshine the Osiris temple proper but rather the two were complementary to each other. Seti's temple was not a *hewt netjer* – a deity's temple, like Osiris' temple – but a royal *hewt*, akin to the similarly named royal mortuary temples of Thebes. As with the latter, Seti's Abydos temple was treated as a dynamic entity, identical to Seti himself.

The temple itself was called 'Menmaatre (i.e. Seti) Happy in Abydos', and the Osireion or dummy tomb behind it was named 'Menmaatre Beneficial to Osiris'.

These names, as well as others applied to individual parts of the temple, had dual significance. They present Seti, the living king, as the dutiful servant of Osiris and other deities; but also as one who, having become a deceased and transformed ruler, is seen as lord of the cosmos upon whom other deities depend. At Abydos, Seti achieved this latter status through his posthumous identification with Osiris, just as at Thebes the king's deification depended upon identification with Amun-Re. Since Amun-Re was lord of the living and Osiris of the dead, Seti's mortuary temples at Thebes and Abydos, respectively, provided his posthumous, cosmic kingship with the widest possible authority.

Thus, the lord of Seti's Abydos temple was actually Seti-*as*-Osiris. Given this, and the Abydos locale, it is not surprising that Osiris and his divine kinfolk are prominently featured in the temple. For example, at the rear was an 'Osiris Complex' celebrating Osiris' 'mysteries' (his cycle of death, regeneration and rulership) and their relationship to Seti's own posthumous transformation. In front of this complex seven large 'barque chapels' stretched across the entire width of the temple. A barque chapel was designed to house the boat-shaped palanquin in which an image of the relevant deity was paraded during processional rituals in and outside of the temple. Four of the chapels were dedicated respectively to Osiris, Isis and Horus, and to Seti as a counterpart to the latter. The other three were for the gods Amun-Re, Re-Horakhty and Ptah. They were not only Egypt's chief deities at this time, but also depended upon Osiris for their regeneration. In total, the seven deities (including Seti) were identified as 'the conclave of deities which resides in Seti's temple'.

The complementary relationship between Osiris' temple and Seti's was further emphasized by textual references celebrating their proximity, Seti's being described as 'alongside Wennefer [Osiris], magnate of eternity'. Although in reality the two temples are almost 1 km (0.62 miles) apart, this was as close as Seti's vast temple could actually be placed. Otherwise, it would have drastically intruded upon earlier royal monuments and the large cemeteries lying between Osiris' temple and Seti's. Seti presumably shared with his son, Ramesses II, the latter's explicitly attested sensitivity as to the inviolability of these earlier structures.

A Visit to the Seti Temple

Seti's temple excites the visitor today as it is exceptionally well preserved, and yet it also intimidates through its vast size and complex artwork. Indeed, the temple's plan was so grandiose that it had to be completed by Seti's son and successor, Ramesses II. In describing this work, Ramesses unexpectedly reveals himself as the first of Abydos' many archaeological observers. Commenting on Abydos' then visible archaeology, he noted that 'the chapels and mortuary

14 *Portrait of Seti I; a relief carving from his temple at Abydos.*

15 *Part of the temple of Ramesses II at Abydos. While completing the temple of his father, Seti I, Ramesses built a smaller one for himself next to Seti's.*

monuments' of earlier kings at Abydos were 'part of them still under construction, [part covered] with soil, their walls lying unfinished'.³ The actual reasons for the half-ruined state of these earlier monuments were multiple; some were incompletely built, but others had been partly demolished, or had simply decayed while sand and debris accumulated over them. Ramesses, however, found a simpler, more uniform interpretation. Whenever, he stated, a king's 'son arose in his father's place, none of them restored the monument of him who begot him'. Nevertheless, he – Ramesses – would so complete and equip Seti's temple that he would be praised 'for ever and ever'.

Indeed, the modern visitor might feel that Seti and Ramesses had succeeded all too well. The temple's once-high pylon and the tall walls that originally defined its courtyards have largely disappeared, but its large roofed area is well preserved. Occupying over 0.53 ha (1 acre) in area, it presents seemingly endless vistas of attractive, brightly painted yet bafflingly arcane scenes and texts extending in every direction.

Well-trained guides do their best, in the limited time available, to explain the meaning of this art. And until recently some tourists were provided with unusual insights by the late Dorothy Edie, an Englishwoman who lived in the nearby village of Arabeh. Locally known as 'Umm Seti', or 'the Mother of Seti', she was a vivacious, intelligent woman combining Egyptological expertise with a profound belief that she had been, long ago, herself a priestess in Seti's temple. Umm Seti genuinely thought of herself as an ancient Egyptian. She once showed me the tomb prepared for her in the backyard of her house at Arabeh. At one end of the underground chamber the appropriate ancient offering formula was inscribed in hieroglyphs upon the wall. Unfortunately, ancient beliefs and modern bureaucracy conflicted when she died. Township regulations forbade burial in residential zones, and Umm Seti was eventually interred in a modern Coptic cemetery. However, her wish to be associated with Abydos' deities was at least partially fulfilled, for this cemetery is set within the much older North Cemetery, itself part of 'the Terrace of the Great God, Osiris' proclaimed in ancient texts.

For the benefit of the modern visitor to Seti's temple, it is perhaps best to first describe and explain the plan of the temple and its environs, and then turn to the complexities of the scenes and texts displayed upon its walls.

The plan of the Seti temple at Abydos is a unique variation of what became the fairly standard layout of Ramesside (*c.* 1292–1075 BC) royal mortuary

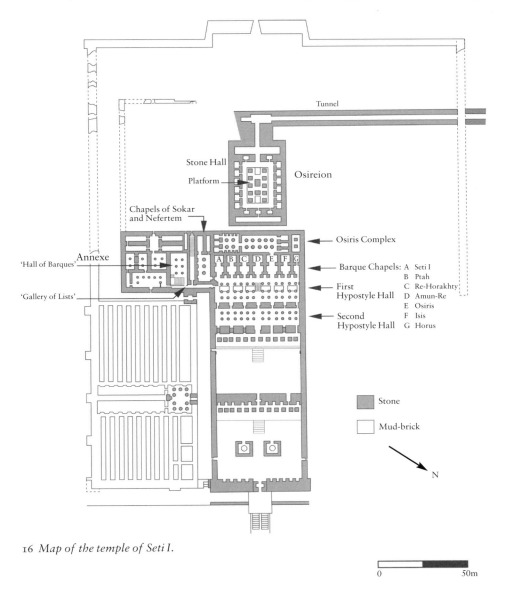

16 *Map of the temple of Seti I.*

temples at Thebes. Seti's Abydos temple deviated from the Theban model for two reasons. First, its precincts included a royal cenotaph, or dummy tomb – the Osireion – which is not the case at Thebes; and second, the incorporation of seven barque chapels into a row stretching across the temple's width required a substantial modification of the Theban model.

Thus, Theban mortuary temples were usually surrounded on three sides by large brick-built magazines, which filled much of the precinct. These were intended for grain and other materials delivered from the large estates which, throughout Egypt, supported the economy of any major temple. But, while Seti's Abydos temple probably had magazines on either side, the precinct area behind it was seemingly left clear of major structures because the Osireion lay below it. Some suggest a mound was intended to mark the Osireion's location, but in fact there is evidence only for a grove of trees at ground level. The Osireion itself was never fully finished and apparently stood at the base of an open pit which, according to the original plan, should have been filled in.

The Theban model might also have suggested a ceremonial palace attached to the local south side of the first court, and apparently such a palace existed at Abydos. In his Theban tomb, a scene shows Nebwenenef, High Priest of Amun, being appointed by Ramesses II while the latter was in the palace at Abydos. The displacement of magazines into this area, however, must in turn have required the palace to be built elsewhere, perhaps further to the southeast.

Traversing Seti's temple from front to rear is physically challenging. In front is a quay, opening to a harbour which has long been filled in. Such harbours were typical of temples: linked to the Nile by canal, they initially facilitated the delivery of building materials and later of supplies, and were also locales for water-borne festival progressions of the temple's deity. At Seti's temple, the stairway-cum-ramp leading up from the harbour is exceptionally large and steep, indicative of the fact that the temple is not only built on a series of ever-higher platforms, as was usual, but also runs up a gently rising but very definite slope.

As noted earlier, the massive two-towered entryway, or pylon, and the two successive courts beyond have largely disappeared, so the approach to the roofed area is open and windswept. Most of the temple was built of locally quarried limestone, but sandstone from southernmost Egypt was used for the roof slabs, and elsewhere.

A traverse of Seti's temple reveals to the visitor that it has a unique, L-shaped plan, for attached to the southeast side of the roofed component (which has an area of 3,465 sq. m or 37,186.5 sq. ft) is a substantial annexe (about 1,900 sq. m or 20,444 sq. ft). This results from the drastic modifications made to the Theban mortuary temple plan in Seti's Abydos temple. By extending barque chapels continuously across its width (access to which could not be blocked), Seti's builders had to move other components which would normally have been incorporated into a Theban mortuary temple into an annexe. These displaced elements found in the annexe at Abydos included other divine chapels, further sacred barque depositories, a treasury, and a nominal 'slaughterhouse' and other rooms for food preparation and storage.

The roofed component is entered by a façade – the southwest side of the second court – originally pierced by seven doorways, corresponding to the seven barque chapels found deeper within the temple. Ramesses had four of these blocked up. Moving through the central doorway, the visitor then traverses two densely columned and lofty halls, the ceiling being about 6.65 m (over 20 ft) above floor level. As was originally the case in all temples, these halls are very dimly lit: there are no windows and, with the doors closed, light entered only via slots cut in the roof.

At the rear of the second hall the seven barque chapels run across the entire width of the temple, each provided with a large and formally articulated doorway. In each chapel was originally housed a boat-shaped palanquin used, as elsewhere, to carry an image of the relevant deity during the processional rituals. Each chapel is about 12.6 sq. m (135 sq. ft) in area, and has a seemingly vaulted ceiling rising to a total height of 5.80 m (19 ft). Windowless, each chapel was completely dark once its doors were shut.

The central chapel, on the axis of the temple, is Amun-Re's; on the right, or northwest, are the chapels of Osiris, Isis and Horus (in that order) and on the left, or southeast, those of Re-Horakhty, Ptah and the deified Seti himself. Thus, Amun-Re is seemingly assigned primacy, but his symbolic dominance is subtly nuanced. While in a Theban mortuary temple a sanctuary behind the barque chapel celebrated the union of Amun-Re and the king, in Seti's Abydos temple the Osiris Complex – running behind all the barque chapels, and accessible via the chapel of Osiris, not Amun-Re – celebrated the identification of King Seti with Osiris.

The Osiris Complex has a roof-height equivalent to that of the barque chapels, but unlike them is orientated north–south (actually, northwest to southeast) rather than east–west. In the complex, a centrally located columned hall is flanked at each end by components identical to each other in size and overall proportions, but different in plan. On the southeast a small hall fronts three chapels dedicated to the mystery of Osiris' return to potency after his murder and burial. On the northwest, three larger chapels – for Horus, Seti-as-Osiris and Isis – focus on the identification between god and king. Thus, the Osiris Complex as a whole serves to correlate Seti's posthumous reinvigoration with that of Osiris.

The composition of the annexe has already been noted; for the visitor, the most interesting component is the northwestern half, articulated around a T-shaped set of corridors. One, running northwest to southeast – 'the Gallery of the Lists' (of Egypt's kings and many of its deities) – links the annexe to the main temple. The other – at right angles to the Gallery – leads via a stairway to the open area behind the temple. On this second corridor's northwest side are two chapels, for the funerary deity Sokar and another god, Nefertem, emblematic of rebirth. On the second corridor's southeast side the 'Hall of Barques' housed yet another series of boat-shaped palanquins, separate from those contained in the barque chapels of the main temple.

Finally, behind the temple the Osireion and its access tunnel can still be entered by the visitor. The tunnel, running from northwest to southeast, turned to connect with a massively built stone hall, flanked at each end by a long, narrow room. In the hall, a platform surrounded by a trench, apparently intended to be waterfilled, supported huge granite piers. The latter would have carried a thick stone roof that was never completed.[4] Overall, tunnel and Osireion are a variation on the contemporary form of the royal tomb, as found at Thebes, a similarity reinforced when Seti's grandson, pharaoh Merenptah (c. 1213–1204 BC), had the tunnel decorated with scenes and texts from books depicting the afterworld, such as were found in the Theban royal tombs.

Nevertheless, as with the Theban temples, the Osireion deviates significantly from the Theban prototype. The Theban tombs of Seti I and his three

17 *View of the Osireion, or the tomb of Seti-as-Osiris, at the temple of Seti I.*

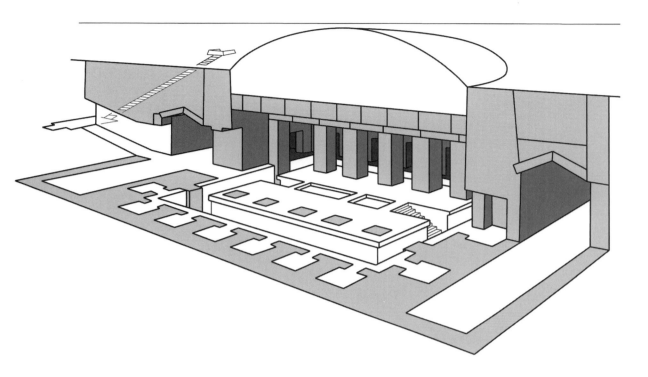

18 *Reconstruction of the Osireion.*

predecessors ran along a single axis, whereas the Osireion, equivalent to the burial chamber in Theban tombs, is at right angles to its access tunnel. Moreover, while the rear chamber in the Osireion corresponds to the area occupied by the sarcophagus in the Theban royal burial chamber, the platform (surrounded by water) is unique to Abydos. It has been suggested it was modelled after the mythical tomb of Osiris himself and, at the least, it seems clear that the Osireion, like the temple, is dedicated to Seti-as-Osiris.

Significant aspects of the plans of both the Osireion and the temple underline the relationship between them. For example, both are L-shaped, and the Osireion's access tunnel is almost exactly the same length as the distance between the temple's pylon and the seven barque chapels, reminding us that both are essentially access routes to a sacred core, i.e. respectively, the barque chapels with the Osiris Complex behind, and the Osireion itself. Moreover, the short 'foot' of the L in both cases (i.e. the Osireion, and the annexe) are almost identical in overall size and proportions, as well as linked in a conceptual way. In the annexe, the cults of Sokar and Nefertem are highlighted, while the burial chamber in a royal tomb (to which the Osireion is an equivalent) was associated with the 'cavern of Sokar' at the heart of the netherworld, and also had scenes celebrating the solar rebirth of the king, an event associated with Nefertem.

19 *View of a hypostyle hall, temple of Seti I.*

The Visual World of the Seti Temple

Understanding the plan of the Seti temple is relatively straightforward, but its visual world is more of a challenge. A 'programme' consisting of scenes and texts endlessly unfolds along the temple's walls, columns and ceilings, so that each hall and chamber is akin to a gallery hung from ceiling to floor with brightly painted scenes. These scenes capture the visitor's attention, but are frustrating in their arcane and often seemingly repetitive subject matter.

To understand and appreciate the complex programme of scenes and texts displayed in Seti's temple we need to realize that this programme has several coexistent and complementary levels of meaning. It records rituals and documents the legitimacy of the cult; it celebrates kingship and its central role in Egyptian life; and finally it is a kind of materialized hymn, manifesting and confirming the wondrous nature of the divine being to whom the temple is dedicated.

The most comprehensive, if in part theoretical analysis of the ritual dimension of the programme is that attempted by Rosalie David.[5] From the ritual perspective, scenes and texts are best described from front to rear, along the path actually followed by the ritualist. Notionally this was the king (the only performer of ritual shown in the programme), in practice usually the temple's chief priest. Many, though not all, of the rituals depicted, however, actually took place in the temple.

Little survives of the scenes and texts of the pylon, and the two courts. Enough exists to show that the programme in the first court depicted the king's victories over foreign enemies, while in the second rituals were depicted and perhaps actually took place. Along both faces of the wall separating the two courts, built and decorated under Ramesses II, are unusual depictions of many of his sons and daughters (he had over 100!) in procession.

In the well-preserved hypostyle hall, scenes of ritual, such as the king making offerings to individual deities, are very common. But other events, remote in time and space from the temple itself, are also depicted. In this way the cycle of

20 *Scene from the temple of Seti I; the kneeling king offers to the enthroned god Horus.*

kingship is repeatedly referred to, as in most temples, in order to affirm that the deities had created an ideal form of governance for humankind, and hence merited the cultic attention this temple exemplified. Relevant scenes include coronation and other ceremonies, and even the processes which brought the king into being. Thus on the southeast wall of the first hall the king's conception within his mother's womb is symbolized by a representation of two gods literally shaping him on a potter's wheel.

Other scenes related more to the ritual and legal correctness of the processes that led to the building of the temple and the maintaining of its cult. Thus on the northeast wall of the first hall (near the north corner) the foundation ceremonies preceding the building of the temple are illustrated, since they were – amongst much else – essential for a temple's legitimacy. Left of the second doorway from the north corner, the king throws white gypsum along the ground to outline the temple's plan, while right of the doorway he interacts with Seshat, the goddess of planning, and above traces out the foundation trenches with a hoe.

Rosalie David has shown that, especially in the second hall, the scores of ritual scenes are actually organized so as to define specific ritual routes relevant to the appropriate deity and leading up to his or her barque chapel. These chapels, in their turn, display on their walls the 'daily service ritual' actually performed in them.

In each chapel, the ritual acts are shown in a sequence. This begins northwest of the doorway, where the first six episodes shown include veneration before the closed chapel, and then the unbolting and opening of its doors. The subsequent series of ritual acts are shown first along the northwest, then along the southeast walls. The penultimate episodes are depicted on the southwest, or rear wall, on either side of a false door that links the temple to the divine world. The final rituals are shown southeast of the doorway, adjacent to the point of exit. The king, as priest, brushes away the traces of his footprints as he leaves, then performs a final purification of the chapel before its doors are again closed. This daily service ritual is analogous to the treatment of an awakened king or nobleman. Like them, the deity's image is cleansed, anointed, dressed, equipped and offered food and drink. But these ritual acts also correspond to the 'coming into being' of the deity, so that he or she literally becomes embodied in the cult statue.

According to Rosalie David's interpretation, the foods, drink and other materials used in the daily service in the barque chapels were then re-allocated as offerings in the 'Ritual of the Royal Ancestors'. This ritual successively involved the barque chapel of Seti I, and – in the annexe – the chapels of Sokar and Nefertem, as well as the Gallery of Lists. In the latter, the chief beneficiaries were a huge number of Egypt's deities (listed on the northeast wall) and all pharaohs before Seti who were considered legitimate (listed on the southwest wall, but excluding 'inappropriate' rulers such as the female pharaoh Hatshepsut and the 'heretic' monotheist king Akhenaten).

Further, sometimes spectacular ritual acts are depicted on the walls of the corridor and stairway set at right angles to the Gallery of the Lists. They include the lassoing of a huge wild bull by Ramesses II and other activities more appropriate to open-air locales than to the temple itself. Rosalie David believes these rituals were traditional and maybe no longer occurred, but it is worth remembering that this corridor led to a vast area behind the temple where some ceremonial form of such rituals could actually have taken place.

The scenes and texts of the Osiris Complex, behind the barque chapels, do not relate to the daily service. Rather, the episodes depicted (many obscure and almost impossible to interpret) celebrate the mysteries of Osiris, including his return to potency after death, embalming and ritual. Indeed, in the central of the three chapels on the southeast Osiris is shown inert on a bier, yet sexually aroused and impregnating Isis, who hovers over him in the form of a bird. The programme of the chapels on the northwest focuses on the 'holy family' produced by these events: Isis; her son by Osiris, Horus; and the rejuvenated Osiris, ruler of the dead, himself. In the central chapel, Osiris and the deified

21 A relief scene in the temple of Seti I showing Ramesses II preparing to lasso a wild bull, assisted by one of his sons, who grasps the bull's tail. The significance of this ritual is uncertain.

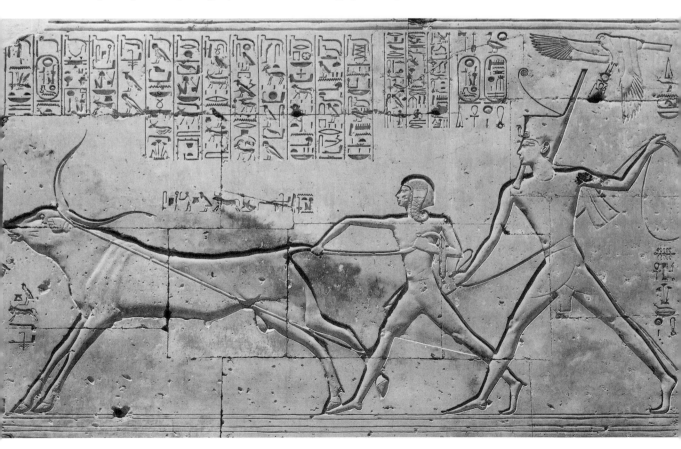

Seti are shown in intimate interaction, emblematic of the being – Seti-as-Osiris – to whom the entire temple was dedicated.

Rosalie David believes that the rituals in the Osiris Complex occurred only once a year and were connected with Osiris' own annual festival. Indeed, it is possible the barque-palanquins of Seti's temple were carried forth to Osiris' temple to join that god in his procession out to Umm el Qa'ab.

So far we have considered the ritual and royal aspects of the programmatically structured scenes and texts of the Seti temple. To understand their ultimate level of meaning, however, we need to completely reverse our perspective on them, i.e. read the meaning of scenes and texts from temple rear to temple front, rather than from front to rear. This is necessary because the primary audience for the programme consisted of the deities themselves, whose statues stood in the rear-lying chapels and sanctuaries.

From this perspective the temple's programme was like an enormous document laid out before the deities, an impression reinforced in the Seti temple by the light-coloured, papyrus-like tones often favoured as the background to the brightly painted hieroglyphs and figures. The purpose of this document was to assure the deities that temple and cult were fully legitimate and effective, and that they could therefore risk the vulnerable process of moving from the divine world into their statues set in the danger-filled world of humankind.

Thus, the depiction of the foundation rituals attested the temple was properly built and a pure place, while the innumerable offering scenes, complemented by texts referring to equipping and endowing the temple, confirmed that its economic basis was both sound and legitimate. Equally reassuring were the repeated depictions of correctly performed and hence effective ritual on the part of the only qualified priest, the king himself.

Moreover, the programme also provided magical protection so that the deities invoked would feel safe from the intrusion of malignant and chaotic forces. Images such as the domination and war scenes on the pylon and in the first court, or the scenes of chaotic natural beings like the wild bull dominated by the pharaoh along the annexe's access corridor, ensured that the vulnerable entry points were protected against penetration by supernatural evil.

I *(opposite) Part of a colossal royal statue from the so-called 'Portal' temple of Ramesses II, assigned to the University of Pennsylvania Museum by the Egyptian authorities in 1969.*

II *(overleaf) View of the façade of the temple of Seti I.*

III *(overleaf) A fecundity figure depicted in the temple of Seti I; arranged in long rows below the major reliefs, such figures represent the abundance bestowed on Egypt by the gods.*

IV *(overleaf) Scene from the temple of Seti I: the kneeling king offers to the enthroned god Horus.*

V *(overleaf) Seti I erecting a Djed pillar in honor of Osiris; relief in the Seti temple.*

II ▲ III ▼

IV

V

Most powerful of all the entire temple, through its form and programme, was a complete microcosm of the macrocosmos. Since the latter's divinely ordained order and processes rendered it invulnerable to chaotic force, so too was its miniaturized version, the temple itself.

Yet the highest and most valued level of the programme's meaning was not protective and reactive, but positive and celebratory. The programme was in effect a materialized hymn of revelation and praise about the deities of the temple. Each was celebrated in its own right, but also as a manifestation of the creator, the sun-god and the cosmic ruler. These identifications were made possible, indeed obligatory, by the statue cult which, in order to empower deities to become embodied in their statues, invoked the tremendous powers of the processes that brought about cosmos (through the creator) and daily renewed and controlled it (through the sun-god and cosmic ruler).

The entire programme is shaped by these beliefs. Like other temples, Seti's was decorated and articulated so as to represent the structure of cosmos (heaven, earth and netherworld) and its divine and human inhabitants. But at the same time the programme was laid out so as to represent the processes that created, renewed and governed that cosmos.

The rearmost units (the Osiris Complex and barque chapels) correspond cosmologically to the formation or re-formation of the deity as it acquires or regains cosmological effectiveness. The hypostyle halls, for their part, represent the cosmos conceptualized by the deity, but not yet vitalized. And the temple's courts correspond to the point at which the deity emerges from the temple as an ascendant sun-god embodying the creator, the cosmos' renewer and the cosmic ruler. As such, he or she transformed the conceptualized cosmos represented within the temple into the vitalized cosmos actually surrounding it – the sky or heaven overhead, the earth stretching off in every direction and the mysterious netherworld below.

Thus the Abydos temple of Seti reflected and documented his ritual transformation into a specific deity, Seti-as-Osiris, but also into those all-powerful beings, the creator, renewer and ruler of cosmos. His immortality achieved through this deification, Seti could indeed believe, as the inscriptions in his temple assured him: 'the deities approach you, you are one of them'.

VI *(opposite) View of a hypostyle hall, temple of Seti I.*

PART II Life Cycle of a Sacred Landscape

CHAPTER FOUR

THE REDISCOVERY OF ABYDOS

Genesis

The rediscovery of Abydos, mentioned in Section III of the Introduction, actually began in far-off Nubia, south of Egypt. Throughout the early 1960s an enormous Nubian salvage campaign took place, coordinated by the Egyptian and Sudanese governments in collaboration with UNESCO. It was prompted by the impending flooding of northern Nubia because of a new dam at Aswan, but the salvage campaign was important to archaeology in Egypt proper as well. For a variety of reasons, excavation by foreign institutions had sharply diminished in Egypt after World War II, but now – to encourage foreign participation in Nubia's salvage – Egypt promised such institutions site concessions in Egypt later. This generous policy has in fact led to much expanded excavations in the country by foreign and Egyptian institutions alike, including those at Abydos.

Moreover, our expedition's original sponsors, the University of Pennsylvania Museum and Yale's Peabody Museum, were well situated to receive an Egyptian concession. Their combined expedition to Nubia, directed by William Kelly Simpson, had been successful and productive while Froelich Rainey, the charismatic director of the University of Pennsylvania Museum, had played an important part in securing support from the United States for the salvage campaign in general. Moreover, Kelly Simpson and Rainey secured a substantial US government grant for their Nubian expedition, and its remaining balance could be used to fund excavation in Egypt proper.

For my part, I too was in Nubia (1961–63), participating in two major projects of the Egypt Exploration Society of the United Kingdom. Directed respectively by Bryan Emery (University College London) and Harry Smith (Cambridge University), these projects were a demanding but exciting introduction to Nile Valley archaeology, and provided me with skills and insights I would apply to our work at Abydos. Emery's excavation of a vast Middle Kingdom Egyptian fortress at Buhen demonstrated for me how a large site could be explored comprehensively yet selectively, if a long-term commitment

22 Reis Ibrahim at Abydos.

was made to the process. Smith's survey of Egyptian Nubia provided me with invaluable experience in locating and mapping (often very slight) surface archaeology and showed me that such archaeology alone could reveal much of a site's history, as well as providing guidance for actual excavation.

Nubia also contributed to my as-yet-unanticipated connection to Abydos in a more specific way, for while in Nubia I was interviewed by Rainey for a position in the University Museum. I met him on the deck of a houseboat moored close to the feet of the four stupendous colossi of Ramesses II fronting the temple of Abu Simbel, a setting so overwhelming I have never been able to recall a word of the discussion! In the event I was appointed, with the understanding that I would seek a site in Egypt for the Pennsylvania-Yale Expedition.

My recommendation of Abydos, after an extensive field survey of many sites, was accepted. Kelly Simpson in particular was enthusiastic; his wide range of interests includes major and unique cult activities at Abydos during the Middle Kingdom.

My reasons for recommending Abydos were several. The site still had enormous archaeological potential, despite much earlier work. From a methodological perspective in which any site is seen as paradigmatic of larger processes involving much of Egypt and its ancient society as a whole, Abydos was of special interest. It combined in an almost unique way the characteristics of both major national and regional centres, and hence promised increased insight into both levels of state and society. Moreover, sites like Abydos, remote from those in and around national centres such as Memphis, Thebes and Tell el-Amarna, had rarely received the comprehensive and long-term archaeological attention we intended to give, although this is less true today, when sites such as Tell el-Da'aba and Elephantine are subject to the same kind of approach.

Of course, Abydos, as a complex site with a long history, was also of great intrinsic, as well as paradigmatic, interest. In both regards, I was convinced after reviewing the publications of earlier excavators and comparing them to the in situ field situation in each case that even already excavated areas were likely to yield a wealth of new information. This prediction has been amply confirmed by several of our projects, as well as by Günter Dreyer's excavations at Umm el Qa'ab.

Expanding Horizons

With permission from the Egyptian Antiquities Organization (now the Supreme Council for Antiquities) we began work in 1967. The earliest seasons were especially hectic, in part because I still had much to learn as an expedition co-director. These earlier initiatives, however, were much strengthened by the participation of Kelly Simpson, and of Barry Kemp (Cambridge University), then at the outset of his distinguished career.

An immediate need was for an appropriate 'dig house', for the local villages did not have accommodation suitable for the residential, work and storage requirements of a large expedition, and earlier dig houses at Abydos rarely

23 *William Kelly Simpson at Abydos.*

survived. Petrie in fact demolished his once his work was over: the wooden elements became cases for antiquities and the mud bricks were resold to the villagers who had supplied them!

One dig house had endured. Built by John Garstang early in the 20th century it had been an imposing structure. An early photograph shows a broad façade with a central tower from which the Union Jack flies, with Garstang in front (in plus-fours) playing 'desert golf'. Used by later excavators, and then by Amice Calverly while she and her associates recorded the Seti temple reliefs, the house had unfortunately fallen into ruin by the 1960s.

Nevertheless, the location at least was approved for modern construction by the Antiquities Organization and we therefore demolished the ruins and built a replacement – constructed of local materials by local craftsmen – which has served us well. Relatively simple, the house has been affectionately regarded by its numerous inhabitants over the years, although its identity has proved fluid. Often it is locally called 'the American House'; for a brief period when Umm Seti and I were out of sorts with each other, she identified it to all and sundry as 'O'Connor's Kremlin'; and sometimes local people refer to it as 'the Sheiks' Tombs'. Both this latter designation and Umm Seti's were inspired by the high corbel vault over each bedroom, reminiscent of the shrines built over holy men's tombs throughout the Egyptian countryside, and of the Kremlin's domes.

Equally important for our success has been the collaboration of the local Supreme Council of Antiquities (formerly the Antiquitites Organization) officials, who have provided many facilities and solved many logistical and

24 *The Pennsylvania-Yale-Institute of Fine Arts, New York University expedition house at Abydos in 2002. The house has much expanded to accommodate the increasing number of affiliated excavation projects at Abydos.*

administrative problems for the expedition. In these propitious circumstances the expedition's activities have both expanded and intensified over the years, particularly as our cohort of younger project directors developed. From 1967 to 1969 my own work focused on the environs of the ancient town in the north corner of Abydos. A tense security situation in Egypt prevented activity at Abydos through the early 1970s, but our excavations resumed in 1977. Thereafter, my interests have been divided between the town and temple site

25 *Excavations at Abydos; the site of the First Intermediate Period town, 1979. In the background, behind the date palms, is the village of Beni Mansur.*

26 *The Last Supper at Abydos, with apologies to Leonardo da Vinci. This light-hearted moment includes several future project directors at Abydos: third from right, Stephen Harvey; centre, Matthew Adams; fourth from left, David Anderson; second from left, Josef Wegner.*

and the great royal mortuary cult enclosures of the 1st and 2nd Dynasties nearby. Kelly Simpson has concentrated upon publishing inscriptional material produced by earlier work and our own, in the form of two major monographs,[1] while my colleague at the University of Pennsylvania Museum, David Silverman, has recorded and studied the epigraphic aspects of an important temple of Ramesses II adjacent to the town.

The development of newer projects, much expanding our coverage of Abydos, is due to our younger project directors, whose work I will list here, and discuss in more detail below. In 1982–83 Diana Patch carried out the first thorough archaeological survey of the Abydos region, for a distance of 20 km (12.4 miles), respectively north and south. Such regional surveys had rarely been attempted in Egypt until more recent times. In 1986, Janet Richards initiated her continuing survey, excavation and analysis of the enormous North and (since 1997) Middle cemeteries, the latter sponsored by the University

27 *Janet Richards excavating the shaft of an Old Kingdom tomb in the Middle Cemetery.*

of Michigan. These formerly sporadically and often superficially excavated cemeteries have now become the basis for one of the most sophisticated applications of current theory and practice concerning mortuary archaeology extant in the Nile Valley.

Several other important projects began slightly later. In 1991 Matthew Adams developed a much-expanded excavational programme at the ancient town and temple site that has provided extraordinary insight into the urban process in Early Bronze Age Egypt, during the Old Kingdom and First Intermediate periods (c. 2675–1980 BC). Stephen Harvey began his excavations at the mysterious pyramid complex of Ahmose in 1993, and has already made discoveries that not only enhance our understanding of this unique monument, but have also revolutionized the history of narrative art in Egypt. His work was subsequently sponsored by the Institute of Egyptian Art and Archaeology of Memphis State University, Tennessee, and later by the Oriental Institute of the University of Chicago. In 1994 Josef Wegner embarked on the re-excavation of the valley temple of Senwosret III, the basic form and nature of which has become much more intelligible as a result. In addition, Wegner's work on a nearby town that served the ritual, administrative and economic needs of the cult is, along with comparable excavations at Elephantine and Tell el-Da'aba, opening up new perspectives on urbanism in Middle Kingdom Egypt. Wegner's work is now sponsored by the University of Pennsylvania Museum.

Since 1996, Mary-Ann Pouls Wegner of the University of Toronto has undertaken the comprehensive survey, excavation and analysis of the major cultic zone providing the interface between town and cemetery in North Abydos. She is currently focused on the excavation and analysis of a once superbly decorated small temple dedicated to the famous pharaoh Thutmose III (c. 1479–1425 BC). The temple is unique in plan, and the quality of its reliefs is a good indication of the importance Abydos held for its royal patrons.

Even more recently, Laurel Bestock (now at Brown University) has made intriguing discoveries about the Early Dynastic and later periods in North Abydos, while Michelle Marlar (Institute of Fine Arts, New York University) is revealing much that is new about the Osiris temple itself, the ritual centre of ancient Abydos.

The Expedition is also completing, in collaboration with colleagues at the German Archaeological Institute, Cairo, the first detailed topographical and archaeological map of the 5 sq. km (almost 2 sq. miles) covered by the site of Abydos.

In addition to the projects listed above, David Anderson has commenced excavations (on behalf of the Department of Anthropology of the University of Pittsburgh) at the well known prehistoric site of Mahasna, not far from Abydos, and has already discovered an extraordinary cache of prehistoric figurines; and a major project focused on Paleolithic remains on the Abydos high desert has been initiated by the University Museum and the Anthropology Department of the University of Pennsylvania. The latter project is co-directed

28 *From left: David O'Connor, Mary-Ann Pouls Wegner and Deborah Vischak at the Western Mastaba Early Dynastic Enclosure at Abydos in 1997.*

by Harold Dibble, Deborah Olszewski and Shannon McPherrson. They are studying prehistoric adaptation to the high desert about one million years ago, with particular reference to the dispersal of humans out of Africa into the rest of the Old World. The sites located so far represent virtually intact accumulations across the landscape and probably include habitation sites.

Neither the Seti temple, nor that of Ramesses II nearby, fall within the scope of the Pennsylvania-Yale-Institute of Fine Arts, New York University Expedition's activities, but they have not been neglected in recent years. Peter Kuhlmann[2] has prepared a publication on the Ramesses II temple, while John Baines of Oxford University has added to the epigraphic recording of Seti's temple begun by Amice Calverly. Recently, the University of Pennsylvania Museum has sponsored an on-site survey (directed by Steven Snape, Liverpool University) of the Seti temple's conservation needs, as well as some small-scale excavations. The latter have been followed up by Ahmed Issawy, Bahai Issawy and James Westermann, under the sponsorship of Sohag University in southern Egypt. The Seti I temple project has owed much to the enthusiastic encouragement of Bruce Mainwaring, Chairman Emeritus of the University Museum's Board of Overseers; and while the Pennsylvania-Yale-Institute of Fine Arts, New York University Expedition has been funded via many sources, it is important to note here that Mainwaring's generosity has made possible the crucial mapping of all Abydos.

29 *Excavating the First Intermediate Period town in 1979; house walls and other features are revealed in the units.*

CHAPTER FIVE

THE EVOLUTION OF
A SACRED LANDSCAPE

Abydos and its Landscape

Abydos is best understood as a sacred landscape, as Janet Richards[1] has shown, albeit one with important administrative and economic dimensions as well. The concept of landscape is a complicated one. Archaeologists have found it a powerful tool for the analysis of individual sites, and of sites distributed throughout a region, but often disagree about definitions. As Robert Layton and Peter Ucko[2] point out, landscape needs to be considered both as 'an environment, generally one shaped by human action', and as 'the expression of an idea' of the ways in which ancient peoples read or interpreted landscapes that they used or viewed.

In the case of Abydos then, we need to consider its ecology and topography in relationship to the beliefs, attitudes and activities of the Egyptians. This presents us with two problems: first, the time-span covered in the second half of this book is long (*c.* 2600 BC to AD 500) and excavations have never been exhaustive, so there are many gaps in our knowledge of the site; second, how reliably can we reconstruct the complex and changing meanings that Abydos had for the Egyptians?

In this latter regard, the Egyptologist is better off than the prehistorian, but worse off than the anthropologist. The former may detect, through archaeology, significant patterns of interaction between terrain and society but, since the communities involved were non-literate, the prehistorian must invent (to greater or lesser degrees of plausibility) the ancient meanings ascribed to environments. The anthropologist, however, can directly interrogate living communities, although their responses may involve different perspectives, misunderstandings, and even mendacity and evasion.

Ancient Egyptians cannot be interrogated, but they are by no means mute. A relatively rich textual and art-historical record conveys much about general Egyptian concepts of landscape, as well as (usually rare) reference to the meanings of the environments of specific sites. Such data can be misinterpreted, but they offer significant insight into places like Abydos.

One important general conclusion from such data is that Egyptians interpreted every form of landscape – national, regional and local – as appropriately scaled-down microcosms of the macrocosmos, i.e. the universe as the Egyptians imagined it. This cosmos incorporated heaven, earth and netherworld and can be envisaged, in James Allen's evocative words, as a kind of 'bubble' of air and light within the otherwise unbroken infinity of dark waters.[3] The latter refers to an endless liquidity surrounding the cosmos, a chaotic formlessness that both sought to overwhelm and annihilate cosmic order, yet paradoxically was the very source of the life that energized the universe.

For Egyptians the Nile Valley and its environs comprised a prototypical landscape suffused with intermingled cosmological and societal meaning. River, floodplain, and low and high desert seemed to be a study in contrasts – order versus chaos, life versus lifelessness – yet conceptually they overlapped in important ways. The Egyptians vividly celebrated the life an ever-flowing Nile brought to a rainless land, yet the annual inundation seemed to threaten re-engulfment in the liquidity of chaos. The floodplain supported the Egyptians, so they could reproduce generationally, yet here they experienced also relatively harsh living and working conditions, illness and ageing, and painful break-downs in social order. There was, however, another community dwelling beneath the arid yet life-giving deserts: the dead, magically self-regenerating and free from want and danger.

Above, day and night, sun-filled or star-studded, stretched the vast firmament. Reassuringly it attested the presence of the deities dwelling therein, upon whose benevolence humanity depended. Challengingly, this required reciprocation in cult places on earth, into which the remote deities could be tempted only by immense ritual effort and a substantial investment of resources. Finally, caverns and tombs provided the living with a glimpse into an otherwise inaccessible realm for which they hoped to be destined, an enormous netherworld at the heart of which was Osiris, simultaneously the embalmed source of cosmic, as much as human, regeneration and the enthroned ruler providing nourishment, protection and eternal ease to the countless dead.

Yet like all deities, Osiris also had specific places or 'residences' in the terrestrial realm – for him, Busiris and Abydos – each of which related in meaningful ways to an ever-expanding series of landscapes: its own local one, the regional and national landscapes, and ultimately the cosmos itself. What do we know about Abydos in these regards?

The cosmological dimension has already been described, and the local and regional landscapes will be discussed below. As for the national, Abydos held a paradoxical position, reflective of its seemingly unique status among Egyptian central places. From a narrow historical perspective Abydos was ranked with provincial centres in general, not with the most prestigious cities, and its history seems less varied (and less painful) than many of its peers. From a broader perspective, however, Abydos had a symbolic value and emotional power far exceeding that of most centres, and hence was among the most historically significant of Egyptian cities and towns.

Like most of these significant towns, Abydos was never a national centre or 'royal city' where political life was filled with far-reaching initiatives and continual intrigue, occasionally resulting in the assassination of even a 'god-king' like Amenemhet I (c. 1938–1909 BC) or Ramesses III. Moreover, in itself Abydos had little strategic value in military or economic terms, and did not experience the sieges and sackings that many towns endured during the more turbulent periods of Egyptian history, although its unusual symbolic value may also have rendered it sacrosanct.

Once, some scholars suggest, Abydos did experience some degree of devastation, during a sustained civil war between a northern, Herakleopolitan kingdom and a southern, Theban one in the First Intermediate Period. However, the ravaging shamefacedly admitted on behalf of a Herakleopolitan ruler comprised the plundering of cemeteries in the 8th Southern Egyptian or Thinite nome (the Greek term later applied to Egypt's provinces) in which Abydos lay, and need not necessarily have involved Abydos itself. Of course, it is possible that during times of foreign invasion the towns and even temples of Abydos might have been sacked. In 631 BC, for example, an Assyrian army plundered the great temple of Amun-Re at Thebes, and might have treated other temples similarly, while Egypt's first Persian overlord Cambyses (525– 522 BC) reputedly also plundered some Egyptian temples.

The official status of the Osiris temple at Abydos is impossible to determine for most periods, for – as Alan Gardiner accurately observed – the historical record needed to establish this is 'a collection of rags and tatters',[4] woefully uninformative about most towns, at most periods. Yet, it is striking that the pious rulers of the 20th Dynasty (c. 1190–1075 BC) regarded Abydos' Osiris temple as equivalent not to the great temples of Egypt, but to other provincial temples in terms of land-holdings and royal benefactions. The metropolitan temples of Thebes, Memphis and Heliopolis far outstripped all others in terms of lavish royal gifts and enormous estates supporting their cults and personnel.[5]

Yet even if the Osiris temple's official status was relatively low at some, or even all periods, another database – mortuary texts much richer and better preserved than the historical record – reveal that in the national landscape Abydos had a much higher symbolic value than most centres. Here, its only rival in importance was Heliopolis, the cult centre for Re, the sun-god.

Of course, ideas about Abydos in such mortuary texts (both royal and elite) change and develop over time, but there are also very strong continuities. Perhaps most importantly, although Egyptians hoped to transfer successfully to the afterlife via their locally based mortuary cults, these were seen as equivalent to, and indeed empowered by, a larger process. In this, the dead flowed towards Abydos which, as Osiris' cult centre, provided unique access to both the subterranean and celestial manifestations of the *Duat* or afterlife. Quite literally, the Egyptians believed (according to the *Coffin Texts*), at Abydos they would pass through the portals of Geb, the earth god, into the netherworld and thus be rendered capable of ascending into the night sky, to become identified with the circumpolar or 'imperishable' stars, never setting and hence emblematic of eternal life. At Abydos, the dead were promised, their hearts could be at peace like that of Osiris in the west, i.e. the netherworld, and they would 'ascend to the top of the high hill' and 'travel around the celestial expanses'.

This nationally significant idea about Abydos generated yet another striking image. Entry into the afterlife involved the ritual empowerment of the deceased, but also a judgment as to their individual moral worth (failure here invoked the 'second death' or complete annihilation); moreover, chaotic forces always sought to abort a successful transition from death to eternal life. The difficulty of the process found vivid expression in the notion that the dead swam to Abydos like a great school of fish and in passing into the afterlife had to escape, through moral worth and ritual power, a gigantic net – its floats in heaven, its weights on earth – wielded by the divine 'fishermen of Abydos' to trap those unworthy of entering Osiris' realm.

Abydos and the Osirian cult it housed were also extrapolated onto the national landscape. A whole series of cult centres, primarily dedicated to other deities and extending through Northern and Middle Egypt, were presented as integral elements in the Osiris legend, in both ritual and mythological terms. These centres included Heliopolis, Letopolis and other northern towns, as well as Rosetau (Memphis' cemetery zone), Herakleopolis and nearby Nareref, in Middle Egypt. Each was associated with a very specific component of Osiris' myth, such as his death by drowning, his embalming, the mourning over his body, and the justification of Horus that led to Osiris' full revitalization as a divine ruler. Presumably, each mythic component found ritual expression at the relevant centre, but these centres also formed a kind of assemblage of powers which, in terms of the national landscape, provided both protection and assistance to Osiris in his travail and triumph. Indeed, each dead person, identifying with Osiris, not only sought to reassemble his family and dependents around him, but saw them as distributed in similarly protective and supportive roles among these same cult centres.

These circumstances raise an interesting question. Osiris was venerated at many places, but was Abydos itself *directly* linked, via festival processions, or water-borne progresses, to cult centres elsewhere? This was certainly a feature of some (maybe many) Egyptian cults. For example the annual Valley Festival of Amun-Re at Thebes involved a round trip, from east to west and back, of at least 10 km (6.2 miles), and perhaps much more, while in Ptolemaic times at least, Horus of Edfu paid an annual ceremonial visit to Hathor of Dendereh, a round trip of over 300 km (186 miles).

Moreover, the dead are sometimes described as accompanying Osiris during the ritual trip from Busiris to Abydos, hinting at a processional progress linking the two centres, which are over 550 km (341 miles) apart. In any event, the extension of Osiris over the national landscape is a recurrent theme. Combined with the sun-god (a union the two actually achieved in the netherworld), Osiris was a divine being who was a 'great god in Heliopolis, whose soul is in Busiris, whose dignity is in Herakleopolis and awe of whom is in Abydos'.

Archaeology and the Abydos Landscape

Treating Abydos as an evolving, fundamentally ritual landscape provides us with a comprehensive approach to otherwise very disparate materials and raises issues that can guide further research, as Janet Richards has shown. It is also important to realize that Abydos is in significant ways a paradigmatic site, where we are able to explore archaeological remains that reflect broader, Egypt-wide phenomena. For example, from Abydos we can learn much about types of temples extant in different periods, and about religious practices in and around temples. Moreover, careful excavation and analysis of both mortuary and settlement remains at Abydos is already enriching our understanding of societal complexity and urbanism over the entire span of Bronze Age Egypt, from c. 3000 to 1000 BC, and providing alternatives to some of the current thinking about these issues.

Abydos' local landscape gains some of its meaning from the broader, regional one. Abydos lay in the 8th Southern Egyptian or Thinite nome, or province. Diana Patch's 1982–83 survey of most of its mortuary remains, on the low desert, indicated that the province had a number of diffuse and relatively small settlements in prehistoric times, but by c. 3000 BC and thereafter displayed a much more nucleated settlement pattern. As Patch observes: 'By the late Old Kingdom, when state-level society is clearly established, the Abydos-Thinis region has a settlement pattern whose complexity matches the central government's requirements for a province.'[6] The archaeological prominence of Thinis, the capital (over 17 km or 10.5 miles northwest of Abydos), and Abydos indicate they were probably the dominant towns. At least six others, however, are textually attested by the New Kingdom, one going back as far as the Old Kingdom.

The Thinite province was relatively wealthy, but given the strong links between government and economic exploitation the benefit was more likely to have accrued to Thinis than Abydos. Diana Patch suggests that timber and cattle were especially important products and there were close links with western desert oases, via which trade goods from Nubia flowed and which provided products of their own.

Osiris did not dominate the province's cults. Around Thinis, the tutelary deities were Onuris and his lioness consort Mehyet, while Khnum may have had a cult centre in the southern part of the province. The capacity for regional deities to flourish in the vicinity of a deity of national importance is indicative of the deep local roots underlying the Egyptian religious system.

For Abydos itself, the initial cultic, societal and economic dynamics shaping the landscape were generated by the Early Dynastic royal tombs and the ritual and other services they required (see Part III). In the Old Kingdom royal burials were far away, in the north, and yet Abydos continued to flourish, perhaps because Osiris' cult and its annual festival were already established there and created a fresh source of national interest and economic benefit. The Pyramid Texts on contemporary royal burial chamber walls firmly locate the episodes of Osiris' myth (later re-enacted in his festival) at Abydos and the Thinite province, while the *neshmet* barque – the type of boat-palanquin peculiar to Osiris – is referred to at Abydos (in a person's name) at this time.

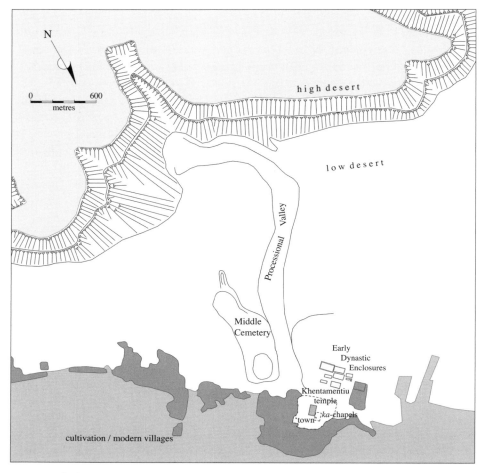

30 *Map of Abydos in the Old Kingdom and First Intermediate Period.*

As far as the Old Kingdom is concerned, the evidence from the temple and town at Abydos' north corner is complex and ambiguous (and will be discussed further below); evidence from the contiguous cemeteries, however, is more clear-cut. A small elite cemetery of the 4th Dynasty lay northwest of the town, while during the 5th and 6th Dynasties another one spread over a high desert eminence near the town's south corner. The latter (the Middle Cemetery) was exceptionally large; some individual excavations revealed literally hundreds of graves, while its highest ground was occupied by especially important tombs. Ransacked, then neglected since Mariette's day, these important tombs are being exhaustively re-excavated by Janet Richards who is also, through survey and excavation, bringing the entire Middle Cemetery into clearer historical perspective.

The elite burials in the Middle Cemetery included a large number of unusually prestigious officials, forming a markedly heterogeneous group unlike the more homogenous cohorts of hierarchically ranked local officials typical of a provincial cemetery. Indeed, the governors of the Thinite nome – the leaders of local society – were not buried here, either being excluded or preferring the protection of the deity of the provincial capital. Middle Cemetery burials included members of the central or national government, such as Weni, the Overseer of Southern Egypt, and Djau, a vizier or prime minister, who was very well connected (of Thinite origin, his two sisters married King Pepi I, and were, respectively, mothers of kings Merenre and Pepi II). Others buried here also had prestigious titles – including vizier – but may have been provincial officials (not necessarily from Thinis) of the highest rank. For all of them, burial at Abydos seems especially desirable, since several include in their mortuary texts unusual phrases specifically referring to the boon of having 'a tomb chamber in Abydos'.

The presence of these officials therefore suggests an unusual, extra-regional interest in Abydos at this time; while the hundreds of lower-order tombs may reflect the substantial service population required to build and equip elite and other tombs, and service temple and mortuary cults. Janet Richards has found that the elite tombs of the Middle Cemetery apparently retained significance for an extraordinarily long time. Some had Middle Kingdom votive chapels in their vicinity; and later large tombs of the Saite Period (664–525 BC) were situated around them so carefully as to suggest the earlier tombs were still considered prestigious and important.

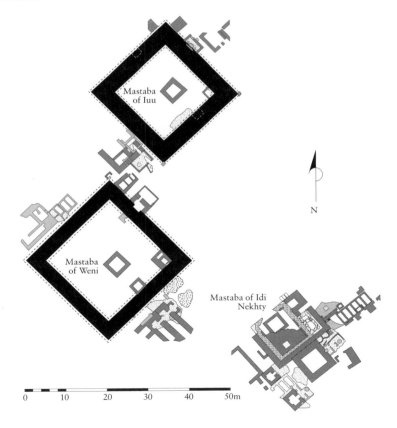

31 *Map of the mastabas of Weni and others in the Middle Cemetery, Abydos.*

Recently, Janet Richards, on behalf of the University of Michigan, has made a spectacular discovery in the Middle Cemetery. Mariette located the tomb of Weni 140 years ago, removing various inscribed and decorated elements from its chapel. These included Weni's long autobiography, for which he is famous amongst Egyptologists. Carved upon a monolithic limestone slab, the autobiography described Weni's career and listed impressive gifts for his tomb supplied by King Pepi I (6th Dynasty) – a great limestone sarcophagus from the Turah quarries near Memphis – as well as 'its lid, a doorway, lintel, two door-jambs, and a libation table', most of which were actually recovered by Mariette. However, he did not provide details about the specific archaeological context, and the tomb itself soon became unidentifiable.

Through meticulous excavation, Janet Richards relocated Weni's tomb in 1999. Its mud-brick superstructure or 'mastaba' occupies 841 sq. m (9,049 sq. ft) and was over 5.5 m (18 ft) high. Richards was able to identify the precise contexts for the items removed by Mariette, and discovered much important additional inscribed and decorated material that his workmen had overlooked. Moreover, in a 'serdab' or chamber originally hidden within the sand filling of the hollow superstructure, she discovered a masterpiece: a beautifully carved

32 *The chapel of the 4th Dynasty official Weni, discovered in the Middle Cemetery by Mariette and re-located and re-excavated by Janet Richards. In front is a courtyard, with the once-roofed chapel behind, abutting the tomb superstructure or mastaba. Many items and inscriptions had been removed by Mariette, but a surprising number of the decorated limestone slabs lining the chapel had survived.*

33 (left) Statue of Weni. The brick-walled superstructure or mastaba of Weni's tomb had been filled solid; concealed within it was a hidden chamber, or serdab, once containing at least 30 statues; most were wood and little survived, but a superb limestone example depicted Weni as a child. Tomb statues sometimes depict their owners at different stages of their life, but this particular statue may refer to Weni's anticipated 'rebirth' in the afterlife.

34 (right) A representation from a corner pillar from the mastaba of Iuu. It shows Weni the Elder (on a smaller scale) venerating his father, the vizier Iuu.

statue representing Weni as a child, perhaps with reference to his anticipated 'rebirth' via burial and mortuary ritual. Finally, in 2001, Richards found the most important of Weni's royal gifts, the great sarcophagus itself, still lodged within the burial chamber. Once again, Abydos manifests its incredible historical and archaeological richness, despite some 150 years of excavations. Richards has established that Weni's father was the vizier Iuu, a position she found Weni himself achieved near the end of his career. Moreover, excavation and magnetic (sub-surface) survey has revealed a societally significant pattern: Weni's tomb and a few others of similar size form a prestigious core, from which many smaller graves 'radiated out initially in neat rows … communicating a controlled pattern of growth and hierarchy'.[7] The rich array of skeletal and mummified materials from here and elsewhere in North Abydos is being studied by Brenda Baker of the Department of Anthropology of Arizona State University.

For the Old Kingdom and First Intermediate Period, the evidence of the town and temple site, while problematical, contributes excitingly to current debates about urbanism and the status of temples throughout Egypt in these periods. Today, the town site is much denuded, but still has great potential for illuminating major aspects of Egyptian society and culture in the later 3rd millennium BC. According to surviving remains, such as a dense bed of sherds overlying the site (left as a result of the removal of nitrogen-rich occupational debris by farmers or *sebakhin* for use as fertilizer), there was once a substantial town mound, with significant strata of the Middle, and maybe New Kingdoms, as well as of the Third Intermediate and later periods, into Roman times. Except for an unusually elevated area in the west, all have been stripped away, but everywhere, below modern ground level, are relatively undisturbed strata and building levels extending from the First Intermediate Period back into prehistoric times. This accessibility makes Abydos one of the most potentially important of known sites for the history of early urbanism in Egypt.

Early excavations by Petrie, together with nearby unexcavated surface remains, clearly, if approximately, fix the town's cultic centre, for probably all periods. Here, material later than the 3rd millennium survived because in Egypt cultic areas, while often rebuilt, retained a ground level lower than the town mound rising around them. Thus Petrie was able to reveal a series of superimposed (and, in each case, relatively denuded) cult structures. These begin in the Old Kingdom, extend through the Middle and New Kingdoms, and conclude with one for pharaoh Amasis (570–526 BC) of the 26th Dynasty. Immediately adjacent, on the southeast, are the unexcavated remains of a large, stone-built temple dedicated presumably to Osiris by pharaoh Nectanebo I (381–362 BC), a date recently confirmed by the excavations of Michelle Marlar.

Cult structures and temple are the focus of a lively debate, the significance of which extends well beyond Abydos. The superimposed cult structures, which are relatively informal and irregular in appearance, are often thought to signify,

35 The temple and town site (Kom el Sultan) at the northern corner of Abydos. The pool is the depression created by Petrie's early excavations here; his spoil heap is evident on the right.

or incorporate, the actual temple of Osiris (or Khentamentiu) at the various periods represented. Barry Kemp, for example, has proposed a general theory that provincial temples would often have been modest and informal during the Old Kingdom, and only gradually replaced by larger, more formal ones in the Middle Kingdom. Moreover, in an important archaeological reanalysis of Petrie's data[8], he further suggested that Abydos' Osiris temple complex (as attested by Petrie's cult structures) retained this informal character into the New Kingdom and beyond, because 'the full wealth of the Egyptian state was reserved not for these essentially "popular" centres of worship and pilgrimage, but for those temples which honoured Osiris in the form of the lately deceased king' (e.g. at the Senwosret III, Ahmose and Seti I monuments of Abydos).

However, I and others consider that an equally probable alternative (in terms of currently available evidence) is that Petrie's cult structures comprise not a temple complex, but rather royal *ka*-chapels from the Old and Middle Kingdoms, and their equivalents from the New Kingdom (and presumably for Amasis also). Royal *ka*-chapels were independent structures, set up near temples. They housed statues of kings (and others favoured by them) so that the life forces of the individuals represented could receive, through 'redistribution', offerings presented initially to the deity of the nearby temple. The sizes and plans of Petrie's structures are appropriate for such *ka*-chapels; and not only are Old Kingdom royal *ka*-chapels inscriptionally attested to Abydos, but one of Petrie's structures (early Middle Kingdom) was actually labelled as such, on a plaque from its foundation deposit.

Thus the Khentamentiu or Osiris temple, successively razed and rebuilt over the millennia, may actually lie under or near the Nectanebo temple, a possibility now being explored by Michelle Marlar. If sufficient material remains (temple foundations can be deep and remove the traces of earlier ones), even

36 *A map of the Old Kingdom and First Intermediate Period remains at the temple and town site (Kom el Sultan) at the northern corner of Abydos; the cult buildings/ka chapels are the structures excavated by Petrie and thought to include the temple of Khentamentiu, but the latter's remains may lie under the site of the Late Period temple, which is currently under excavation.*

OK Large Building

OK Cult Buildings/ *ka*-chapels

OK Enclosure wall

Late Period Temple of Osiris

OK/FIP Large Building

N

Faience production area

OK/FIP Houses 1991 excavations

0   100m

37 *Excavating the First Intermediate Period town in* 1991.

the Old Kingdom temple may prove to be comparatively impressive. Dieter Arnold has recently suggested that a few provincial temples of this period may have had 'monumental proportions, matching or even outshining the royal mortuary temples' attached to the pyramids of Giza, Saqqara and elsewhere.[9]

The town surrounding the temple in the First Intermediate Period and earlier is an extraordinarily rich source on early urbanism, as excavations by myself and – on a much expanded scale – Matthew Adams, have shown. Settlement sites of any period are rarely excavated in Egypt, and published evidence on Old Kingdom and First Intermediate Period urbanism is mostly restricted to 'pyramid towns'. Attached to, or developing near pyramids, these are specialized in function and hardly representative of urbanism or settlement types as a whole.

Visible town remains in North Abydos cover about 8 ha (almost 20 acres), but may continue for a considerable distance under adjoining modern villages. For example, recently a very extensive Old Kingdom settlement was located under a modern town at the foot of the Giza pyramids. So far, we have excavated only a small part (*c.* 1,000 sq. m or 10,760 sq. ft) of the Abydos town, but the results have been almost overwhelming in terms of good preservation of the great societal complexity revealed, as well as a wide range of other materials.

38 *Burials of young children and even infants are a feature of the First Intermediate Period town. Here two children, one much younger than the other, are found buried under a corridor floor.*

Matthew Adams' meticulous excavations were combined with close study of a multitude of complex microstratigraphies, as well as full recovery of all artifacts and large-scale sampling of debitage, and faunal and botanical remains. His ongoing research is reflected in the following information, supplemented by some observations of my own.

Adams has identified all or parts of nine houses, nearly all built at about the same time, early in the First Intermediate Period, and continuing in use into the early Middle Kingdom – an impressive span of over a century. The functions of many parts of these houses (bread-baking, animal-penning, workstations, etc.) can be identified with a specificity rare in Egyptian archaeology. Here, however, I would like to focus on the issues of societal complexity and historical significance.

39 *Plan of the excavated (1979, 1991) area of the First Intermediate Period town. Nine individual buildings or houses have been identified. Despite much variety in size and internal plan, the regularity of the layout is evident in the similar orientation of each house.*

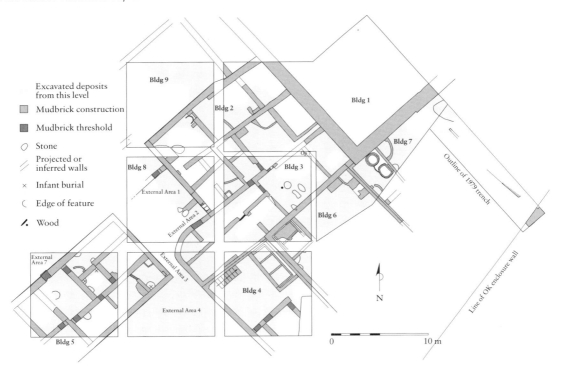

Unlike some pyramid towns, the houses are not laid out according to a regular and highly repetitive pattern. Built of mud brick, the houses are densely packed together, many sharing party walls, with communication via narrow, irregular, almost alley-like streets. Some houses are rectilinear in outline, others much less so. Internal plans are complex, second storeys may have existed in some cases, and an open court was usual. In two cases the court contained excessively large granaries, suggesting that the households were engaged in entrepreneurial grain-trading, or were responsible (perhaps administratively) for supplying lower-order households in the vicinity.

The houses were built around the south corner of a large enclosed area of perhaps 1,000–1,400 sq. m (10,760–15,064 sq. ft). Its interior is occupied by habitations, of a possibly more formal character than elsewhere. The other houses are divisible into groups averaging 190 sq. m (2,044.4 sq. ft) and 160 sq. m (1,721.6 sq. ft) in area (estimates, since only two houses have been fully revealed), while the smallest house covered 89 sq. m (957.6 sq. ft) and was later subdivided into two separate components. This societal complexity probably extended throughout the town, except for administrative, storage and industrial areas. Adams has also begun to expose one of the best-preserved faience manufactories ever located in Egypt. Faience, an artificial composition, was much used for beads, amulets, figurines and small containers, and the manufactory's proximity to the temple area suggests they were made here as votive objects, or items the pious could take away.

Inscriptional evidence from Abydos indicates a complex community corresponding to the archaeology just described. There was a hierarchy of priests and administrators for the temple of Khentamentiu, and a large service population, including servants, artisans and agriculturists, is to be expected.

Historically, as Adams has emphasized, these urban remains are important because they belong to what seems a highly disturbed period, yet no deterioration in living conditions is to be seen, and materials were imported from other parts of southern Egypt. It may well be that the wars and political conflicts that impressed the elite in the First Intermediate Period had little direct impact on most communities, although it is possible Abydos had an unusually sacrosanct status. Several houses were involved in a widespread and most likely accidental conflagration, akin to those occurring in Abydos' closely packed villages today, where the spread of fire is inhibited by the municipal fire brigade – a convenience not enjoyed by the ancient Abydenes!

The appearance of the town and temple in Abydos' north corner, towards c. 2000 BC, could then be sketched as follows. The picture is necessarily hypothetical, but relates to the archaeology described above, as well as other archaeological data discussed by others, especially Barry Kemp in his important 1977 article.[10]

According to the interpretation I prefer, a large, brick-walled enclosure, occupying perhaps 3.6 ha (almost 9 acres) had as a centrally located feature a temple of significant, if as yet unknown, proportions. It is likely that the temple

40 *Details of the First Intermediate Period urban architecture at Abydos; the circular features are granaries.*

had a large courtyard in front, and may have had its own defining enclosure wall. The north quadrant of the larger enclosure was occupied by a cluster of royal *ka*-chapels, themselves walled off and provided with their own entrance and exit, though they were perhaps also connected to a relatively open area in front of the temple. The nature of the west quadrant of the enclosed space is unknown, but southeast of the temple was a densely packed zone of houses. All the residential and service areas may have been directly connected to the temple, its cult, administration and material needs.

Northwest of the temple precinct, as reconstructed above, was another walled area, which extended along the northeast side of the temple enclosure as well. Almost completely unexcavated, this area's most conspicuous feature is a massive brick structure that was in existence in the Old Kingdom and has been exposed by the activities of the sebakhin. It could be interpreted as a storage unit, an administrative headquarters (for the town, rather than the temple as such) or both.

The entities described cover an area of roughly 6 ha (14.8 acres), and might comprise the greater part of the ancient town. Yet their seemingly specialized functions, and the large population implied by the cemetery, suggest that further urban remains might have extended to the northeast, running under the floodplain, and await identification through coring and selective excavation.

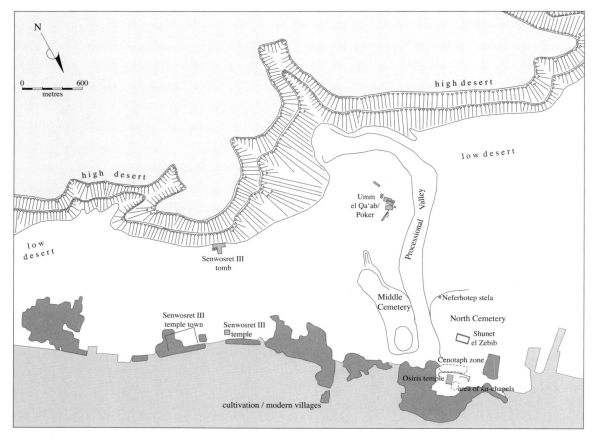

N

0   600
metres

high desert

high desert

low desert

low desert

Umm
el Qaʿab/
Poker

Senwosret III
tomb

Processional Valley

Middle
Cemetery

○ Neferhotep stela

North Cemetery

Senwosret III
temple town

Senwosret III
temple

Shunet
el Zebib

Cenotaph zone

Osiris temple

area of ka-chapels

cultivation / modern villages

41 *Map of Middle Kingdom Abydos.*

CHAPTER SIX

THE EXPANDING LANDSCAPE OF THE MIDDLE KINGDOM

Royal and Private Cult in Middle Kingdom Abydos

The landscape of Abydos was completed in the 2nd millennium BC, in the sense that the site's monuments and other structures experienced their greatest dispersion over the terrain at this time. Significant additions and modifications were later set within this 2nd millennium landscape. This expansion requires us to think about Abydos' landscape in some kind of structured way. Umm el Qa'ab and the town and temple site at Abydos' north corner define the core area, with the town, its environs and adjacent cemeteries representing a more intensively developing inner core. Expansion took the form of partial radii moving over time towards the southeast. The first is marked by the Senwosret III complex, the second and last by pharaoh Ahmose's. The Seti temple (and that of Ramesses II) can therefore be seen as a return to the core area, or as the ultimate expansion of the inner core.

Abydos' history is particularly rich and intriguing during the Middle Kingdom – later 11th Dynasty (c. 2060–1938 BC), 12th Dynasty (c. 1938–1759 BC), and early 13th Dynasty (c. 1759–1700 BC). Moreover, thanks to studies by William Kelly Simpson,[1] we have been provided with fascinating glimpses of the administrative and economic life of the Thinite province (to which Abydos belonged) in this period. The unusual documents involved are all administrative records on papyrus and were discovered near Thinis itself. One set of records relates to the building of a temple, perhaps at Abydos itself, although Kelly Simpson thinks Coptos more likely. Other documents concern the workshop of a royal dockyard at Thinis, and indicate the incessant traffic travelling along the river (serving Abydos, like other major sites); while yet others relate to agricultural and building activities, again including a temple, now perhaps at Thinis. All these remind us that Abydos was part of a far-flung web of relationships throughout its province and beyond.

As for Middle Kingdom Abydos itself, relevant inscriptional and archaeological data are extant, and more will be recovered in the future; however, major issues still await resolution. For example, the inner core shows an intermingling of royal, elite and 'popular' piety that seems to many scholars to be uniquely generated by Osiris' cult, yet similar patterns may have existed at other, less well-explored provincial centres. Does Abydos in this regard display a prevalent pattern but on an unusually large scale? At the same time, the Senwosret III mortuary cult complex indicates that a specifically royal area, ritually linked to Osiris' cult yet located far from the piety of the core, was considered desirable. This seems not to be represented at any other provincial centre.

Focusing first on the core area, it is likely the Old Kingdom temple survived through the First Intermediate Period without being rebuilt, since such royal initiatives were rarely undertaken during this period of internal political fragmentation. Egypt was finally reunited by the Theban ruler Nebhepetre Mentuhotep. He and his successor Sankhkare Mentuhotep both built what I would interpret as royal *ka*-chapels (Sankhkare Mentuhotep's was specifically labelled as such) in the vicinity of what was now called – in Nebhepetre Mentuhotep's chapel – the 'temple of Osiris Khentamentiu'. This subtly changing terminology for what was still essentially the Old Kingdom temple is again suggestive of the long-standing relationship, and even identification, between the two deities.

Soon after the 12th Dynasty began, however, the old temple was razed and an entirely new one built in its place. Several stelae set up for officials of Senwosret I (*c.* 1919–1875 BC) refer obliquely to this event, the reality of which was confirmed later by an official of the 13th Dynasty king Khendjer (absolute dates uncertain) who recorded that he cleansed the temple of Osiris Khentamentiu 'on the outside and on the inside' and had his painters and plasterers renew the scenes originally carved under 'King Kheperkare [Senwosret I]'.

One might guess then that while the Abydos temple may have been rebuilt once in the Old Kingdom (perhaps in the 5th or 6th Dynasty), and again at the outset of the 12th Dynasty, it then survived unscathed until the early 18th Dynasty, at which time it was most likely razed and rebuilt again. This would be a typical pattern for Egyptian provincial and other temples that were dedicated to a god or goddess. Rebuilding a temple was possible, and evidently at the appropriate moment desirable, especially at times (such as during the early 12th and 18th Dynasties) when there was a strong sense of national renewal after extended periods of disunity and internal conflict.

Nevertheless, it was no light matter to intrude so drastically on the earthly dwelling place of a deity, and so complete rebuildings were relatively rare. Rather, kings, their officials and others concentrated on building additions to temples, replacing cult equipment, adding further income-producing endowments, and periodically undertaking major renovations. Temples could become dilapidated, unauthorized structures could intrude upon them and their precinct, and as the town mound rose around them (for temple precincts maintained a relatively low ground level) other problems ensued. Thus, the female pharaoh Hatshepsut (*c.* 1473–1458 BC) observed that the chief temple of the important provincial town of Cusae (modern Kis) had begun to fall into ruin; its sanctuary was being swallowed up by the rising ground level around it, which also meant that houses, inappropriately located, were so close and at such an elevated level that children could play upon the temple roof!

Given its national significance, it was not likely that the Abydos temple of Osiris would have experienced this degree of neglect. Sporadic inscriptional evidence suggests that throughout the 12th and earlier 13th Dynasties, officials acting on the king's behalf periodically had new images and *neshmet* barques made; renewed and expanded the offerings presented to Osiris and others according to a regular schedule; refurbished chapels set up for various deities within Osiris' temple; and even 'renewed' the 'great altar of cedar wood' that stood before the god Osiris himself.

Incomplete examples of royal statuary and fragments of inscribed and decorated architectural elements recovered from the precinct of Osiris' temple at Abydos also attest to the activity of rulers such as Senwosret I, Senwosret II, Amenemhet III and, in the 13th Dynasty, the kings Neferhotep I, Khendjer and Khaneferre Sobekhotep IV. However, these items could have come from any or all of three types of structures: the temple itself, which was demolished early in the New Kingdom and its Middle Kingdom masonry and statuary dispersed and reused; cult buildings complementary in some way to the temple; and, as before, royal *ka*-chapels probably clustered near the north corner of the temple. The latter unfortunately seem to have been completely demolished – probably because they were at the time still standing, maybe even functioning structures – in order to make room for similar chapels dedicated to New Kingdom pharaohs.

Most of the architectural fragments recovered by Petrie and others are therefore ambiguous as to the type of structure they came from. Yet, colossal royal statues in red granite depicting kings Senwosret I and Senwosret III in Osirian form are on a scale commensurate with a temple, rather than a *ka*-chapel or other subordinate structure – some were 4 m (13 ft) high. Originally, they were probably arranged around the sides of the temple court.

The Middle Kingdom temple of Osiris at Abydos then was probably a relatively large, imposing and richly equipped building. As such, it was in startling contrast to the other major focus for Osiris' cult at Abydos at this time, the ancient royal cemetery at Umm el Qa'ab, far out in the desert to the south.

By the Middle Kingdom, almost 800 years after the latest royal tomb was built there, Umm el Qa'ab would have seemed a rather desolate site. The 1st and 2nd Dynasty tombs had been plundered early, so now the site was characterized by large sand-filled depressions, spoil heaps on the surface and increasing amounts of wind-deposited sand. It was still considered a very ancient, indeed primeval, royal cemetery.

In the Middle Kingdom, probably all of the early tombs were re-excavated and one tomb (King Djer's) was re-roofed and provided with an access stairway, being evidently regarded as Osiris' own 'tomb'. This is proven by an impressive basalt statue representing the recumbent Osiris impregnating

42 *The late Middle Kingdom representation of Osiris placed in his supposed tomb at Umm el Qaʿab, the royal cemetery of the 1st and 2nd Dynasties. This statue was found in the tomb, and presumably was used for cult purposes well into the Late Period at least. The statue represents the inert Osiris impregnating his consort Isis, who has taken on the form of a kite.*

the bird-shaped Isis, and dedicated by the 13th Dynasty king Khendjer, which Amélineau found in Djer's tomb.

Unfortunately, although the episodes described for the 12th Dynasty festival of Osiris involve ritual movement through a landscape, which includes named places, these data in themselves do not prove that the association of Umm el Qaʿab with Osiris' tomb goes back to the beginning of the Middle Kingdom. As described, the mythical landscape involved might have been ritually traced out in and around the temple itself.

More significant is, first, the fact that a substantial stone offering-table dedicated to Sankhkare Mentuhotep (11th Dynasty) by Senwosret I was recovered (not in situ) at Umm el Qaʿab, indicating cult activity there at this time; and, second, that the lower end of the shallow valley leading from the temple to Umm el Qaʿab was left completely free of graves and other structures through the Old and Middle Kingdoms (and indeed later), despite a very large cemetery on either side (Middle Cemetery, Old Kingdom; North Cemetery, largely Middle Kingdom). Normally, graves would certainly have also filled in the valley and their absence implies a deliberate, official policy, the only apparent purpose of which was to keep the valley as an unobstructed processional way from the temple to Umm el Qaʿab.

This inference is made all the more likely in that King Ugaf (early 13th Dynasty) had conspicuously large stelae set up, one each at the four corners of the part of the valley traversing the cemetery fields. These were later rededi-cated by a successor, Neferhotep I. Each stela apparently proclaimed (only one survived) that this 'holy land' (i.e. the valley) could only be entered by priests carrying out ritual duties, and tombs were explicitly forbidden. In the cemeter-ies on either side of the valley, however, people could freely 'make tombs for themselves and be buried'.

These circumstances indicate that Umm el Qaʿab was identified with Poker, the mythical region in which Osiris' tomb lay and towards which Osiris' annual festival procession was directed. So far, we have been tracing out the ritual and sacred landscape of Abydos via its archaeology (with textually derived infor-mation as an important but less precise background), but the identification between Poker and Umm el Qaʿab provides us with rare direct insight into Egyptian ideas about a specific landscape. Strikingly, despite its ritual impor-tance, Umm el Qaʿab in the Middle Kingdom seemingly contained no substantial surface monuments, and was not even the locale for repetitive offer-ing rituals. The latter are attested in later periods by deposits of pottery and other items at Umm el Qaʿab and in its environs. Thus, the Middle Kingdom Egyptians sought to maintain this intensely sacred site with as natural a desert landscape as possible, perhaps because Osiris' myth required or implied just such a setting for Poker. Indeed, as Anthony Leahy has suggested,[2] this mythi-cal place name may derive from the Egyptian word (approximately *pega*), explicitly meaning an open place, valley mouth or plateau, i.e. a natural, not built landscape.

The circumstances described above suggest, very tentatively, specific relationships between the landscape and the processional festival that traversed it. The festival opens with a 'procession of Wepwawet', interpreted as a progress by Osiris' image in the form of the living king he once was, and hence preceded by the jackal deity Wepwawet who overthrows and subdues all potential enemies. This segment might correspond to the rather sharply defined, lower (northern) part of the valley, the area delineated by Neferhotep's stelae and associated specifically with Wepwawet in the decree inscribed upon those stelae.

Beyond the lower valley the topography becomes more diffuse and less sharply defined, forming a wide if irregular open area, in the southern part of which is the elevation upon which Umm el Qaʿab lies. After the procession of Wepwawet, the events of the Osiris festival focus more sharply on Osiris himself, and refer implicitly or otherwise to his death, the search for his body and the mourning over his remains. Perhaps these events were ritually enacted according to a cir-cuitous route around or through this second area, rather than the more strictly linear progress imposed by the narrower northern end of the valley.

Ultimately, the procession reached Umm el Qaʿab, and Osiris' image was presumably placed in the refurbished tomb of Djer. The 13th Dynasty statue mentioned above shows that the image's sojourn here was equivalent to Osiris' embalming, his return to sexual potency and, perhaps, his revitalization via the eye of Horus, his son and champion.

43 *The excavation of the Middle Kingdom 'cenotaphs' or memorial chapels on the scarp overlooking the Osiris temple. In the foreground is the side of the 'portal' temple of Ramesses II, behind which are the mud brick memorial chapels, originally covered by the temple. In the background is the Middle Cemetery and, to the right, the shallow processional valley leading to Umm el Qa'ab and the supposed tomb of Osiris.*

A very important part of the landscape of the inner core, around Osiris' temple, became archaeologically known for the first time through the (then) Pennsylvania-Yale Expedition. During the Middle Kingdom a dense mass of 'cenotaphs' (false tombs or, more properly, memorial chapels) developed along the desert scarp overlooking the Osiris temple. The existence of such chapels had been long inferred from hundreds of stelae removed from them during unsupervised or poorly-run excavations in the 19th century, but their architectural and archaeological contexts, being unrecorded and subsequently buried, were unknown to modern scholarship.

The expedition's contribution to a much enriched knowledge of these chapels, which are important manifestations of the more popular aspects of the Osiris cult, has been twofold. First, in 1974 Kelly Simpson published a seminal and most influential study of the stelae removed so many years ago, and showed that many of them could be assembled into related groups of stelae that were once displayed in a single monument, or in several contiguous and related ones. Kelly Simpson also emphasized the basic function of the chapels

44 *Some memorial chapels were small and modest, and so were the associated stelae. This irregular flake of limestone (18 cm or 7 in high) is in appearance an ostracon, but originally was set in some small chapel. The dedicatee is a certain Inyotef (his figure is shown seated), but also commemorated are his mother and father, two brothers, his wife and 'his beloved friend'.*

from which the stelae had come: each dedicator wished to provide himself and his family with 'an eternal association with the mysteries of the local deities', especially the annual festival of Osiris, and 'a share of the offerings made after they had been used by the gods'.

Coincidentally but serendipitously, I had commenced excavation (in 1967) of a ruined and enigmatic temple or 'portal' of Ramesses II on the desert scarp overlooking the Osiris temple. The temple had been built over a large number of these Middle Kingdom memorial chapels (that were therefore exceptionally well preserved), which could thus be archaeologically recorded for the first time. Kelly Simpson and I had therefore brought together epigraphic and archaeological evidence about these unique cult structures in a way not possible before.

Unfortunately, it will probably never be possible to directly match known stelae to any of the excavated chapels; many have stelae niches and recesses preserved, but the stelae themselves are often very similar in size, so quite a few might 'fit' any particular niche. Moreover, although the excavated area contains many chapels (about 150), which vary considerably in size, it is not necessarily fully representative. Nevertheless, much of what we see probably represents patterns typical of the entire memorial chapel zone.

The desert scarp overlooking the temple is a highly disturbed area, most of which still requires controlled excavation, but Mary-Ann Pouls Wegner's

45 *A typical group of memorial chapels, bringing out well the variety they exhibit in type and size. On the left, a large chapel (with its door bricked in) set in a spacious walled court; to the right a smaller chapel, its vault intact. In the lower right, part of a 'chapel' which is of solid mud brick, with deeply recessed external faces.*

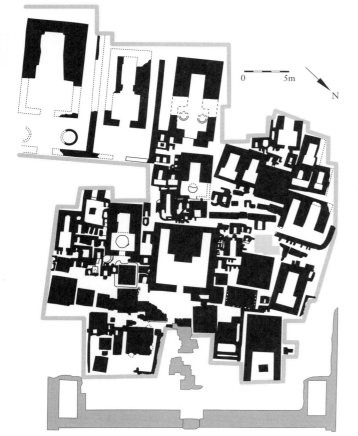

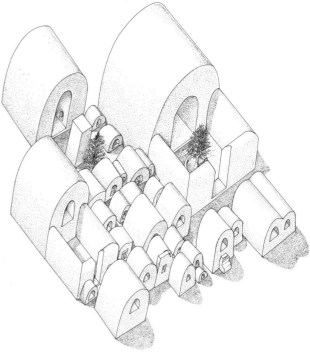

46 *(left) Map of the excavated cenotaphs or memorial chapels.*

47 *Reconstruction of a group of memorial chapels.*

exhaustive survey of its surface archaeology indicates the chapels were concentrated in an area west of the Osiris temple, and outside its precinct. Given the often-expressed wish that those imaged in statuary, relief and painting in the chapels could literally kiss the ground before Osiris and see the beauty of Wepwawet during the great processional festival described above, it is likely the processional route ran up the scarp from the temple, turned along the front of the chapel zone, and then ran down to the entrance of the valley leading to Umm el Qa'ab or Poker. What lay between the memorial chapels and the valley, in the Middle Kingdom, is as yet uncertain.

The excavated chapels (occupying about 1,000 sq. m or 10,760 sq. ft) evidently developed over time through the Middle Kingdom and eventually presented a picture of great complexity. All are built of mud-brick, which was then plastered and whitewashed. Most consist of a single-chambered chapel (in many cases with a vaulted roof), often with a low-walled forecourt, which contained one or two symmetrically arranged trees. A significant minority (about 15 per cent) were built of solid brick and without an internal chamber; they must have had stelae displayed on one or more of the upper faces. All were orientated to face the temple, and the assumed processional way, because those commemorated in them wished to see the festival, and also to benefit from the daily and other offering services performed in and around the temple. In addition to stelae, statues and statuettes of those commemorated stood in the chapels, but probably were not taken out to 'join' the processional festival; in fact, at least some chapels had their entrance walled in, for security reasons, with a stone-framed window supplied so the images within could still 'see' out.

In the excavated area, and presumably elsewhere, it seems initially a number of relatively large chapels were built, some adjoining, but most with considerable open space between them. These were probably for quite high-ranking individuals and their families. The largest excavated averaged (excluding courtyards) 33 sq. m (355 sq. ft); the largest of these was 46.2 sq. m (497 sq. ft), while the next size down averaged – with remarkable uniformity – about 12 sq. m (129 sq. ft). Over time, these larger chapels were flanked and fronted by often much smaller ones, and eventually the intervening space became filled in an almost impenetrable way. Nevertheless, alleys and spaces were maintained to a degree indicating that priests or others were expected to visit some of the large and small chapels on a regular basis.

Clearly, many socio-economic levels are represented by these chapels, although it is likely that there was usually some link to the owners of the larger chapels involved. This relationship need not have been one of kinship, for amongst the few stelae we discovered in situ one commemorated a 'butler', presumably servant to one of the larger chapel owners. It is likely that these practices are not unique to Abydos. Inscriptional or other evidence indicates that such chapels existed near other provincial temples at this time e.g. at Asyut, but perhaps at Abydos the custom was on an especially large scale, and certainly included the commemoration of individuals who lived, and were buried, far from Abydos itself.

The cenotaph or memorial chapel stelae published by Kelly Simpson also provide an opportunity to study larger issues relevant to Middle Kingdom religious practice and social structure. Kelly Simpson himself, for example, utilized some (along with texts from elsewhere) in a fascinating study (1974b) indicating that the Middle Kingdom elite likely practised some degree of polygamy, even though Egyptologists tend to think this practice was virtually non-existent in pre-Ptolemaic Egypt.

Thus far, I have sketched out the developing landscape of the core area and suggested (as have many) that Umm el Qaʿab is equivalent to Poker, and that the lower (northern) and upper (southern) portions of the processional valley related to different mythological episodes as re-enacted in Osiris' festival procession. For their part, Middle Kingdom inscriptions name a number of different areas making up the landscape of the inner core, around the Osiris temple in particular, but the exact locations of these on the ground is hard to determine. Particularly intriguing is a feature often referred to as 'the terrace of the great god [Osiris]', at which the memorial chapels are said to have been built. For this, the rising scarp behind the temple and town seems the likely candidate (as Kelly Simpson suggests), but others have different interpretations. Indeed, the 'terrace', if at times used in a more expansive sense, might refer to most of the landscape, the elevated low desert that contains Poker and extends back to the high cliffs.

There is also a significant connection between the memorial chapels and the more distant landscape. The chapels are in no way tombs; no actual or imitation burial chambers exist, although the stelae and statuary are very similar to those set up in actual tomb chapels at Abydos and elsewhere. The memorial chapels are often called *mahats*, which at Abydos was unlikely to be applied to actual tombs, as it is sometimes elsewhere. However, Osiris is also said to have a *mahat*, in Poker, by which presumably his tomb-like sanctuary in the erstwhile tomb of King Djer is meant. Possibly, therefore, even at Abydos *mahat* involved the notion of a tomb in a very special way: each individual had a specific chapel, or *mahat*, near the Osiris temple, but all shared a *single* tomb or *mahat*, that of Osiris himself at Poker. Here, the owners of the memorial chapels were identified with Osiris and like him experienced regeneration in his mysterious 'tomb'. If this notion is correct, yet another ritual linkage is established that both defines and enriches the evolving landscape of Abydos.

The Senwosret III Complex

We turn now to the first known expansion of the core area, the mortuary complex built for King Senwosret III about 2.3 km (1.4 miles) southeast of the Osiris temple. Heavily denuded, this complex was once one of Abydos' most impressive monuments. Organized along an axis of over 0.5 km (0.3 miles), it has at the southwestern end a gigantic subterranean tomb (as well as some surface structures) and at the northeastern end a large temple. Both components were

48 *The excavated site of the temple of Senwosret III. In the foreground, the white limestone flooring and foundation platform of the otherwise completely razed temple with, on either side, brick-built blocks of storerooms and priests' residences.*

explored between 1899 and 1902 and their general character established, but new surveys and excavations by Josef Wegner, for the University of Pennsylvania and under the aegis of the Pennsylvania-Yale-Institute of Fine Arts, New York University Expedition, are producing a flood of new data and insights, far exceeding the results of the earlier work.

Under Josef Wegner the southwestern end of the Senwosret III complex has been resurveyed. Here, at the foot of the high cliffs, a large T-shaped area defined by brick enclosure walls contains a 25-m (80-ft) deep shaft leading to a well-constructed, rock-cut tomb (explored by Currelly in 1901–1902). Over 270 m (885 ft) long, it is larger than the actual royal tombs of the Middle Kingdom, under their respective pyramids near Memphis or the Fayum.

Thus far, Wegner's excavations have been concentrated mainly on the temple (and a nearby town) at floodplain edge. More recently, he has initiated a re-excavation of the tomb, while Dawn McCormack has begun a study of nearby mortuary remains. Wegner's meticulous methods, full recovery of all artifactual and other data and probing analyses of the materials have proved extremely productive. The stone-built temple itself had been razed down to the foundation platform on which it had been built, and the plan generated by an earlier excavation was almost unintelligible. However, by careful observation of crucial details, such as incised guidelines and corner marks still surviving on the platform and intended to guide the laying out of walls, and by recovering the thousands of usually quite small architectural and decorated fragments

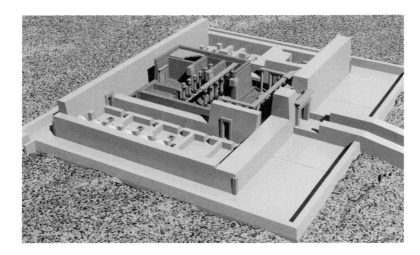

49 *Computerized reconstruction of the temple of Senwosret III. Central to the temple is a stone-built temple and court and on either side are store rooms and priests' residences.*

ignored in earlier work, Wegner has been able to recreate the three-dimensional reality of this unique monument.

Built of white limestone, the temple stood on a platform and rose perhaps 5 to 6 m (16 to 19 ft) above the court in front of it, which had a colonnade on three sides. Almost square in plan, the cube-like temple – at 231.5 sq. m (2,491 sq. ft) – is similar in scale to the mortuary temples attached to later 12th Dynasty pyramids, such as that of Senwosret II at Illahun, and Senwosret III at Dahshur. Indeed, the overall Abydos complex is quite similar in scale to the most fully articulated (in archaeological terms) Middle Kingdom royal complex, the pyramid and valley temple of Senwosret III at Illahun, although of course no actual pyramid existed at Abydos. Clearly, the Abydos complex was one of the major building initiatives of the 12th Dynasty and its name, discovered by Wegner, was 'Beautiful is the *Ka* of Senwosret III'.

The Abydos temple's façade was decorated with large-scale relief representations of the king. Within, the devastation makes it hard to reconstruct the interior plan. Wegner suggests that two successively placed, rectilinear halls – both columned – may have fronted three equally sized, sanctuary-like chambers set side by side at the rear of the temple. The interior decoration had included offering scenes focused on the deceased Senwosret III as well as others typical of royal mortuary buildings attached to pyramids; but there were also a significant number of scenes illustrating the veneration of Osiris, and the relationship between him and the king. These are more unusual, and a product of the temple's specific Abydene setting.

Work and materials were of the highest quality, yet this jewel-like building was almost entirely hidden and masked. It was not intended to delight the populace, but to be an immensely pleasing gift to the dead king's *ka* and its protector Osiris, and for their delectation only. Thus, its court and façade were masked by a massive brick pylon, probably rising higher than the temple, and an enclosure wall, also relatively high, surrounded the other three sides of the temple. Moreover, the temple was flanked on the northwest and southeast by well-built blocks, which would have hidden much, though not all, of the temple exterior. The northwest block housed hierarchically ranked priests (their residences varied in scale) serving for a specified period in the temple; the southeast contained supplies and items needed for the cult.

Wegner, after a thorough comparative analysis of contemporary and earlier royal pyramid complexes, suggests that Senwosret III's temple at Abydos is an 'expansion' of the Abydene royal *ka*-chapel (as found near the temple of Osiris) into a 'full mortuary complex complete with a burial place for the deceased king'. Like other experts, such as Dieter Arnold, he believes Senwosret III was actually buried at Abydos, not under his pyramid at Dahshur. Indeed, a well-made granite sarcophagus was found in the Abydos tomb – it had been plundered, and no trace of the body or its adornments had been located, but the early excavation was not exhaustive.

Present evidence, however, permits an alternative interpretation, derived from the larger landscape of Abydos. Cult structures near the Osiris temple were probably one source of inspiration, and royal mortuary complexes surely another. Yet strikingly there was no pyramid over the tomb (clearly the resources to build one were available) and, although Wegner suggests the high cliffs immediately behind the tomb were visually read as a pyramid, this process still involves the transformation of a built landscape into a natural one. Indeed, there seems to be no substantial surface structure of any kind associated with Senwosret's tomb, as was also the case with the royal tombs of New Kingdom Thebes. However, this desire not to intrude upon the natural landscape with either a built pyramid or cult structure is also very reminiscent of the Middle Kingdom attitude towards Umm el Qa'ab, or Poker, where Osiris' own 'tomb' lay. Here too, the surface area was left in a relatively natural state.

Implicitly, a processional route may have linked the tomb site to the Senwosret temple, just as Poker was linked to the Osiris temple. However, Senwosret's temple might not have been inspired by the royal *ka*-chapels (of which almost nothing has survived for the Middle Kingdom) clustered near the north corner of the Osiris temple. Another kind of royal temple or chapel developed at Abydos in this period, exemplified by a 'seat of eternity' for Senwosret I, and a 'god's temple' for Amenemhet III (although the latter might have been at Thinis). These and others as yet undocumented were perhaps royal equivalents to the *mahat* or private memorial chapel described above, as Kelly Simpson suggests, and possibly lay southeast of the latter, closer to the mouth of the processional valley. Indeed, these possible royal *mahats* could have extended even further southeast. Some kind of a chapel dedicated to the 13th Dynasty king Khaankhre Sobekhotep once stood near the area later occupied by the Seti I temple.

Nevertheless, any such royal memorial chapels – so located – would still, like the private ones, be close enough as to relate symbolically to the tomb-like *mahat* of Osiris at Umm el Qa'ab. However, if Senwosret III's temple is equivalent to a memorial chapel, its remoteness from the core area, together with an apparent desire to create a new, specifically royal zone within the Abydos landscape, required that it be provided its own remote and – at surface – visually modest tomb. The latter, equivalent to Osiris' tomb at Umm el Qa'ab, would have been for Senwosret-as-Osiris, and hence a cenotaph, the king actually being buried under his Dahshur pyramid, as tradition and self-interest would demand.

Thus, Senwosret's complex most likely should be seen as not only an extension of the core landscape, but as a replication of it. It is even possible that ritual linkages existed between the two, with Senwosret's image being processed to the Osiris temple to participate in Osiris' annual festival, and perhaps Osiris himself visiting Senwosret's temple in an expanded version of that festival.

This new royal zone may have developed further. The building of another great cenotaph or false tomb (of the late 12th Dynasty?) was at least begun near Senwosret's, and in the vicinity of the latter's tomb are two unusually large mastabas, with elaborate subterranean components, that Wegner suggests may have held royal 13th Dynasty burials. Indeed, the actual burial places of all 13th Dynasty rulers after the 27th king of that line are unknown. Because of the disturbed conditions of northern Egypt, these rulers were apparently not buried there. Their presumably modest tombs could have been at Thebes, but since no trace of them has yet been located, Abydos remains a good second possibility.

The Societal Dimensions of the Abydos Landscape

The landscape of Abydos was generated by ritual and symbolism, but inevitably included other societal dimensions. Cult required ritual structures and substantial, income-generating estates (many probably located on the nearby floodplain) and hence also priests, administrators and large service populations. Transient but perhaps large-scale visits by 'pilgrims' also had needs to be met while, like any large provincial town, Abydos intermeshed with the regional government, which most likely had permanent representatives at Abydos.

These larger societal aspects of Abydos are particularly well documented for the Middle Kingdom, as the work of Janet Richards and Josef Wegner has shown. Moreover, their results – like so many others at Abydos – have paradigmatic significance as well, for from them we can generalize about societal phenomena possibly typical of much of Egypt at this time.

In 1986, Richards carried out the first comprehensive archaeological and topographical survey of the vast North Cemetery (about 14.8 ha or 36.5 acres), followed up by selective excavation of a representative range of Middle Kingdom burials. Wegner, since 1994, has been excavating an orthogonal ('grid-iron') town developed to service the cult and endowments of the Senwosret III complex, which was called 'Enduring are the Places of Khakaure (Senwosret III) in Abydos'. The town is known to cover between 4.5 to 6 ha (11 to almost 15 acres) and may be even larger, if it runs under the modern floodplain.

Richards' aim was to explore social complexity at Middle Kingdom Abydos, insofar as it was documented by mortuary remains; and to compare the results with a current theory that the state at this time sought to create a 'prescriptive society' of great simplicity – two-tiered, it ideally consisted of the elite, and all others as a homogeneous mass. Proponents of the theory realized the reality was probably more complex. Indeed, Richards' analyses of the Abydos material (and

50 *Excavating Middle Kingdom tomb shafts in the North Cemetery.*

other data from cemeteries in northern Egypt) revealed that throughout the 12th Dynasty, and presumably throughout much of the country, there was a 'widely differentiated, "unprescribed" society and a flexible economic system which functioned at least partially outside a regimented government umbrella'.[3]

Richards' sophisticated analyses of mortuary material provided many important, societally significant observations about burial practices of the period. For example, the sizes and types of graves on the one hand, and grave wealth on the other, were to some degree independent variables, rather than inextricably related as one might have thought. Either variable could be chosen to express social status. Intact burials in large, labour-intensive shaft and chamber graves could be very modest in grave wealth, whereas surface burials – much less labour-intensive – incorporated not only wooden coffins, but also significant amounts of valuable materials such as amethyst, carnelian, gold and copper.

Apart from its specific significance, Richards' work (alongside that of a few others, such as Stephen Seidlmayer) is also important in that it is bringing historic mortuary material – abundant in Egypt yet long-neglected for social analysis – back into mainstream Egyptian archaeology.

Wegner's work on the Senwosret III town is also significant with regard to larger issues, such as Egyptian urbanism, and functional differentiation within households. Three hundred metres (984 ft) southeast of the Senwosret temple, the town is revealing that Middle Kingdom 'official', i.e. state-sponsored, settlements do not always adhere to the two-tier social model mentioned above.

The Abydos town's closest analogy is a larger settlement (about 13 ha or 32 acres) built to service the ritual and administrative needs of the pyramid

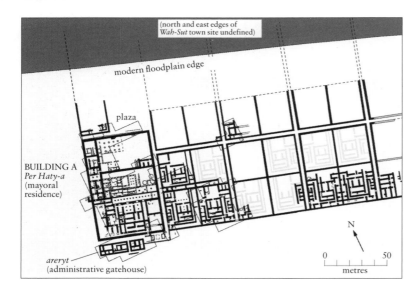

modern floodplain edge

plaza

BUILDING A
Per Haty-a
(mayoral
residence)

areryt
(administrative gatehouse)

N

0   50
metres

51 *Plan of the town servicing King Senwosret III's temple at Abydos. The great regularity of its layout is typical of several Middle Kingdom towns and fortresses; the houses shown were intended for the mayor of the town (Building A) and for subordinate, but still elite officials, who resided in houses uniformly sized but not as large as the mayor's. Smaller houses must lie in other, as yet unexcavated parts of the town.*

complex of Senwosret II (Senwosret III's immediate predecessor) at Kahun. The latter inspired the two-tier model, for its elite families were housed in 11 very large and identically planned and sized houses, each about 2,500 sq. m (26,900 sq. ft), while everyone else lived in much smaller ones. The Abydos town, Wegner has shown, was substantially different. Like Kahun, it had an elite component (attested in part by numerous seal impressions), a mayor or *haty-a*, and a hierarchy of priests and senior administrators. Yet one exceptionally large house (including an office) of over 4,200 sq. m (45,192 sq. ft) was assigned to the mayor (in situ seal impressions confirm this), while the next rank of at least 16 houses were identically sized at about 840 sq. m (9,038 sq. ft), but much smaller than the Kahun elite house. Yet they were also much larger (about five times) than the typical Kahun small house, many examples of which presumably lie in the as-yet-unexcavated parts of the Abydos town. These important differences suggest that the societal differentiation displayed within Middle Kingdom planned settlements has more to do with local circumstances than with an overarching policy of a 'prescriptive society'.

Despite the relatively early excavation of Kahun, and later of Middle Kingdom fortified towns in Nubia, the vital issue of functional differentiation within individual households (elite and other) has been difficult. Our best opportunity for a comprehensive study of the phenomenon was missed in 1888–91 when Petrie recovered a great deal of artifactual and inscriptional material from Kahun, but did not locate it for us in terms of specific houses, rooms or rubbish dumps. More recent excavations of Middle Kingdom settlements at Elephantine, Tell el-Da'aba and elsewhere are providing much better data as to functional differentiation, but the Senwosret III town at Abydos is proving especially valuable. This is due in part to the preservative effects of its low-desert setting, in part to its relative simplicity and comparatively short life-span (Senwosret III into the late Middle Kingdom).

For example, Wegner has established the largest house belonged to the mayor, as noted above. Although as yet only partially excavated, Wegner has already identified the house's residential core (partly by its plan, partly by its exceptionally clean condition); a courtyard in the western quadrant shown, by in situ debris, to be for short-term food storage and preparation and associated with 'the house-attendant Senwosret' (28 seal impressions with his name had been discarded in a nearby room); a set of offices in the rear; and a very large granary north of the residential component. More recently, a segment of the house set aside for women has been identified, the principal occupant of which was a royal princess, perhaps wife to the contemporary mayor. The excavations here yielded a unique decorated birth brick, originally one of a set that women would squat on while giving birth. When the work of Wegner and of members of his team is completed, we shall have perhaps our best data available on functional variation within Middle Kingdom households, individually the basic components of every town or village.

The Pennsylvania-Yale-Institute of Fine Arts, New York University Expedition has then revealed much more than earlier excavators about the complexities of the Abydos landscape in the Middle Kingdom. In this period the Abydos landscape was restructured into one dominated by two long ritual axes, far apart in space yet implicitly mirroring each other in important ways. Each axis was associated with a substantial town; these towns are difficult to compare with each other except in obvious ways, for example the relatively short life-span of Senwosret's town clearly contrasts with the continuing one of that around the Osiris temple.

The Middle Kingdom components of the latter town have long since disappeared: were they larger and more important than Senwosret's town, or were the two roughly equal in size or importance? The large size of the North Cemetery, adjacent to the Osiris temple and town, might suggest it was substantially larger, at least in population, than Senwosret's town. But perhaps many of the latter's inhabitants were buried in the North Cemetery because of its close association with Osiris. In any event, the expansion of the Abydos landscape was to continue into the New Kingdom.

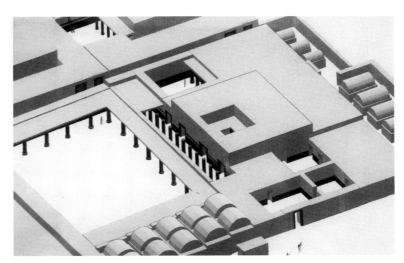

52 *Computerized reconstruction of the mayor's house in the Senwosret III town: behind the colonnaded courtyard is the house proper, the central portion rising to a greater height and provided with a light well.*

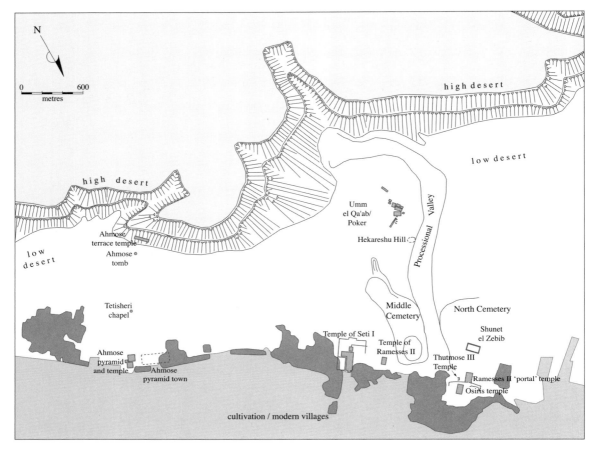

N

0 ___ 600
metres

high desert

high desert

low desert

low
desert

Ahmose
terrace temple
Ahmose
tomb

Tetisheri
chapel

Ahmose
pyramid
and temple
Ahmose
pyramid town

Umm
el Qa'ab/
Poker

Hekareshu Hill

Processional Valley

Middle
Cemetery

North Cemetery

Shunet
el Zebib

Temple of Seti I

Temple of
Ramesses II

Thutmose III
Temple

Ramesses II 'portal' temple

Osiris temple

cultivation / modern villages

53 *Map of New Kingdom Abydos.*

CHAPTER SEVEN

THE LANDSCAPE COMPLETED: ABYDOS IN THE NEW KINGDOM

The Last Royal Pyramid

The Abydos landscape experienced its greatest expansion at the beginning of the New Kingdom, an expansion defined by a unique monument, the last royal pyramid to survive from ancient Egypt. This pyramid was incorporated into a mortuary complex built for pharaoh Ahmose (*c.* 1539–1514 BC) and located almost 1 km (0.62 miles) to the southeast of Senwosret's. About 50 m (164 ft) high and covering over 0.4 ha (1 acre), the pyramid – encased in white limestone – was a prominent addition to the landscape. Somewhere at Abydos, however, must be the remains of an even later royal pyramid. No New Kingdom pharaoh after Ahmose had a pyramid attached to either Theban mortuary temple or tomb, but a stela from the Osiris temple records that Thutmose I (*c.* 1493–1483 BC) ordered the local priesthood to 'provide for my pyramid' at Abydos.[1] Moreover, as Stephen Harvey has discovered, Ahmose himself definitely had smaller pyramids built at Abydos for the cults of his grandmother, Queen Tetisheri (*c.* 1550 BC) and probably for his sister-queen Ahmose-Nefertari.

Like Senwosret's, Ahmose's monuments are distributed along an axis extending from cliffs to floodplain for over 1 km (0.62 miles). At the cliff's foot is an extensive terraced platform, northeast of which is an enormous, subterranean rock-cut tomb. Then, half-way between the terraces and Ahmose's pyramid and its attached temple is the in-part pyramidal shrine for Tetisheri, described as a 'pyramid temple' in an in situ text. Ahmose's pyramid and temple (as well as the adjacent chapel and perhaps pyramid for Ahmose-Nefertari) are today close to the floodplain edge, but the latter was probably further away in ancient times. The entire complex was originally explored (in part somewhat superficially) between 1899 and 1902, but since 1993 Stephen Harvey has renewed excavations there with spectacular results. Recently, sub-surface survey by Tomasz Herbich near Ahmose's temple has revealed the archaeological situation to be even more exciting and complex. It includes an additional temple (perhaps for Queen Ahmose-Nefertari) measuring 27 × 57 m (88.56 × 187 ft) and with a massive, 40-m (131.2-ft) wide pylon.[2]

While the entire set of monuments has been resurveyed, Harvey's principal focus so far has been the temple in front of the pyramid. This temple had in the past experienced savage destruction and subsequent denudation, but through

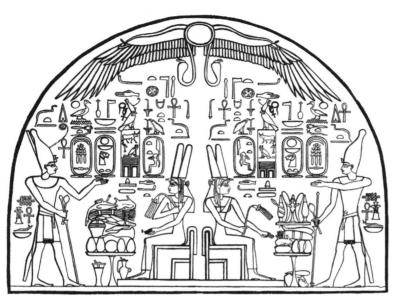

54 (left) A limestone stela 1.98 m (6.5 ft) high was found in a pyramid chapel at Abydos forming part of King Ahmose's mortuary complex and dedicated to the cult of his grandmother, queen Tetisheri. A scene in the stela's lunette shows Ahmose performing offering cults for Tetisheri, and the text describes a conversation between Ahmose and his queen in which his intention to provide Tetisheri with a 'pyramid and temple' at Abydos is quoted.

55 The remains of King Ahmose's pyramid at Abydos. In the foreground, the cultivated flood plain; centre, the rubble core of the pyramid, partially collapsed after its stone casing was removed, and further distorted by large-scale excavations by various excavators fruitlessly seeking a burial chamber beneath it.

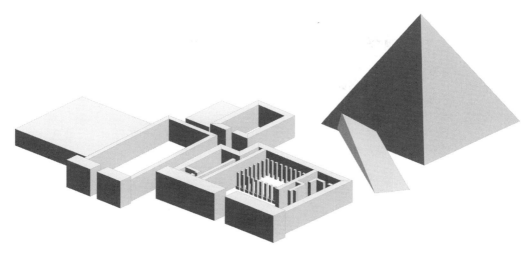

56 *A reconstruction of King Ahmose's pyramid, the temple in front of it, and the structure dedicated to his queen Ahmose-Nefertari and additional temples nearby. The remains of a brick ramp leading to the pyramid apparently relate to its construction. This reconstruction is based on the discoveries of the British excavations and those of Stephen Harvey. At the moment, some key features are necessarily conjectural.*

meticulous excavation and close analysis Harvey has been able to reconstruct much of the temple's architectural form and decorative programme, reveal its unexpectedly complicated history, and highlight major new issues to be pursued by his future excavations. Ahmose's complex has begun to emerge as one of the most significant of early New Kingdom building projects and cultic institutions, while more generally the new data provide important insights into the history and art of the New Kingdom.

Scale alone is an index of the importance of Ahmose's complex. With an area of over 2,000 sq. m (21,500 sq. ft) Ahmose's pyramid is approximately comparable to some of the smaller ones of the Old Kingdom (average 3,780 sq. m or 40,143 sq. ft) and Middle Kingdom (average 2,670 sq. m or 28,355 sq. ft). Ahmose's temple occupied at least 2,600 sq. m (27,612 sq. ft) and perhaps as much as 4,200 sq. m (44,604 sq. ft); at Abydos the impressive temple of Ramesses II covered 2,745.8 sq. m or 29,160 sq. ft (4,335.5 sq. m or 46,043 sq. ft including its now gone first court). Finally, the rock-cut tomb, approximately 135 m (443 ft) long, is similar in scale to the large Theban royal tombs in the New Kingdom.

Harvey has established that the form of Ahmose's temple can be reconstructed in either of two ways. In both instances, a massive mud-brick pylon fronted an open court with a colonnade of stone piers at the far or southwestern end; on either side, brick structures may have been comparable to the priests' residences and magazines of the Senwosret temple. From this point on, reconstruction can differ. There is a large space between the excavated area and the pyramid, and at some point the area immediately behind the colonnade was walled off from this space, and a ramp built against the northeast face of the pyramid. Harvey interprets the ramp as connected to the building of the pyramid, indicating no temple structure was built in the area in its vicinity.

The temple site is covered by thousands of small decorated or inscribed stone fragments generated by the temple's destruction, and almost completely ignored by earlier excavators. Harvey's analysis of these has revealed that while the reliefs in the court (on stone cladding along the brick walls) and on the colonnade were carved during Ahmose's reign, the roofed structure further to the southwest (wherever its exact location) was decorated under his son and successor, pharaoh Amenhotep I (c. 1514–1493 BC). Indeed, Amenhotep is depicted as a recipient of cult (presumably alongside Ahmose) and, as we have seen, queens Tetisheri and Ahmose-Nefertari also had cult chapels in the complex, so Ahmose's monuments were as much for the royal family as for Ahmose himself. Ahmose-Nefertari's monument, near the east corner of Ahmose's pyramid, may have included a subsidiary pyramid that was completely unsuspected until Harvey's excavations.

Some, perhaps all, of the cults remained active for a long time. A festival procession of the deified Ahmose at Abydos (during which it delivered an oracular decision or resolution of a dispute more typical of Amun-Re's cult at Thebes) is attested under Ramesses II. It may have originated from Ahmose's mortuary complex, which was certainly still active under pharaoh Merenptah (c. 1213–1204 BC) according to an inscription recovered there by Harvey. Indeed, even after the dismantling of the pyramid had begun, the front part of the temple – now walled off at the rear – was remodelled so that the cult could continue. A sturdy stone pavement was laid down behind the colonnade, evidently to support a new cult building of some kind.

Harvey has shown that Ahmose's monuments have substantial paradigmatic and extra-regional significance, especially in terms of history and art. A careful contextual and comparative study of some 50 small decorated fragments has enabled him to reconstruct the subjects of several contiguous scenes once displayed on the southeast wall of the court. These scenes provide unique historical data about Ahmose's reign, and lead to a major revision of the history of narrative art in Egypt. They seem to be the first known pictorial record of momentous events involving Ahmose. Before his reign, Egypt had long been divided between a Theban kingdom in the south, and a 'Hyksos' kingdom in the north, the latter ruled by a semi-Egyptianized dynasty of Canaanite origin, still strongly connected with the Levant. Ahmose's immediate predecessors began a war of liberation and reunification against the Hyksos (during which Ahmose's father, King Sekenenre Tao II, was killed in battle). But it was Ahmose who captured Avaris (*Hat Waret* in Egyptian), the Hyksos capital in the eastern Delta, reunited Egypt and carried the war into Canaan itself.

Harvey interprets these scenes as probably relating directly to these circumstances. Occupying a wall space about 6 m (19.7 ft) long and 3 m (9.84 ft) high, he speculates that the scenes consist of two in an upper, and two in a lower register. The lower left depicted Ahmose's royal ship and others sailing 'north', presumably from Thebes to Avaris; the upper left showed a superhuman Ahmose in his chariot riding down Canaanite enemies, with – further left – the

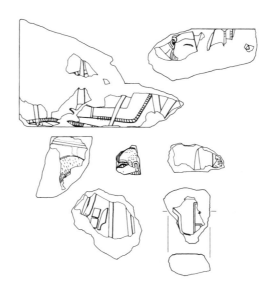

57 Drawings of fragments of painted relief from the court of Ahmose's temple. They belonged to scenes depicting Ahmose's victory over Levantine enemies, and show such 'historical narratives' existed much earlier in New Kingdom art than previously thought. The upper fragments show part of a bearded head, and the arm of a prostrate Levantine foe, wearing a typically long-sleeved garment. The two lower fragments record the name Apepi (left) perhaps a reference to a ruler or leader of the Hyksos; and – from a stela, rather than a wall relief (right) – 'Hat Waret' or Avaris, the name of the Hyksos capital in northern Egypt.

siege of a fortified town. This is probably Avaris, since a stele once set up in Ahmose's temple specifically referred to that city. On the upper right is a further battle scene, concluding perhaps with a triumphal celebration, while below a royal thanks offering before the sacred barque of Amun-Re presumably signals the return of the victorious king to Thebes.

The art-historical significance of these scenes is also considerable. Complex historical narratives in pictorial form are relatively rare in Egyptian art, and are generally believed not to have developed until the late 18th Dynasty, finally reaching fruition in the Ramesside period. But Harvey has shown that elaborate and large-scale examples of such narratives existed in Ahmose's time. Whether they were invented in his reign or based on earlier, as-yet-unknown prototypes, Ahmose's scenes at Abydos (and elsewhere?) were crucial in the transmission of historical narrative in art.

Harvey's comparative study of Ahmose's complex leads him to suggest that its designers intentionally fused architectural traditions from both Memphis and Thebes, and referred to both the Old and Middle Kingdoms, in order to emphasize and symbolize the national reunification Ahmose had achieved. Harvey also of course recognizes a strong connection to the Osiris cult at Abydos, and I see this as the major factor affecting Ahmose's complex, which met for him a compelling personal need – deification and immortality – achieved here at Abydos by the identification of Ahmose with Osiris. Indeed, the bricks of the temple are stamped 'Nebpehtyre (Ahmose) beloved of Osiris'.

The fundamentally Abydene character of Ahmose's complex is, I think, indicated by its relationship to the larger Abydos landscape. A primary model was Senwosret's complex, celebrating Senwosret-as-Osiris and active as a cult at least into the early 17th Dynasty (c. 1630–1600 BC), hence likely still to be standing in Ahmose's day. As already noted, the two complexes are similar in their components (cenotaph, cult temple) and axial arrangement. Moreover, the front part of

Ahmose's temple, i.e. the excavated area, is reminiscent of Senwosret's temple in plan – large pylon (identical in scale in both temples), open court with some form of side colonnades, a rear cult building and flanking service blocks.

Senwosret's complex was itself modelled upon the axial and cultic relationship between the Osiris temple and Osiris' tomb (*mahat*) at Umm el Qa'ab, and hence so was Ahmose's. Both complexes reinforce this relationship by keeping the environment of the royal tomb relatively pristine and naturalistic (with no conspicuously large surface structures), as was the setting for Osiris' own tomb at Umm el Qa'ab.

Ahmose's pyramid of course *is* a major innovation, and the best evidence for Harvey's belief that the complex had a Memphite dimension. Nevertheless, as Harvey notes, Ahmose's pyramid can also be related to the admittedly much smaller pyramidal tombs of his immediate royal predecessors (17th Dynasty) at western Thebes; one of these long-lost tombs (originally located in the 19th century) has recently been rediscovered by Daniel Polz. Insofar as his pyramid complex was a grandiose version of theirs, it may have been intended to signal more emphatically than in Senwosret's case that a tomb was indeed present, even if it was far away from the pyramid, in order to conform to the separation between the Osiris temple and Osiris' tomb at Umm el Qa'ab. At Thebes, as earlier, the tomb was under the pyramid.

The Core Landscape and its Royal Monuments

All significant royal monuments at Abydos other than Ahmose's are located, as far as we know, within the original core of the Abydos landscape. Probably to build further southeast than Ahmose would be to make any king's cult uncomfortably remote from Osiris' own temple and tomb. Of those other monuments, the two best preserved, and hence most conspicuous, are the temples of Seti I and, nearby, of Ramesses II.

In the context of the preceding discussion, it is now clear that Seti's temple, with its cenotaph or Osireion, is – like Senwosret's and Ahmose's – modelled on the relationship between Osiris' temple and Osiris' tomb. Seti's cenotaph, however, is adjacent to the temple, not far away – perhaps because to have set the Osireion far back in the desert, on the axis of Seti's temple, would have placed it inappropriately close to Osiris' own. The temples of Seti I and Ramesses II were also perhaps the anchor for a new urban development (to the southeast), which most likely existed for a long time.

Nevertheless, the Osiris temple at Abydos' north corner continued to be the ritual heart of the site. All evidence for the New Kingdom phase of the adjacent town was long ago stripped away (although there are some significant pockets of New Kingdom graves in the North Cemetery), but Petrie's excavations provided much, if tantalizingly ambiguous, evidence for royal activity in and around the Osiris temple at this time. Moreover, the Pennsylvania-Yale-Institute of Fine Arts, New York University Expedition is revealing that the desert scarp overlooking the Osiris temple (where the Middle Kingdom memorial chapels had been located) was rich in royal, as well as other monuments in the New Kingdom. This revelation is largely due to Mary-Ann Pouls Wegner, who has carried out the first detailed archaeological and topographic survey of the scarp, and has begun to follow this up with excavations that are already of extraordinary interest. Moreover, this outer periphery of the Abydos Osiris temple has a much broader significance, in that the outer environs of Egyptian temples have rarely been subject to comprehensive archaeological examination. Pouls Wegner's work at Abydos shows there was significant and complex ritual activity here, linking royalty, the elite and others to the cult of the adjacent temple's deity.

First, however, we shall focus on the Osiris temple in the New Kingdom. As noted earlier, a cluster of structures excavated by Petrie roughly in the centre of the town site is identified by some scholars as the Osiris temple itself, periodically expanding as changes and additions were made over time. However, I believe that the building history of these structures (ably reconstructed by Barry Kemp on the basis of Petrie's data) is to be more persuasively read as the construction of a series of royal cult chapels, each independent of the other and built over a span of time covering much of the New Kingdom.

For this reading, it is important to note that the chapels' building history itself indicates that the space available for them was limited. Some later chapels partially overlay earlier ones, or earlier ones were completely razed, to be replaced entirely by later ones (which, archaeologically, did not always survive). These chapels appear to have stood within an enclosed area, across which a street ran from southwest to northeast. The southwestern and northeastern

58 An adaptation of Barry Kemp's map of the New Kingdom royal structures discovered by Petrie in the Osiris temple enclosure. Kemp and others believe these represent the actual Osiris temple of the New Kingdom, but, as an alternative, it is possible they are royal cult chapels built in the vicinity of an as yet unlocated Osiris temple. As the map shows, the structures were poorly preserved.

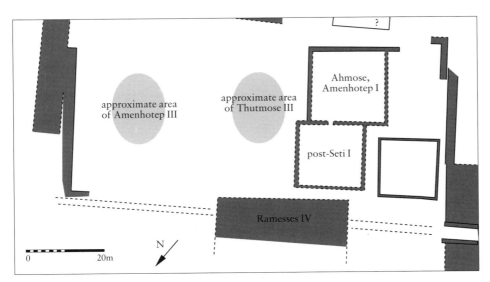

enclosure walls were recovered by Petrie, and the southeastern side would have been defined by the Osiris temple and its enclosure. How far to the northeast the enclosed chapels extended is unknown.

The earliest known chapel, dedicated to pharaohs Amenhotep I and Ahmose, was relatively large, complex in plan, and oriented – in local terms – 'north–south'. Immediately adjacent to it, to the northeast, was a chapel for Thutmose III (c. 1479–1425 BC), largely razed but apparently oriented local 'east–west', hence probably not an addition to the earlier chapel, but an independent structure built next to it.[3] Yet another chapel (for Amenhotep III, c. 1390–1353 BC) had once filled the space between Thutmose's chapel and the northeast enclosure wall. There may well have been other 18th Dynasty royal chapels, but no definite remains of them were found.

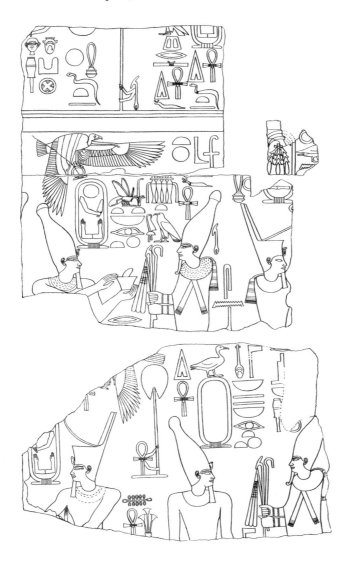

59 Limestone slabs carved in relief, from a structure dedicated near, or in the Osiris temple and celebrating kings Ahmose and Amenhotep I (Ahmose's son and successor). The upper slab shows Amenhotep I offering to Osiris (left) and Ahmose (right) presumably doing the same. The lower shows Amenhotep I on the left (offering to Osiris) and an anonymous king (Ahmose?) confronting Osiris on the right.

Later (after Seti I), another chapel (labelled E) overbuilt much of the Amenhotep I-Ahmose chapel; like the latter, it was oriented local 'north–south' and could be considered an addition, but equally could be an independent chapel seeking space (indeed, it deprived the earlier chapel of its court). Finally, substantial foundations were laid down for a chapel of Ramesses IV (*c.* 1156–1150 BC). This was markedly off-axis to the Amenhotep I-Ahmose chapel, hence not likely an addition to it, and also blocked the cross-street, an indication of how little space was available within the enclosed area. Thus, I believe these New Kingdom royal chapels are equivalent to the earlier royal *ka*-chapels that preceded them on the same spot.

Nearby are the remains of an impressive temple initiated by pharaoh Nectanebo I (381–362 BC), and also contributed to by Nectanebo II (358–341 BC), both members of the last independent Egyptian dynasty, the 30th. These circumstances (the first already suggested by Petrie) have been confirmed by recent, on-going excavations initiated by Michelle Marlar of the Institute of Fine Arts, New York University. Surviving and surface traces of the 30th Dynasty temple confirm its impressive size of roughly 40 × 116 m (131 × 330 ft) or 4,654.5 sq. m (50,035 sq. ft). The extant remains of the foundations of the temple's once massive pylon are also visible. Marlar's skillfully strategized excavations have confirmed the 30th Dynasty temple (which has as yet no trace of significant Ptolemaic or Roman additions) was levelled down to the foundations, and even beyond, at a time yet to be precisely determined. An abundance of inscribed and decorated fragments survive, however, and these are currently under study.

Equally intriguing are the remains of an underlying, earlier structure of well-cut limestone masonry, built on a brick-walled sand bed probably similar to the sand bed provided to the 30th Dynasty temple itself. This earlier structure, insofar as revealed, is in a good state of preservation, and appears to have been deliberately razed down to the blank, or dado, section of its walls. The earlier structure appears to be cultic in nature, and is built on the same alignment as the 30th Dynasty temple; the section excavated so far lies under the rear, or sanctuary, portion of the latter. The date and full extent of this earlier structure remain to be determined, but a number of very well carved reliefs dating to Thutmose IV (*c.* 1400–1390 BC) have been recovered from the debris associated with the 30th Dynasty temple. A block of similar date was reused within the walls of the 30th Dynasty. Further 18th Dynasty items have been discovered in an adjacent, secondary deposition, such as a fragment of a wooden shrine naming King Amenhotep III, with the Amun-component of his name erased, presumably during the reign of his successor, Akhenaten (*c.* 1353–1336 BC).

We may reasonably expect that the Middle Kingdom Osiris temple was razed, and replaced by another early in the New Kingdom, but no specific references to such a rebuilding (or subsequent ones) have survived. That the Osiris temple continued to be of great significance, however, is indicated by texts recording royal gifts (e.g. by Thutmose I) or increased endowments and offerings (e.g. by Thutmose III and Thutmose IV), and the dedication of royal

(Thutmose III, Thutmose IV, Seti I, Merenptah and Ramesses IV) and elite statuary. The last significant building activity known dates to Ramesses III (c. 1187–1156 BC), who built a chapel for himself in or near the Osiris temple and provided the 'temple of Osiris and Horus son of Isis' with a new precinct wall.[4] The temple also incorporated chapels for its own 'ennead', or divine corporation, which protected and collaborated with Osiris; under Thutmose I this ennead consisted of two forms of Khnum, Thoth, and two forms of Horus and Wepwawet, respectively – seven in all.

Equally importantly, it is clear that the processional festival linking the Osiris temple and Umm el Qa'ab continued throughout the New Kingdom. It is referred to directly or obliquely in a number of inscriptions from Abydos, and is the focus of Chapter 169 of the Book of the Dead, a collection of funerary spells often deposited with the dead throughout Egypt during the New Kingdom and later. As before, the desert valley serving as the processional route continued to be left free of graves or other obstructions. And finally, there is considerable evidence for New Kingdom cultic activity at Umm el Qa'ab itself.

As before, no substantial surface structure seems to have been built at Umm el Qa'ab, but the tomb of Osiris (i.e. King Djer's tomb) was certainly of cultic interest, and so were other early royal tombs, such as those of kings Den and Qa'a. Eight metres away from the former, for example, were two pits containing votive offerings left by an 18th Dynasty official, Kenamun. These included shrines in wood and copper, and faience and wooden shabtis or funerary figurines representing Kenamun. Generally, however, both earlier and the current German excavations indicate that New Kingdom votive offerings were relatively rare at Umm el Qa'ab itself.

In contrast, a low hill about 300 m (984 ft) north of Umm el Qa'ab, at the head of the processional approach, became a popular place for offerings, especially in the 18th Dynasty and later in the 25th Dynasty. A modest structure, perhaps approached by a ramp, was built on this elevation: conceivably, it might even have been a barque shrine, where the boat-shaped palanquin of Osiris may have been placed before it entered, and after it left Umm el Qa'ab. Recent reinvestigation of this site – which Petrie called 'Hekreshu Hill'– by the German Archaeological Institute has revealed pottery mainly of types specifically used for ritual purposes. The scholars involved suggest that most participants in the annual festival procession would have halted here, and only a small group continued on into the much more restricted Umm el Qa'ab, where Osiris' 'mysteries' were celebrated.

The 'Terraces of the Great God' in the New Kingdom

The desert scarp overlooking the Osiris temple (which may be the 'terraces' of Osiris referred to especially in the Middle Kingdom) evidently continued to be of great cultic significance, probably because – as earlier – it was traversed by the annual processional festival of Osiris on its way up the desert valley to Umm el Qa'ab. The area covered by the scarp and its immediate hinterland is substantial at about 5 ha (over 12 acres), but its appearance today belies its ancient importance.

For the archaeologist, this zone is a dismaying wasteland, which seems to offer almost overwhelming challenges to interpretation and excavation. Its northeast side is marked by a massive brick wall (part of the Osiris temple precinct enclosure in relatively late times), and on the southwest it gradually merges into the North Cemetery. The zone's northwestern half was savagely and deeply pitted by antiquities seekers in the 19th century and, as Pouls Wegner has shown, displays as a result classic 'reverse stratigraphy', with the earliest material now at the modern surface. Roughly central to the scarp area is a large and badly destroyed stone temple of Ramesses II – scoured by Mariette's workmen, partially excavated by Petrie, and more comprehensively explored under my direction in 1967–1969. Finally, the

60 *Map of the area identified by some as the feature ancients called 'the Terrace of the Great God (Osiris)'. On this 'terrace' or scarp, overlooking the lower-lying site of the Osiris temple, is the so-called 'Portal' temple of Ramesses II and the chapel of King Thutmose III discovered by Mary-Ann Pouls Wegner.*

61 *(right) This magnificent sandstone statue, perfectly preserved (82.5 cm or 32.5 in high) was discovered in situ in the tomb of the owner, Sitepehu, in the North Cemetery at Abydos. Sitepehu was Overseer of Priests in the Thinite Province during the reign of the female king Hatshepsut of the 18th Dynasty.*

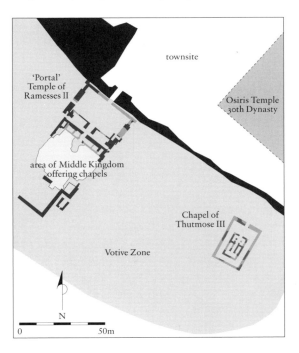

southeastern half of the zone has a markedly irregular topography and an equally desolate appearance.

This scarp – along with the town site and Osiris temple – is probably the most complex and archaeologically challenging of Abydos' remains, but Pouls Wegner is a project director well qualified to meet the challenge. Already, in the early stages of her work, she has provided a coherent, if necessarily tentative, interpretation of the entire zone, and has begun an excavational programme with already spectacular results.

Pouls Wegner has suggested that the Middle Kingdom cenotaphs were confined to the northwestern two-thirds of the scarp, an area continuing in use (presumably for cultic purposes) down into Ptolemaic times. The southeastern third, however, seems to have had a mix of royal chapels and private offering places in the New Kingdom and then experienced successive waves of tomb construction – Third Intermediate Period (c. 1075–656 BC), Saite (664–525 BC) and Ptolemaic (305–30 BC).

Although *mahats,* or memorial chapels, are rarely referred to in the New Kingdom, it is likely that many private offering places developed along the scarp at this time. Pouls Wegner has found archaeological evidence for them, and many New Kingdom stelae – often depicting Osiris but rarely referring directly to his festival – recovered along the scarp probably came from such cult chapels.

But now, for the first time to our knowledge, royal temples and chapels also appear on the scarp, most notably a small, hitherto unsuspected temple of Thutmose III, discovered by Pouls Wegner, and that of Ramesses II, mentioned above. As Pouls Wegner shows, the Thutmose temple is seemingly unique in plan, and had a painted relief programme of great beauty. Built of limestone, it had been largely destroyed, yet Pouls Wegner's meticulous excavations have recovered thousands of inscribed and decorated fragments, and they and others, she believes, will ultimately enable the programme to be fully reconstructed – which is not the case with other royal temples, such as those of Senwosret III and Ahmose.

The Thutmose temple, although relatively small, seemed monumental in appearance and was laid out with impressive regularity. A brick-walled enclosure, with a large pylon in front, occupied about 485 sq. m (5,213 sq. ft) and surrounded a stone cult building measuring 140 sq. m (1,505 sq. ft). Externally, it was a simple cube-like structure, with cavetto cornices above and torus mouldings running down the corners; yet inside it was surprisingly complex in plan. A two-columned vestibule gave access to an inner doorway flanked by two large statues of the king in Osiride form. Beyond this a central corridor led circuitously to two apparent sanctuaries, one on each side and facing local west. As Pouls Wegner points out, the temple therefore relates to both the Osiris temple, on its north, and Umm el Qa'ab and Osiris' tomb, far to the south. Clearly, it links the king both to regular cult in Osiris' temple, and the annual processional festival of that god.

Pouls Wegner has also shown that the reliefs included large-scale depictions of ritual interactions between Osiris and Thutmose III; scenes of offering-bearers

62 *Painted relief block from Thutmose III's temple showing a deity's palanquin being carried in procession.*

and assemblages of food and flowers; and, most intriguingly, a depiction of priests carrying 'a shrine or barque on a sledge' that may 'actually be a representation of the annual festival of Osiris'.[5] Much of the relief work was of the highest quality, as was the often exceptionally well preserved painting, all comparable to that of important buildings of Thutmose III at Thebes itself. Evidently, his links with Abydos were quite important to this ruler. Thutmose III is famous in his own right, but is also noted for initially being junior co-ruler with Hatshepsut (*c.* 1473–1458 BC), one of the very few women to achieve pharaonic status and, in her case, power. Hatshepsut too was likely to have had a temple on the scarp, for bricks stamped with her name – perhaps from the enclosure wall of her temple – were found in the ruins of the Ramesses II temple.

This latter temple, 65 m (213.2 ft) northwest of Thutmose's, was in fact initiated by Seti I, whose name is stamped on some bricks in a massive retaining wall underlying the temple. But its construction largely occurred under Ramesses, the chief recipient of the cult indicated by the surviving texts.

Like Thutmose's temple, Ramesses' linked the ruler to Osiris, but the two temples have different relationships to the landscape of the core area. The Thutmose temple, by position, relates directly to the Osiris temple, and also to the mouth of the processional valley further to the southeast; in addition, Pouls Wegner has shown that a complementary chapel also of Thutmose III stood on the other side of the valley mouth. The Ramesses temple (begun by Seti) lines up with the enclosed area containing royal chapels adjacent to the Osiris temple, and was probably directly linked to them by a street. Perhaps Seti desired an equivalent cult building so large in scale it would have been too intrusive in the chapel area. The Ramesses temple on the scarp occupied at least 2,000 sq. m (21,500 sq. ft), and maybe as much as 3,000 sq. m (32,250 sq. ft).

Most of Ramesses' temple had disappeared, but like Thutmose's it clearly displayed an unusual form and (perhaps) pattern of orientations. Petrie had

63 *The so-called 'Portal' temple of King Ramesses II during its excavation in 1967–1969. The traces of a brick-built pylon and forecourt were located, but the only parts of the stone-built temple to survive were the lower sections of its columned portico and front wall, visible in the photograph. To the rear is the 2nd Dynasty brick monument, the Shunet el Zebib.*

thought it was a 'portal', a monumental gateway opening to the North Cemetery, but our discovery of a court and pylon in front makes this unlikely. However, the first hall of the temple, immediately behind a columned portico on the southwest side of the court, seems to have been unique in form. An elaborate programme of engaged statuary ran around its surviving walls, and presumably originally around all of them. Relatively large Osiride figures (perhaps of Osiris himself) were set in niches recessed in the wall surfaces; projecting *from* the wall and supported by a low platform presumably running around the entire hall were colossal figures of Ramesses in Osiride form. These were either flanked or alternated with the Osiride figures in the niches. Beyond this point the temple has disappeared, but the close relationship between Osiris and Ramesses is clear.

This relationship is also evident from the surviving texts and scenes, studied by David Silverman, who directed the epigraphic recording of the temple; he notes that Osiris' name 'occurs many times in the inscriptions'. As for orientation, Silverman observed that adoring baboons depicted on the entrance way in the portico face west, 'the area sacred to Osiris',[6] whereas they normally face east towards the rising sun in Egyptian temple art. This suggests that the Ramesses temple, like Thutmose's, had an external orientation towards the east, but an internal orientation to the west, and – locally – to Umm el Qa'ab and Osiris' tomb.

Finally, Ramesses' temple has contributed to our knowledge of New Kingdom Abydos in yet another way, for reused in its foundations were the typically small stone building blocks used in structures built by Akhenaten (*c.* 1353–1336 BC), the 'heretic' king who tried to impose monotheism on the polytheistic Egyptians. Some of these blocks were inscribed and decorated and have been published by Kelly Simpson (1995). Such reused Akhenaten material is not uncommon in early Ramesside structures, and often came from Akhenaten's two main building sites: Thebes and Tell el-Amarna. Silverman, however, has found a textual indication that our material may have come from

64 *The 'Portal' temple of King Ramesses II had been mostly destroyed in antiquity. However, parts of one of its colossal statues of Ramesses II survived, and were assigned to the University of Pennsylvania Museum by the Egyptian authorities in 1969. Here, the composite parts are being reassembled at the University of Pennsylvania Museum. (See colour plate I.)*

a relatively small structure at Abydos itself.[7] Whether Akhenaten built cult structures at sites other than Thebes and Tell el-Amarna is disputed, but maybe Osiris and Abydos were a special case. Osiris, like other traditional deities, was banished from official Amarna religion, but even Akhenaten had his shawabtis or funerary figurines made in the traditional mummified 'Osirian' form.

65 *An intriguing discovery at the 'Portal' temple of Ramesses II was that its foundations included re-used stone blocks from earlier structures, presumably also at Abydos. These included a number of decorated or plain 'talatat', the distinctively proportioned blocks typical of structures built for King Akhenaten, the monotheistic 'heretic' king. The talatat above depicts Akhenaten receiving life from the sun-disc or Aten. The talatat below depicts a temple, with a columned portico incorporating statues of Akhenaten and his queen.*

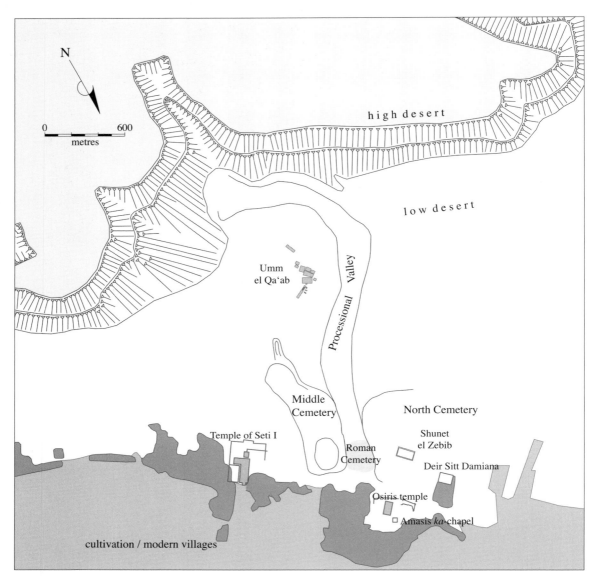

N

0   600
metres

high desert

low desert

Umm
el Qa'ab

Processional Valley

Middle
Cemetery

North Cemetery

Temple of Seti I

Shunet
el Zebib

Roman
Cemetery

Deir Sitt Damiana

Osiris temple

Amasis *ka*-chapel

cultivation / modern villages

66 *Map of Late Period Abydos.*

CHAPTER EIGHT

THE CLIMAX OF THE OSIRIS CULT

Turbulent Times

For Abydos, the New Kingdom – however productive – was but one chapter in a story that still had some 1,500 years to run. Moreover, during that time the Osiris cult, important as it was earlier, seems to have climaxed in terms of its significance and pervasiveness. Jaroslav Černy remarked on 'the slow and continuous penetration of Osiris into the realm of the living' since the New Kingdom and noted: 'With the expansion of Osiris, the cult of the sun-god Re vanished, and his personality became more and more absorbed by Osiris'.[1] Thus Osiris now dominated both the world of the living and the dead. He and Isis were immensely popular and chapels dedicated to them in and around the temples of other deities became more prominent than before. Moreover, Isis and Osiris (often in his special Ptolemaic form, Serapis) were among the very few Egyptian deities who became popular abroad – with the ancient Nubians and Sudanese, the Greeks and the Romans, and others.

The later phases of Egyptian religion, of which the processes just described were a part, are often seen as a period of decline in both spiritual and historical terms, but in fact Egyptian religious ideas and theories now reached a level of sophistication which drew upon, but in some ways surpassed, earlier tradition. Scholars are also put off by such late phenomena as the veneration, mummification and burial of sacred animals and birds, although these are simply one particular manifestation of very ancient Egyptian beliefs and customs. As at other sites, cemeteries for such creatures occur at Abydos in post-New Kingdom times, specifically for ones linked to deities associated with Osiris, i.e. hawks (Horus), dogs (Wepwawet and Anubis) and ibises (Thoth). Glimpses of religious practice in Egypt provided by Greek and Roman observers also disconcert scholars because of their somewhat 'lower-class' manifestations of enthusiasm, and religiously sanctioned license. As Dominic Montserrat observes, not only did men and women participate equally in Egyptian religious festivals but to outside observers 'what goes on at them is excessive and unrestrained, be it eating, drinking, sex or all three at once'.[2] Here again, however, we are probably seeing the continuation of much earlier practices that were not so clearly revealed in earlier sources.

Naturally, Abydos benefited from the increased importance of Osiris, and Barry Kemp has suggested that the Third Intermediate and Late periods (c. 1075–332 BC) 'saw the most important development of Abydos as a national cemetery'.[3] The temple of Osiris also continued to flourish, and the names and titles of many of its priests and other personnel – especially during the Late and Ptolemaic periods (664–30 BC) – have survived. Like other major temples, that of Osiris had an elaborately arranged hierarchy of priests, headed by four levels of senior priests. There was also a multitude of other functionaries, ranging from overseers of the god's buildings, estates and treasuries, to lower-level individuals, such as gardeners and a man called Tjawtaw, a 'barber of the domain of Osiris' in the 7th century BC. The latter seems incongruously highlighted, until we remember that priests, in order to be ritually pure, had to be free of all body hair!

. Given this dynamic situation, the sacred landscape of Abydos continued, over the next 1,500 years, to change and develop, although two features of this development should be noted. First, whereas earlier each major historical period was marked by substantial additions to the Abydos landscape, with new temples, new cemetery fields and even new settlements, from c. 1000 BC to AD 400 it continued to be structured to a surprising degree by surviving New Kingdom structures, large and small. Secondly, sometime before c. 1000 BC the landscape, having previously been an ever-expanding one, in fact contracted severely. Senwosret's monument was not used after c. 1500 BC, and Ahmose's temple ceased to be used for a cult after the New Kingdom. Finally, some time after 300 BC Umm el Qa'ab seems to have ceased being part of the ritual life of Abydos, and that axial relationship between Osiris' temple and his tomb at Umm el Qa'ab, which had so strongly influenced the structure of the repeatedly expanding Abydos landscape, ended.

Despite this contraction, the old core area of Abydos – defined by the Osiris temple, the Seti I temple and, for a long time, Umm el Qa'ab – was ritually active over some 1,500 years; years which, for Egypt, proved to be exceptionally turbulent. As background to Abydos' continuing development, Egypt's history during this period now needs to be described briefly, for it is complex and often unfamiliar. Many readers are so familiar with the historical pattern of earlier times in Egypt – the relatively stable and prosperous Old, Middle and New Kingdoms, interspersed with brief phases of political fragmentation and conflict (the First and Second Intermediate periods) – that I have virtually assumed that knowledge up to this point. This I cannot do after c. 1000 BC.

After this date, Egypt oscillated more violently, and for longer periods than before, between high levels of societal stress and phases of relative stability and prosperity. Moreover, it was gradually transformed from being an independent, core state to a peripheral one, and a dependency of larger entities such as the Assyrian, Persian and Roman empires. For a period (c. 760–656 BC) Egypt was even subordinate to its erstwhile colonial subjects, the Kushites of Nubia.

The Third Intermediate Period (c. 1075–656 BC)[4] was an extraordinarily long phase of ever-increasing political disintegration for Egypt. First, two successive dynasties (the 21st and 22nd: c. 1075–712 BC) received nominal recognition throughout Egypt but, being based in the Delta, both found that southern Egypt – centred at Thebes – either had to be kept loyal via intermarriage with the royal house and the appointment of royal kin or supporters to important positions at Thebes, or be allowed to become virtually independent. Indeed, some scholars argue that Thebes was eventually ruled by its own line of kings (most of those identified as the 23rd Dynasty: *c.* 830–712 BC), although not all would agree.

By *c.* 750 BC the situation was becoming even more complicated. A new principality (ultimately ruled by the 24th Dynasty: *c.* 730–712 BC) was rising in the western Delta, and the Nubian kingdom of northern Sudan was expanding northwards into Egypt, eventually securing full control over it (as the 25th Dynasty) for almost a century (*c.* 747–656 BC). These Nubian rulers were effective throughout Egypt, but did not end its underlying fragmentation; the country comprised some 11 petty states, headed by kings, 'Great Chiefs' of Libyan tribes and others, serving as the vassals of the 25th Dynasty.

This dynasty ended violently, after a series of invasions and short-lived occupations of Egypt by the expanding Assyrian empire – in *c.* 671, 667/666 and 664/663 BC. But, for external reasons, the Assyrians soon gave up control of Egypt, to be replaced by a native Egyptian dynasty – albeit probably of Libyan origin, like some of those preceding it – the 26th Dynasty (664–525 BC). These rulers brought back prosperity and political unity to Egypt, but increasingly found themselves at violent odds with the latest great power of the Near East, the Persian empire. Eventually, Egypt became a province of that empire for over a century (525–404 BC; the relevant Persian kings were identified as the 27th Dynasty). There followed a period of Egyptian independence, comprising three dynasties (28th to 30th: 404–341 BC), of which the last was particularly powerful and prosperous. A brief return to Persian rule (341–332 BC) was terminated by the conquest of Egypt by Alexander the Great, who had undertaken the destruction of the entire Persian empire.

From 332 to 30 BC Egypt was first ruled by Alexander, followed by his immediate successors, and then finally, as an independent kingdom, by a dynasty descended from Ptolemy, one of Alexander's generals. The Ptolemies, as they are called, were for the most part good administrators and active imperialists, so Egypt was relatively prosperous for much of this time. However, nationalist resistance to these 'foreign' kings (and the many Greeks serving in the army and the administration) smouldered away in southern and middle Egypt, sometimes flaring into open rebellion, especially in the 2nd and early 1st centuries BC. Royal reaction was severe; for example, one such rebellion ended in 85 BC with – in Idris Bell's words – the 'virtual destruction of Thebes' and its reduction to 'a group of villages scattered among the ruins of her former magnificence'.[5] Abydos itself was besieged at least once during such a rebellion (in the 2nd century BC).

Finally, in 30 BC, Egypt became a province of the Roman empire, and later of the eastern Roman empire ruled from Constantinople. By the time Egypt came under the control of the Muslim Arabs (AD 641) its people had become fully

Christianized. Nevertheless, traditional Egyptian culture continued for a long time during the Roman period, as the emperors, like the Ptolemies before them, had actively supported the religious system that remained the dynamic core of Egyptian society, even if pharaonic kingship had ceased to be a reality. Only gradually did Christians become the majority and older religious systems fall into disrepute, but these processes were irreversible. In AD 390 emperor Theodosius I decreed the closing of pagan temples throughout the Byzantine empire. Up to this point, it is likely that Osiris' temple at Abydos had continued to function, although eventually the cult must have become extremely attenuated.[6]

'Thirty pints of wine ... daily to the altar of Khentamentiu'

This phrase, uttered by the official Paftuaneith in the 6th century BC, is but one of many hundreds of inscriptions which epitomize the vigorous support given to the Osiris cult at Abydos by royalty, elite and the populace at large during the long period of interest to us here. As before, support and devotion found expression through the core components of the Abydos landscape: the Osiris temple, the tomb of Osiris at Umm el Qa'ab, the processional route between the two, and the large cemeteries – the Middle and North – flanking that route on either side. However, attempting to reconstruct patterns of activity and change over this vast area (which also includes the Seti I temple) is like trying to assemble a jigsaw puzzle from which most of the pieces are missing and many of those that remain are small or fragmentary – fragments of statues and stelae from temple and cemetery; shawabtis and coffin fragments from unknown or sketchily recorded tombs; and, from Umm el Qa'ab, often quite tiny items, such as wind-worn sherds from jars once containing offerings dedicated to Osiris under rulers whose names were written hastily in ink.

Despite these difficulties, the story that emerges is a fascinating one that highlights many important issues and problems to be explored through new excavations and survey. An especially prominent feature of that story is the surprising degree to which New Kingdom monuments, rather than being replaced, continued to be major or significant features of the landscape and were still used for cultic purposes.

This is perhaps least surprising for the massive temple of Seti I, which could not easily be replaced by another. It was, as Barry Kemp notes, 'a centre for pilgrimage and tourism' into the 3rd century AD.[7] The deity venerated was no longer Seti but Osiris himself and, in particular, in Ptolemaic times a special form of Osiris called Serapis, or in Egyptian 'User-Hape' (Osiris the Apis Bull). This suggests that the Seti temple was particularly important under the Ptolemies, and may explain why they did not replace the existing temple of Osiris, further to the northwest, with a new one (even though they did build new temples in the region, as in the case of the goddess Hathor at Dendereh). Serapis was a deity intended by Ptolemy I (305–284 BC) to be a new national god for Egypt – a striking example of Osiris' increased importance, which was further reflected in the immense popularity Serapis in fact came to enjoy among Greeks; Egyptians continued to venerate Osiris in his older, more traditional form. Strangely, in the Roman period, Serapis was replaced by Bes as the deity of Seti's temple. Bes was a significant but lesser being.

More striking examples of the continuing use of New Kingdom structures involve the smaller temples along the scarp overlooking the Osiris temple at the north corner of Abydos. On that scarp, the temple of Ramesses II continued in use, apparently for ritual purposes, well into the Third Intermediate Period and perhaps beyond. In fact, we recovered from its ruins many sherds from pottery bowls dating to that period and evidently used for ritual purposes. Almost unique to Abydos, and indeed to this particular temple, these bowls were inscribed with the varied ingredients for incense and were often decorated with finely drawn representations of deities, especially of Osiris and his ennead. For her part, Mary-Ann Pouls Wegner has shown that the small temple of Thutmose III seems to have been used continuously for ritual into the Ptolemaic period. Indeed, she observed that the last planting of two trees in front of the temple was dated to Ptolemaic times by the sherds in the dirt surrounding their roots.

Even the Osiris temple itself may have been essentially a New Kingdom structure for much of the next 1,500 years, although one continually embellished with new shrines, sacred barques and statuary as time went on. I have surmised above that the Osiris temple had been completely rebuilt – maybe more than once – during the New Kingdom, although we have as yet no direct, unambiguous proof for this. It could be argued, on present evidence, that the latest New Kingdom temple survived until replaced by one built by Nectanebo I (381–362 BC), almost 700 years later.

67 *During the Late Period, rituals were practiced in the so-called 'Portal' temple of Ramesses II. One by-product of these practices were unbaked mud figurines of a variety of animals or birds emblematic of specific deities, the exact use of which is as yet unknown. Especially common were ram's heads, evocative of the god Amun, but vultures (Mut or Nekhbet), cobras (Wadjiyet) and others also occurred.*

Abydos and the Osiris temple were evidently quite important in the Third Intermediate Period, including the 25th Dynasty. Throughout this period, royal activity (but not necessarily building activity) is attested in the Osiris temple's vicinity, and a number of high-ranking Theban officials also held positions in Osiris' Abydos cult, as priests or temple scribes. In addition, some princesses of the 21st Dynasty were priestesses of Osiris, Horus and Isis in Abydos.

A number of other high-ranking individuals, many resident at Thebes, were buried or commemorated in the Middle and North cemeteries, south and southwest of the temple and town. They included Psussenes, son of the Theban High Priest of Amun Menkheperre (c. 1045–992 BC); Iuput, a Theban High Priest who was a son of King Shoshenk I (c. 945–924 BC); no fewer than four Kushite royal women, at least two of whom were the wives of 25th Dynasty kings; and a vizier or prime minister Nespamedu who was so powerful that the Assyrian conquerors of Egypt in c. 671 BC identified him as 'the king of Thinis', where he apparently resided, rather than at Thebes (the more usual case for southern viziers).

It is also clear that the practice of setting up statue cults for kings and elite individuals in relationship to the Osiris temple continued. King Takeloth III (c. 754–734 BC) apparently had such a cult in or near the Osiris temple, while a stela describing the establishment of a similar cult for a local ruler of Bubastis in the Delta – the 'Great Chief of the Mashwash (a Libyan tribe), Nimlot'[8] – is extraordinarily revealing about the economic and administrative arrangements that in one form or another must have been involved in such cults all the way back to the Old Kingdom.

Nimlot was one of a line descended from Libyan prisoners of war settled as hereditary troops by Ramesses III at Bubastis. By the reign of Psussenes II (c. 959–945 BC) these leaders were well connected to the royal house and Nimlot's son and successor, Shoshenk (who himself became King Shoshenk I), petitioned the king to secure from Amun-Re at Thebes a decree authorizing a statue cult at Abydos for the deceased Nimlot. With approval granted, Nimlot's statue travelled in state from Thebes to Abydos, where it was ritually vitalized and purified in the temple of Osiris before being 'caused to repose in the sanctuaries of the gods for ever and ever'. The relevant text is also very specific about the endowment for the cult, and reminds us how much of Abydos' landscape is hidden from us, for – in the form of endowment-supporting estates – it extended over much of the regional floodplain, and even to other parts of the Nile Valley as well. Thus, Nimlot's endowment included large local estates north and south of Abydos but, in order to ensure that his statue cult's needs would be met in perpetuity, its support was also firmly linked to the 'treasury of Osiris'. The harvest of the estates was delivered to the treasury for storage, processing, ritual use and ultimate redistribution, while the treasury was paid silver to ensure some of its personnel would always be allotted the task of ensuring Nimlot's cult received regular supplies of honey, incense, oil ('for the lamp of…Nimlot'), bread and beer. In addition, the king and Shoshenk made

68 (right) A well-carved limestone stela of the Third Intermediate Period (mid-6th century BC). Below the winged sun disc, it shows a person called Nepthys-tekhti venerating the sun god Re. Below, Osiris is asked to provide Nepthys-tekhti 'a fine burial in the necropolis'.

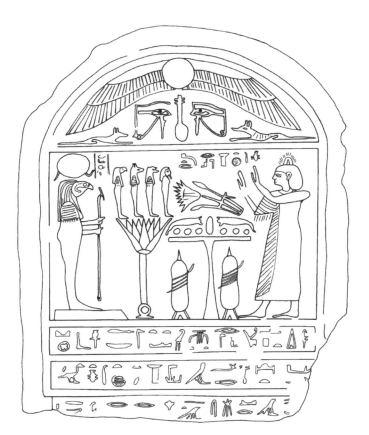

69 In 1967 a large and surprisingly almost unplundered burial chamber was excavated near the so-called 'Portal' temple of Ramesses II; as was often the case in the Late Period, it was a family tomb containing multiple burials, packed around or above each other. Some were in finely decorated cartonage coffins, but insects had destroyed much of the organic material. The tomb was originally constructed for a man called Redi-Anhur (late 25th or early 26th Dynasty), a man of importance whose official title and status, however, are not known.

generous and unencumbered gifts of silver to the Osiris treasury, presumably to provide the incentive for the contractual agreements specified, otherwise the temple made no profit.

Given all of these circumstances, one might wonder why no new temple for Osiris was built in the Third Intermediate Period. But in fact while the 21st–23rd Dynasties were active temple builders at their Delta capital Tanis, as was the 25th Dynasty at its Nubian centres, neither seems to have undertaken major building projects in southern Egypt, even at Thebes, although they did add to existing New Kingdom temples. Thus, Abydos here seems to be part of a general trend.

With the 26th Dynasty, which clearly valued Abydos, a different story might be expected. Egypt was united and prosperous, and the dynasty undertook major temple rebuildings – but again more in the Delta than in southern Egypt. No definite evidence for a rebuilding of Osiris' Abydos temple exists, although a high official of the period was very active in and around the temple during the reigns of kings Apries (589–570 BC) and Amasis (570–526 BC). Paftuaneith[9] was so proud of his achievements that he set up a large statue of himself (1.69 m or 5.5 ft high) inscribed with his activities and standing in or in front of the Osiris temple so that 'you who come from the temple blessed, say: ... may (Paftuaneith) receive eternal bread at the hand of the blessed!'.

The acts described are certainly comprehensive, and include the bold statement that Paftuaneith 'built the temple of Khentamentiu (Osiris)'. But the text also indicates that the temple had become dilapidated, and describes what seems to be more a renovation than an actual rebuilding. Paftuaneith supplied the temple with new cultic equipment, and a granite shrine (fragments of which were found by Petrie), as well as a 'god's boat' built of cedar to replace an existing one of cheaper acacia wood. Paftuaneith's building activities were extensive, but peripheral to the temple – he constructed a new enclosure wall of brick and renewed the 'ruined' House of Life, a typical appendage to temples and described by Miriam Lichtheim as an institution in which 'medicine, magic, theology, ritual and dream interpretation' were 'studied and practiced'.[10]

Perhaps Paftuaneith was also responsible for an impressive stone-built chapel (about 1,650 sq. m or 17,737 sq. ft) which Petrie discovered overlying the site of the earlier chapels of Thutmose III and Amenhotep III. This chapel (of which only the foundations of the enclosure wall and a little of the internal plan survive) was built initially for King Amasis, and some see it as part of the actual Osiris temple. However, I would interpret it as an independent royal cult chapel.

Like their predecessors, the Persian overlords of Egypt do not seem to have been great temple builders in southern Egypt. If the New Kingdom temple had survived the 26th Dynasty, it was likely to have remained until finally replaced by a new one, by pharaoh Nectanebo I of the 30th Dynasty. The 30th Dynasty rulers certainly had the resources to build new temples, and did so in many places in Egypt.

As noted earlier, Nectanebo's temple is still visible as a surface ruin (including a pylon, large court and temple proper) and hence was the last Osiris temple to

Late Period architecture
Earlier phase (New Kingdom?) walls
Earlier phase (New Kingdom?) floors
Mud-brick architecture
Dry-laid mud brick
Loose stone blocks
Excavation units
Probable extent of Late Period temple

0   5   10   15   20m

N

70 *Outline of the Late Period (Nectanebo I) temple of Osiris and remains of an earlier temple phase below it.*

be built at Abydos. It must have been the one visited by Strabo (who was impressed by the absence of singing and music in its cult); the one worked upon, according to an inscription, in the 17th year of Emperor Tiberius' rule (AD 30); the one that perhaps stayed open until the pagan temples were closed in AD 390. Finally, at some point it was savagely destroyed (a fate escaped by contemporary temples not far away, such as Hathor's at Dendereh), thus bringing to a close one of the longest-lived Egyptian temples for which we have direct (if often ambiguous) archaeological evidence.

The Desert Hinterland

We have seen that, for millennia, the core landscape of Abydos had been structured around the axial relationship between the Osiris temple and Osiris' tomb at Umm el Qaʿab – an axis defined by the annual processional festival which was a focus of national as much as of royal interest. This situation continued for much of the post-New Kingdom period, a period which also provides us with some unexpectedly direct insights into the Egyptians' own ideas about sacred landscapes such as that of Abydos, especially insofar as the desert hinterland was concerned.

Thus, in this period (but also as early as Ramesside times at least) the vast cemetery field comprising the Middle and North cemeteries and Umm el Qaʿab was personified as Hapetnebes, 'She who hides her lord', a term peculiar to Abydos. The endless, open desert plain of Abydos was imagined to be a goddess, generated by and embodied in the landscape itself. 'She who hides her lord' was complex in meaning. At one level, this goddess as landscape literally hid and thus protected (e.g. from Osiris' murderer Seth) Osiris himself – buried at Umm el Qaʿab – as well as his countless followers, each one also 'an Osiris', entombed in the Abydene cemeteries. But Hapetnebes was also a more positive force in that Osiris, buried within her, experienced revitalization or rebirth every year (as did all deceased Egyptians, identified with him). In this perspective, 'She who hides her lord' is virtually landscape conceived of as a mother goddess, in whose womb lies the potential for and actualization of life. She thus relates to the subtle interplay of meaning between desert and flood-plain in the prototypical Egyptian landscape, which I discussed earlier. The desert, seemingly dead, generates life for Osiris and deceased Egyptians; and thus relates to those more obvious manifestations of vitality and reproduction, the inundation and consequent vegetation, both seen as manifestations of Osiris' capacity to regenerate.

Another Late Period text which is particularly revealing about Egyptian concepts of landscape is a seemingly mundane decree once inscribed upon one of the cliff faces at Abydos (its exact provenance now unknown). The decree, issued under Nectanebo II (358–341 BC), forbade the quarrying of stone from the cliffs or the desert valleys running back from them. The text states that such quarrying, while recently noted and reported to the king, 'had never been done before',[11] indicating again that the Egyptians sought to maintain the pristine quality of the Abydos landscape, presumably because of its sacred character.

The Nectanebo decree also reveals that the sacred could become manifest in the landscape in a strikingly direct way. It refers to 'the holy mountain' (the high desert plateau behind Abydos) as 'She who hides her lord', thus extending the designation of the low desert cemeteries into the purely natural landscape beyond them; and notes that this holy mountain is visibly 'protected ... by the two falcons', evidently bird-shaped natural eminences. These circumstances are very reminiscent of a coffin type popular in the Late Period: a box-like wooden sarcophagus with a falcon at each corner and often specifically identified with 'the tomb of Osiris'. Moreover, coffins could also be personified as protective and regenerative goddesses and, after the New Kingdom, often had the sky goddess Nut – the mother of Osiris – depicted on the inner face of the lid. Thus, in the Late Period (and maybe earlier) the Egyptians seem to have read the high cliffs of Abydos as equivalent to the falcon-topped sarcophagus of Osiris, a sarcophagus that was also a mother goddess protecting the god and guaranteeing him renewed life or rebirth.

Turning from the symbolism to the archaeology of Abydos' desert land-scape, there is good evidence that the processional route to Umm el Qa'ab, and hence the tomb of Osiris there, was maintained until at least the 30th Dynasty. As we have seen, royal and other chapels along the scarp overlooking the begin-ning of the processional route from the temple of Osiris were maintained and added to throughout this period. Moreover, even the funerary monuments and tombs of high-ranking individuals of the Third Intermediate Period seem to indicate a desire for proximity to significant points along the lower, more nar-rowly defined stretch of the processional desert valley leading to Umm el Qa'ab. Some tombs were clustered at the north corner, near the entrance to this particular stretch, some in Cemetery D at its west corner, where it opened up into the wider area leading up to 'Hekreshu Hill' and Umm el Qa'ab. Finally, it is also important to note that a small cult building, or assemblage of such buildings, had stood at the southern end of the lower stretch of the valley (just south of Cemetery D) since the 19th Dynasty at least. Presumably a way station of some kind along the processional route, this complex included *naoi*, or shrines, dedicated by or to Nectanebo I and II, a clear indication that the processional route had functioned at least up to the end of the 30th Dynasty.

Cultic activity is also attested at and around Umm el Qa'ab itself. Inscribed items show that dedicatory offerings were made there in the names of kings of

71 *Redi-Anhur was provided with a large limestone stela, set in a chapel above the tomb. On the stela (about two-thirds survived) he is shown venerated by his very large family (his sons and daughters). One of the latter was called Sit-Nubt: the third woman from the right. Her burial in the chamber was identified by inscriptions, indicating that it is likely that others in the tomb included some of her brothers and sisters. Redi-Anhur was probably buried in an adjoining chamber, which was completely plundered out.*

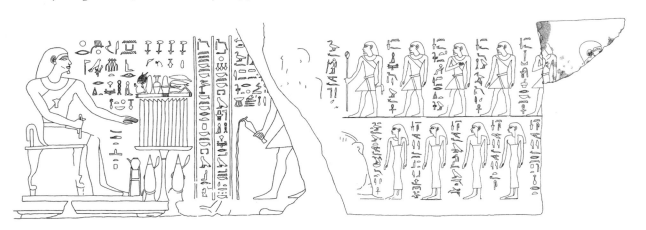

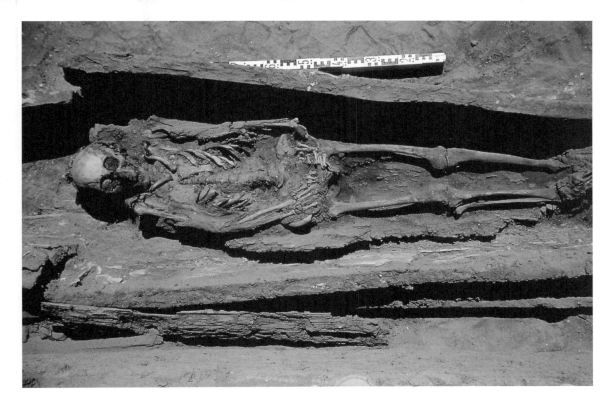

72 *(above) The burial of the lady Sit-Nubt.*

73 *North Abydos was an especially popular burial ground in the Third Intermediate Period and later, and coffin burials of this period are often encountered by archaeologists. A series of burials for both adults and children has been exposed here.*

the 21st (Psussenes II), the 22nd (Osorkon I and II) and the 23rd (Osorkon III) Dynasties, as well as on behalf of High Priests of Amun-Re at Thebes. Both at Umm el Qa'ab and Hekreshu Hill there is much offering pottery of the Third Intermediate Period, especially the 25th Dynasty.

Finally, Paftuaneith, who as we have heard carried out substantial renovations in and around the temple of Osiris, also renovated or rebuilt the 'wepeg-sanctuary' of Osiris, which seems to mean his tomb at Umm el Qa'ab. Indeed, Amélineau and Petrie found at Umm el Qa'ab dated materials of precisely those kings (Apries and Amasis) Paftuaneith served, all probably coming from a shrine set up centrally (according to Petrie's observations of the floor) in the erstwhile tomb of King Djer of the 1st Dynasty. Part of a stela of King Amasis was found in King Den's tomb (41 m or 134.5 ft directly south of Djer's) and a door jamb from a structure inscribed with King Apries' name in the tomb of Queen Merneith (38.4 m or 125.9 ft southwest of Djer's). Both probably came originally from Djer's tomb, material from which was widely scattered by plunderers. Petrie certainly thought this was true of the Apries fragment, for he also found two fragments of the massive bier of Osiris (discovered by

Amélineau in Djer's tomb), one by the tomb of Anedjib (next to Merneith's) and the other 'a furlong (200 m) to the south'.

As earlier, there is no indication of a substantial surface building associated with Osiris' tomb at this time, although Paftuaneith does say that he 'set up its braziers' (perhaps in the tomb) and 'dug its pond and planted its trees', which must have been surface features. Given the difficulty of maintaining them in this remote and arid spot, however, it is not likely that either pond or plantation was very large.

The subterranean shrine of Osiris, accessible to priests and perhaps very distinguished visitors via a stairway, must have been a fascinating place. The floorspace in Djer's tomb was about 156 sq. m (1,677 sq. ft) and the dimensions of the centrally placed shrine are uncertain. Petrie merely observed that 'all the middle of the tomb had been cleared to the native marl for building the Osiris shrine, of which some fragments of sculpture in hard limestone are now all that remain'.[12] In any event, there must have been sufficient space for votive objects to be placed around the shrine.

It seems that the remote past, and the present of Third Intermediate Period Egypt, came together in an even more unique way at Umm el Qa'ab. A 'chief of the Libyan tribe Mahasun and Fourth Prophet of Amun-Re at Thebes' called Pashedbast recorded that in the reign of Osorkon I he was 'strolling about in the desert' of Abydos and discovered a 'stela of the necropolis'.[13] Pashedbast had the stela 'cleaned', or perhaps 're-erected' (in the latter case he must have found it fallen over); provided it with 'boundary stelae', which probably included the extant one, i.e. all would have described Pashedbast's beneficial acts; and endowed it with fields and offerings for 'Osiris Khentamentiu, lord of Abydos'. Indeed, in a scene about the text, Pashedbast (of the scene, only his feet survive) was probably shown adoring Osiris.

This pious act was not as casual as it might seem at first glance. As a high ecclesiastic, Pashedbast was likely to have visited Abydos to participate in the processional festival to Umm el Qa'ab, and it is also likely he found the stela *at* Umm el Qa'ab, for he makes it clear the stela lay or stood far out in the desert, 'beside the cliff of "She who hides her lord"'. At this period, Umm el Qa'ab was the only monument-rich site, set far out in the desert, which would have been visited by festival participants, pilgrims and pious tourists.

The stela itself must have seemed especially significant to Pashedbast, for he went to the trouble and expense of reinstalling it in an appropriate setting, and endowing it with an estate to provide offerings and implicitly to support a priest to make these offerings. The stela was probably relatively large, for Pashedbast's 'boundary stela' was likely 60 cm (2 ft) high, yet its peripheral function implies that the stela that was the focus of cult would have been substantially larger. Finally, Pashedbast himself tries to indicate that the stela was of an unusual, perhaps even unique nature; it was similar to 'those (stelae) which are brought from the necropolis beside Memphis'. The only stelae unique to the latter would be the royal funerary stelae set up next to the pyramids of the Old and Middle Kingdoms and at 2nd Dynasty royal tombs, which suggests that

Pashedbast had actually discovered one of the Early Dynastic royal funerary stelae (similar in some ways to the Memphite ones just mentioned) which Amélineau and Petrie had found scattered, either intact or in fragments, around Umm el Qa'ab. These indeed could be quite impressive. Djet's intact stela, for example, is 2.5 m (over 8 ft) high, and intact stelae of Queen Merneith and King Peribsen were respectively 1.56 m (5.1 ft) and 1.52 m (5 ft) high.

Pashedbast probably did not know the exact significance of the stela he had found, but presumably recognized that it was ancient and royal, and hence associated it with the nearby tomb of Osiris. In any event, if my theory is correct, this was an extraordinary moment in the archaeological history of Abydos.

To return to Umm el Qa'ab as a whole, we have seen that cult was practiced there until the end of the 31st Dynasty. After this, neither inscriptional data nor archaeological material such as datable ceramic types indicates any subsequent activity. The implication is that, in Ptolemaic and Roman times, the annual processional festival no longer made its way to Umm el Qa'ab and the tomb of Osiris there was no longer of significance. Mark Smith has in fact observed that: 'In the Graeco-Roman period ... the tomb of Osiris ... was thought to lie within the god's temple complex'[14] at Abydos, and indeed a large cemetery of the Roman period was allowed – for the first time in Abydos' long history – to block the mouth of the processional valley, a good indication that the path was no longer used.

The annual festival of Osiris was still celebrated, but perhaps in and around the Osiris temple itself. Or possibly, since the Seti temple was upgraded into a temple of Serapis in the Ptolemaic period, the processional festival went *there*, and treated the Osireion, the cenotaph or false tomb of Seti-as-Osiris, as the actual tomb of Osiris. Certainly the Osireion and its access tunnel were open throughout most of Abydos' last 1,500 years, for they display graffiti running perhaps as late as the 3rd century AD.

The Osiris festival of course eventually did end, as did the cult of Osiris itself. Thereafter, apart from sporadic activity in the Christian period, little took place over this vast site. A long silence began as sand blew over the ruined temples, abandoned towns and enormous cemetery fields. The Coptic Christians were direct descendants of the ancient Egyptians, but despite this the latter would have thought that at Abydos and throughout Egypt their world, their cosmos, had come to an end.

Such an end had been envisaged by the ancients themselves, in a way that yet again involved Osiris. Centuries before Abydos and the other pagan centres had finally ended, the creator god Atum is made to prophesy, in the Book of the Dead, Chapter 175: 'The earth will return to the primeval water ... to endless flood as in its first state. I shall remain with Osiris after I have transformed myself into another snake which men do not know and the gods do not see'. As Eric Hornung points out, the snake referred to embodies the 'regenerating non-existence that encircles the world',[15] a world that has itself disappeared. Inherent in this non-existence is the potential (Osiris) and the dynamic (Atum) for cosmic regeneration, for the creation of a new world – but not that of the ancient Egyptians.

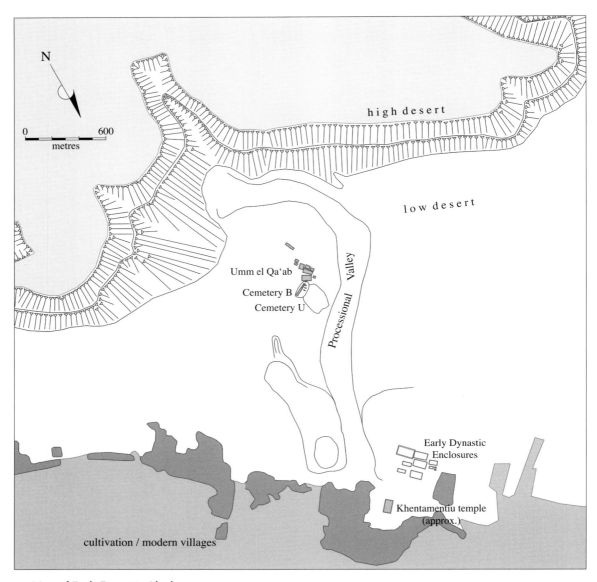

N

0 ————— 600
metres

high desert

low desert

Umm el Qa'ab

Cemetery B
Cemetery U

Processional Valley

Early Dynastic
Enclosures

Khentamentiu temple
(approx.)

cultivation / modern villages

74 *Map of Early Dynastic Abydos.*

PART III Origins of the Abydos Landscape

CHAPTER NINE

THE ROYAL TOMBS OF ABYDOS

Big Fish Eat Little Fish

Abydos had a unique status in early Egypt because all kings of the 1st Dynasty (which began *c.* 2950 BC) and the last two of the 2nd Dynasty (ending *c.* 2650 BC) were buried there. Their large and once sumptuously equipped tombs initiate developments leading on to the pyramids and rock-cut tombs of later kings. Moreover, the royal tombs of Abydos were associated with large enclosures anticipating the later pyramid complexes in important ways. The enclosures are being explored by the Pennsylvania-Yale-Institute of Fine Arts, New York University Expedition; recent discoveries include a cache of large, buried boats that are the prototypes for later royal boat burials such as those found with the Great Pyramid of King Khufu at Giza. Most recently, and unexpectedly, the Supreme Council of Antiquities of Egypt has discovered elite Early Dynastic tombs a little to the south of the Seti temple.

In all, Abydos in the Early Dynastic period (the 1st and 2nd Dynasties) is the most important source we have for the enormous cultural and political changes taking place at this time. It was during this period that Egyptian civilization began to take on its characteristic and unique forms. To appreciate the significance of the early royal tombs, enclosures and boat graves of Abydos, however, we need to glance quickly at the exciting but frustrating issues involved in the origins of Egyptian civilization. Recent books by David Wengrow and Toby Wilkinson, and Walter B. Emery's much earlier but still valuable overview, guide us through the material, but debate remains lively as new discoveries enrich yet complicate our understanding of the story.

This debate reminds me of Pieter Bruegel's wonderful etching depicting scrambling men gutting an enormous fish. It towers above them while from the vast and gaping cut a gigantic stream of smaller fish pours across the beach. Grand theories (as impressive as Bruegel's great fish) are proposed about early culture and kingship in Egypt, but are based on heterogeneous and random archaeological data, akin to Bruegel's variegated little fish. So far, these data are an inadequate foundation for the complex speculations built upon them, for the evidence still has substantial ambiguities and gaps. Yet, the challenge of tracing the origins of one of the world's most brilliant civilizations continues to fascinate us, and Abydos is increasingly important in that endeavour.

The chronological picture at least is fairly clear. After the full Neolithic of the 5th millennium BC, Egypt entered the 'predynastic period' of *c.* 4000 to 3300 BC after a transitional phase dubbed the Badarian culture (*c.* 4300–3800 BC). From the latter, at least partly, evolved the successive prehistoric cultures labelled Amratian (Naqada I) and Gerzean (Naqada II), partially paralleled by a supposedly distinct 'Maadian' culture in the Delta. The latter distinction, however, has recently been called into question. Naqada III, for its part, spans the latest prehistoric and the earliest historic periods (*c.* 3400/3300 BC onwards). Phases a and b cover the earliest, possibly royal tombs identified at Abydos, while Naqada IIIc is the period of the 1st Dynasty royal tombs and their immediate predecessors.

In reconstructing the history of Naqada IIIc much use is made of Egypt's earliest surviving texts, mostly from the royal tombs themselves. Their value, however, is limited, for most relate to the equipment and provisions provided to the tomb, and only incidentally refer to 'historical' events such as royal military campaigns, or the kings' ritual and building activities. Analogies made with later ideas, practices and cultural features are tempting but pose problems. Overall, a more critical approach to current theories is desirable. It is especially important to recognize that the available data are often open to equally valid, if sometimes contradictory, interpretations, although scholars sometimes arbitrarily reject one in favour of another in order to support a specific theory. In such cases, with different but equally valid options, each interpretation should be assigned equal value until debate or new discoveries resolve the issue one way or the other.

In particular, 'civilization' and 'kingship' are slippery terms insofar as early Egypt is concerned. Certainly, by the 1st Dynasty Egypt offers almost a checklist for early civilization. There are kings and bureaucrats, writing, monumental architecture and strongly developed social inequality. Yet evidence about some major issues is almost non-existent. For example, how large could a late prehistoric or Early Dynastic town be, and were they defended by massive, towered walls as one late prehistoric relief suggests? More specifically as regards Abydos, when can we legitimately identify 'kingship' in the archaeological record, particularly insofar as the elite tombs preceding the 1st Dynasty are concerned (see the discussion of Tomb 'U-j' below)?

Another important problem is the possible connection between early Egypt and contemporary civilization in Mesopotamia; there were certainly at least indirect contacts between the two, but some scholars argue Mesopotamia provided crucial stimulation to the development of civilization in Egypt. It has even been suggested that 'the bearers of the Mesopotamian influences were Sumerians who migrated to Egypt and settled in the Nile Valley'.[1]

Yet this issue is still a very open one, especially as far as Abydos is concerned. Günter Dreyer's discovery of the earliest surviving Egyptian written documents (in Tomb U-j, 150 years older than any previously found) is pushing the use of writing in Egypt back towards the date of the appearance of fully developed writing in Mesopotamia. This, then, suggests that the development of writing was independent in these two places. And while distinctive features of Mesopotamian mud-brick architecture seem reflected in the 1st Dynasty elite tombs at Saqqara, the royal mortuary enclosures of Abydos – which now go back to King Aha at the beginning of the 1st Dynasty – seem more free of such influences. Evidently, much remains to be learned about early Egypt, and especially from the royal monuments of Abydos.

The Tombs in Context

Apart from Tutankhamun's tomb and those of a few later kings at Tanis, Egyptian royal graves are usually so severely plundered that virtually nothing of their treasures survives. The burial chamber of the Great Pyramid at Giza, for example, contained only an empty stone sarcophagus when it was first entered in modern times. Surprisingly, the tombs of the 1st Dynasty kings and the last two rulers of the 2nd Dynasty at Umm el Qa'ab have provided much evidence about their original richness, despite having been badly disturbed.

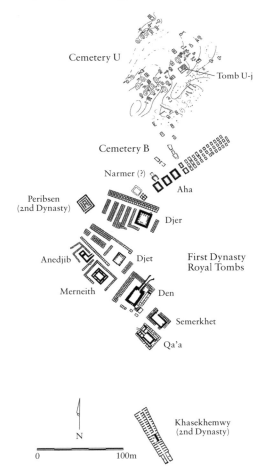

75 *The cemeteries of Umm el Qa'ab. Cemetery U, in the north, is the earliest in what became a continuous development. At first it contained many elite graves (Naqada I and II) but later, in Naqada III, some are large enough, and sufficiently isolated, to suggest they are in some sense 'royal'; tomb U-j is the most striking example. Later, in Cemetery B, the tombs are conspicuously isolated, and some are inscriptionally ascribable to Dynasty 0 kings, such as Qa'a, Iry-Hor and Narmer. Finally, in the south, the tombs of 1st and 2nd Dynasty kings were built.*

Emile Amélineau, then Flinders Petrie, recovered fragments of royal jewelry, bits and pieces of once richly inlaid furniture, exquisitely carved small objects in ivory, wood and stone, and many examples – mostly fragmentary – of what must originally have been vast hoards of well-made stone vases and bowls. Recently, Günter Dreyer has recovered yet more items of these kinds from the ancient plunderers' spoil heaps surrounding the tombs (never investigated by Petrie and Amélineau) and also added to the large number of inscribed objects found by the earlier excavators.

These glimpses of the wealth of Egypt's earliest historic kings are intriguing and exciting, but the principal value of these tombs, and of earlier graves in cemeteries U and B, adjacent to Umm el Qaʿab proper, is their architecture and evidence of burial customs. These provide the basis for much speculation, but the 1st and 2nd Dynasty tombs of Umm el Qaʿab cannot be properly understood without reference to contemporary monuments elsewhere.

Some 1.5 km (0.93 miles) due north of the royal cemetery is a cluster of massive enclosures (sometimes called *Tälbezirke* or 'valley precincts') which were complementary to the kings' tombs. Each was probably related to the relevant king's mortuary cult, although much remains to be discovered about the connection. They are discussed in detail in Chapter 10. Also relevant are the tombs of Egypt's highest elite during the first two dynasties, mostly buried at Saqqara near Memphis. Memphis was clearly Egypt's capital, and 1st and 2nd Dynasty kings probably resided there even though many were buried at Abydos. For a time, scholars thought that in the 1st Dynasty both the Abydos and Saqqara tombs were royal, the former being cenotaphs, the latter the actual tombs, but Barry Kemp and Werner Kaiser have effectively disposed of that idea. The Saqqara elite tombs differ in many ways from the royal ones, but also incorporate features derived from the latter and the enclosures. They can inform us about aspects of the royal tombs of Umm el Qaʿab (and perhaps of the enclosures) which have not survived or are poorly preserved.

Cemeteries U and B, and the adjacent graves of the 1st and 2nd Dynasty rulers, lie atypically deep in the desert, about 1.8 km (1.1 miles) southwest of the floodplain. They extend along a low elevation bordering the east side of a broad, shallow valley which curves off towards the east and finally debouches onto the floodplain near the early town and temple at Abydos' north corner.

Cemeteries U and B, and Umm el Qaʿab proper, developed over time from north to south. The northwest part of the area involved (Cemetery U) is densely filled with Naqada I and II graves, with larger late Naqada II and earlier Naqada III tombs along their northwestern and southeastern peripheries. Further south are a handful of large, widely dispersed tombs of mid-Naqada III, which merge into Cemetery B. The latter comprises three or four double-chambered large tombs (Dynasty 0), and the much larger, triple-chambered tomb of King Aha, first ruler of the 1st Dynasty. South of this extend the massive graves of the other 1st Dynasty kings, and of a queen mother called Merneith. Finally, northwest of the 1st Dynasty tombs is that of

Peribsen, penultimate king of the 2nd Dynasty, while in the extreme south is Khasekhemwy's tomb, dating from the very end of that dynasty.

The other 2nd Dynasty kings (about eight in all) seem to have been buried at Saqqara, somewhat to the south of the Saqqara elite cemetery referred to above. Adjacent, rock-cut subterranean complexes have been ascribed to two of these kings, and the remainder may have been buried in a nearby area now largely covered by the 3rd Dynasty step pyramid complex of King Djoser.

Proto-kings at Abydos

According to a recent and fascinating theory of Günter Dreyer's, not only were 1st and 2nd Dynasty kings buried at Umm el Qa'ab, but so were their predecessors, proto-kings extending far back into prehistoric times. More specifically, Dreyer suggests that the tombs of some 17 proto-kings whose names are attested inscriptionally can be identified in Cemetery U. The tombs in question begin on the south edge of Cemetery U, at the outset of Naqada III, and extend sequentially southwards as far as Cemetery B. The latter consists of King Aha's tomb, and of four smaller ones associated with inscriptions indicating that three, and maybe all, belonged to Aha's immediate royal predecessors (Dynasty 0), including King Narmer. Dreyer's theory would thus much enrich our knowledge of kingship's origins in Egypt, and of early political history as well, for he suggests that this line of proto-kings, with their political centre at Thinis, initiated a process of national unification some eight reigns before Narmer.

Dreyer's carefully argued ideas are persuasive in overall terms; given the presence of Narmer's tomb, and of other rulers immediately antedating the 1st Dynasty in Cemetery B, it seems likely that even earlier royalty were buried in the adjacent Cemetery U. However, in practice the identification of their specific tombs is more difficult than Dreyer's theory would suggest; Cemetery U includes both supposedly royal tombs and very similar, presumably elite, graves, and the distinctions between the two, in archaeological terms, are often not very clear. Moreover, if some of the tombs in question are indeed royal, their similarities with elite tombs in scale, form and content indicate that early Egyptian proto-kings were not as sharply differentiated from the elite as later kings were.

For example, the supposedly royal and otherwise elite tombs of Naqada III in Cemetery U are typologically very similar – relatively large, rectilinear and lined with brick walling. Dreyer sees two or more chambers as indicative of royal status, but this criterion is not applied consistently. Differentiating between supposedly royal tombs and implicitly elite ones is problematical in other regards as well. Thus, on either side of the unusually large and centrally placed Tomb U-j (discussed further below), Dreyer identified seven earlier royal tombs to its northwest, and six to its southwest. However, it is striking, given the other typological similarities, that all 13 'royal' tombs (excluding U-j) overlap considerably with the other, merely elite tombs in scale. At 21 sq. m or 225 sq. ft (average), 38.5 per cent of the 'royal' tombs are the largest in

Cemetery U, but about 60 per cent (averaging 15.5 sq. m or 166 sq. ft, or 9.5 sq. m or 102 sq. ft) are identical in scale with more than half of the other, implicitly elite tombs.

It is true that while the northwestern, earlier group of supposedly royal graves are set within or adjacent to a mass of both earlier and contemporary tombs, the southwestern group is relatively isolated, a circumstance indicating a special, maybe royal status. Nevertheless, even they are accompanied by a few equally large tombs, implicitly non-royal (i.e. elite) in status.

Dreyer's theory is based in part on his belief that numerous inscribed jars in Tomb U-j refer to its owner, his successor, and seven earlier kings whose 'mortuary estates' provided materials to the tomb. Thus, it is natural for him to seek for seven royal tombs within the earlier graves northwest of Tomb U-j. However, Dreyer's reasoning and the comparanda he cites do not conclusively show that the signs inscribed on the pots from U-j refer to kings – they might refer to deities, or to generic royal qualities. They may even, as I suggest below, refer to towns. To this extent also then, the identification of royal tombs prior to Tomb U-j is uncertain.

I have saved until last discussion of Tomb U-j (Naqada IIIa2), one of Dreyer's most spectacular discoveries in Cemetery U. Its size, complexity and richness make it a special case, and the tomb best qualified to be identified as royal and belonging to a proto-king. However, these very characteristics also raise additional problems about the royal status of the other Cemetery U tombs identified as such.

In having a burial chamber of 20 sq. m (215 sq. ft), Tomb U-j in fact is similar to the largest tombs of Cemetery U, which have burial chambers of, on average, 15 sq. m (161 sq. ft) and in one case (Tomb U-d) specifically 19.4 sq. m (208 sq. ft). What is unusual about Tomb U-j is the substantial expansion (as compared to other tombs) of its storage facilities. It has 11 additional chambers all dedicated to the storage of food, drink and other items for the use of the deceased, chambers bringing its overall size to 84 sq. m (903 sq. ft). Dreyer suggests that the supposedly royal tombs later than U-j had similarly scaled storage facilities elsewhere (perhaps close to the later enclosures 1.5 km or 0.93 miles to the north), but in the absence of direct proof for this supposition, one could equally plausibly suggest that modest storage facilities were considered sufficient for even the largest tombs preceding and succeeding Tomb U-j in Cemetery U. This second possibility suggests two alternatives: first, that if U-j is a royal tomb, the others are not, or, second, Tomb U-j is so idiosyncratic that it cannot be used to evaluate the status of the other, supposedly royal tombs.

Nevertheless, it seems probable that Tomb U-j belonged to a proto-king and provides unique insight into the great wealth accumulated by the highest echelon of the elite by Naqada IIIa2 times. Many small tags once attached to individual items, or to groups of items, survived even though the objects or materials were gone. Originally, there must also have been hundreds of pots filled with foods or drink; three of the chambers in fact had once been filled

76 (right) A view of the multi-chambered Tomb U-j after excavation.

77 (below) The plan of Tomb U-j. Most of the chambers had been plundered out, but note the traces of a large wooden 'shrine' in Chamber 1 (the burial chamber) and the small ivory sceptre in the north corner. In Chamber 11 parts of wooden boxes survived, and in Chambers 7 and 10 much of the original pottery.

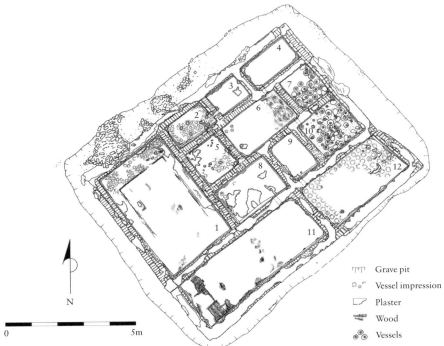

⊓⊓⊓	Grave pit
⌒₀⌐	Vessel impression
◻⟋	Plaster
▱	Wood
◉◌	Vessels

N

0   5m

with wine jars – locally made imitations of pottery typical of Southern Canaan or Palestine, equivalent to some 4,500 litres – indeed a royal send-off!

Egypt's Earliest Writing

Dreyer's exciting discovery of many inscribed objects in Tomb U-j has pushed the existence of writing in Egypt back some 150 years, to about *c.* 3300 BC, according to his chronology. This sharply reduces, although it does not eliminate, the possibility that Egyptian writing was stimulated by an already existing Mesopotamian system. In Mesopotamia writing first occurs in the Late Uruk phase, and thus developed soon after *c.* 3500 BC.

Like the system used in Tomb U-j, the earliest Mesopotamian writing was simple. Hans Nissen notes that its signs were 'in part still highly pictorial' (later, as cuneiform, it became much more abstract in appearance) and used numerals as well as 'written symbols' standing for 'what was being counted (on the documents in question)…(and) personal names'.[2] The inscriptions in Tomb U-j reveal similar characteristics and employ signs not only often Egyptian or African in character, but also rendered in a style setting the norm for the hieroglyphs of the later, fully developed writing system.

The later Egyptian system used many hieroglyphs interchangeably as 'ideograms' (to be read as the item depicted) or 'phonemes' (to be read as having a specific sound value, which could be used to write words unconnected with what the hieroglyphs depicted). Was this the case with the writing system found in Tomb U-j? Dreyer suggests that it was, but can cite only a handful of possible phonetic writings, and all of these might in reality be non-phonetic. For example, he reads an elephant (written out according to him as *3b* in later texts) above a triple-peaked mountain (*ḏw*) phonetically, the resulting word (*3bḏw*) being in his view an early writing of Abydos itself. However, the elephant and mountain could be more persuasively read as Elephantine, and regarded as purely ideograms, not phonemes: in the earlier Old Kingdom writings of Elephantine it is phonetically spelled out as *3bw* (Abu), but its unvocalized determinatives or ideograms are an elephant (*3bw*) and the triple-peaked 'foreign land' hieroglyph.

Whether used at times phonetically or, more probably, always as ideograms, what might the signs on the Tomb U-j objects refer to? They occur either as inscriptions painted on a type of pot which had ledge handles shaped into wave-like forms (at least 133 examples) or carved into small bone or ivory tags (164 were recovered), each pierced near a corner for attachment to an object or container. In each case, the 'text' is very brief, consisting usually of one or two signs, sometimes a few more. Dreyer suggests that apart from a few tags bearing only numerals, most of the inscriptions refer to a relatively complex administrative and economic system, various parts of which were responsible for providing the items and materials involved. Thus, for him a jar with a tree and a scorpion indicates the contents came from a 'mortuary estate or plantation (the tree) of King Scorpion', or a tag inscribed with a falcon standing on a triangular object interpreted as a vulva refers to 'the harem of King Falcon'.

This is one possible way of reading the evidence, but is not confirmed by any contemporary data (it relies heavily on analogies with later materials) and I believe that an alternative interpretation, which is supported by contemporary evidence, is possible.[3] Dreyer notes that some of the tags refer to named towns, not institutions; in particular, two signs (one a most unusual depiction of two men confronting each other) are identical to specific town names recorded on a prehistoric artifact, the so-called 'City' ceremonial palette. While Dreyer believes that references to towns among the inscribed objects (as the sources of items or materials deposited in Tomb U-j) are in the minority, I would suggest

78 Bone and ivory tags from Tomb U-j, bearing early examples of the hieroglyphic script. The label in the upper left has a town name, seen also on the so-called 'Libyan' palette. The elephant standing on a triple-peaked mountain (lower left corner) is read by Dreyer as 'Abdju', i.e. Abydos; but an alternative reading of 'Elephantine' is possible.

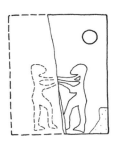

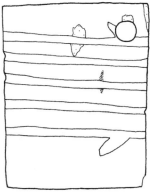

that some and perhaps virtually *all* the signs and sign-groups attested can be read as town names.

This interpretation, insofar as the available evidence is concerned, thus implies a simpler political system than the more complex one envisaged by Dreyer, but is still one compatible with the notion that the owner of Tomb U-j was indeed a proto-king of considerable authority. If some 45 towns contributed to his burial equipment, it was likely because he was their overlord. The territory involved perhaps extended as far south as Elephantine, as I noted above, but its extent north of Thinis is unknown. Dreyer identifies two towns as well-known Delta ones of later times, but these identifications depend upon phonetic readings which are questionable.

As noted earlier, Tomb U-j once contained an enormous number of Palestinian or Canaanite wine jars which must have reached Abydos via northern Egypt but might, of course, have been obtained through trading relationships between Thinis and independent polities in the Delta. These jars bring us to another possible example of an extensive use of writing in found in

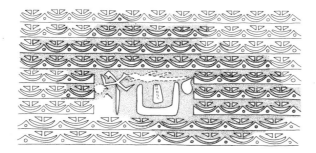

Tomb U-j, for at least 250 of them had mud sealings impressed with cylinder seals, the elaborate decoration of which included many figural elements, potentially yet more signs employed in a writing system.

Ulrich Hartung, pointing out the sealings are probably of Egyptian mud and the cylinders' designs thoroughly Egyptian in content, has indeed suggested that some of these signs refer to administrative or economic institutions involved in securing, storing and distributing the imported wine. However, the form, functions and contexts of these impressions suggest to me that an alternative interpretation, which does not involve writing, is preferable.

The clue is provided by the extraordinary elaborateness of the cylinder seals' decoration, unparalleled in contemporary Mesopotamia or in Egypt itself, although there are some significant predecessors in earlier (Naqada IId) sealings found in Cemetery U. In Tomb U-j, five individual seals are identifiable, and each is markedly different from the others in decoration. In every case, however, a central panel with figural decoration is surrounded or flanked by elaborate, brocade-like geometric patterns that cover a wide area.

Since the cylinder seals themselves were not large, the dedication of so much space to geometric patterning makes the figural panels quite small, yet many signs are crammed into each. In the three best-preserved examples a panel 3 × 1.8 cm (1.2 × 0.7 in) contains 35 figures and elements, and the other two similarly sized seals contain 13 or more, and seven respectively. Recognizable figures are ibexes, birds, snakes, scorpions and, in one instance, a human; but the other elements are very small, highly schematic and seem to act as space fillers more than anything else.

In my opinion, this complexity relates not to informational needs, but to the seals' purposes. As in contemporary Mesopotamia, elaborately decorated seals perhaps served to identify, at least within a limited circle, the individual owner of each, not directly but by association. More importantly, however elaborately and individually decorated, seals enhanced the efficiency of the sealing process, and the security of the materials sealed. Since the seals themselves would be very difficult to duplicate or replicate, because of their elaborate decoration, it was all the harder to tamper with the sealed materials and remain undetected.

Thus, overall I believe that on the tags and the wavy ledge handle jars from Tomb U-j we have a genuine writing system in use, but at this point the decorated cylinder seals are not involved. The writing system is relatively simple, and may not yet employ phonemes and use signs as ideograms or, in some cases, numerals. Nevertheless, even at this level it is an important and powerful means of communication and recording, surely being used elsewhere in early Egypt and laying the foundations for the more sophisticated system used in historic times. Whether one agrees with all Dreyer's interpretations of this material or not, his discovery and presentation of this early writing system is a great milestone in the history of Egyptian language and writing.

The 1st Dynasty, 'The Kings of Thinis'
The identities of potential proto-kings buried in Cemetery U may be debatable, but not those of the inscriptionally identified tomb owners in Cemetery B and Umm el Qa'ab itself. In Cemetery B, the graves of the Dynasty 0 kings Narmer, Iry-Hor and Qa'a lie alongside the grave of Aha, first ruler of the 1st Dynasty; and those of his successors extend off to the southwest, along with that of queen mother Merneith.

Why were the 1st Dynasty kings buried at Abydos, since Egypt's political centre – and probably royal residence – at this time was Memphis? Later Egyptian tradition, recorded by the annalist Manetho in 300 BC, stated that the 1st and 2nd Dynasties were 'of Thinis', in contrast to the 3rd, 4th and 6th Dynasties, all 'of Memphis'. These traditions may not be very reliable; for example, they label the 5th Dynasty, for no known historical reason, as 'of Elephantine'. However, it may be that the 1st and 2nd Dynasties *were* ultimately of Thinite origin, although Thinis itself (to judge from its excavated cemeteries) does not seem of unusual importance at the time. Indeed, elite tombs comparable to those of Saqqara are found in southern Egypt only at

Naqada (in the very early 1st Dynasty), perhaps indicating that Naqada was the political centre of southern Egypt before the shift to Memphis.

Presumably therefore, actual or notional links between the 1st Dynasty and its precursors in Cemetery B and perhaps U encouraged the continuing use of Umm el Qa'ab as a royal cemetery. In this way, Abydos became the locale for initiatives and developments in supra-elite monumental architecture and burial customs that had a perceptible impact upon elite and other tombs throughout Egypt.

The 1st Dynasty tombs of Umm el Qa'ab have experienced a great deal. They were repeatedly plundered, and at one point some were consumed by intense fires, since their substructures were rich in wood and other combustibles. According to Dreyer, all the tombs were excavated in the Middle Kingdom in the search for Osiris' tomb, and some were refurbished in the New Kingdom and later; eventually, yet more pillaging occurred. And all this preceded their rough-and-ready clearance by Amélineau, Petrie's excavations and finally Dreyer's ongoing and meticulous re-excavations!

Yet, surprisingly, enough survives to permit some idea of the impressive royal funerals that took place here. After an imposing procession along the shallow valley running up from the floodplain, the royal corpse was lowered or – via a ramp or stairway – carried into the largely or entirely roofed royal burial chamber. Here, the coffin was set within a large room-like wooden shrine, filling most of the chamber and made probably of aromatic cedar. Once sealed, the tomb's contents were shrouded in impenetrable darkness. Probably a number of ritual acts were involved in the burial, and one was actually encountered by Petrie with an eerie physicality, as the present was interpenetrated by the ancient past. In excavating the ramp leading down into King Semerkhet's tomb, Petrie discovered that the ramp had been filled 'to three feet with sand saturated with ointment; hundred-weights of it must have been poured here, and the scent was so strong in cutting away this sand that it could be smelt over the whole tomb'.

A grisly aspect of the royal funeral, or of anterior preparations, was the internment of royal kin, courtiers and officials in the small subsidiary graves surrounding each royal tomb. All were likely killed so as to be immediately available to their lord. In some cases, their numbers were enormous (Djer's tomb had about 325), but by King Qa'a's time, at the end of the 1st Dynasty, they dwindled to about 20.

Only the substructures of the royal tombs survived, the surface features having entirely disappeared except for occasional examples of the large, twin stone stelae that had stood above each tomb. Nevertheless, these substructures – built on a monumental scale in terms of their period – reveal a fascinatingly complex pattern of continuity and innovation, and of subtle and interrelated changes over time.

This pattern was due to several factors. Ideology, the expression of royal status vis-à-vis the larger population, was one factor which found expression in burial customs unique to royalty, as well as in unusual architecture and the size and richness of the tombs. Religion was another factor: the needs of the dead kings in the afterlife, and their access to mortuary cult, had to be serviced.

80 *Each 1st and 2nd Dynasty royal tomb at Umm el Qa'ab was supplied with a pair of stone stelae naming the tomb's owner. These stelae stood at surface level and varied in material (e.g. limestone, basalt and granite), size and quality of relief work. This basalt stela was for King Qa'a; it is 1.43 m (4.8 ft) high. The dynastic falcon god Horus stands on a 'serekh', representing an enclosure or palace, and the king's name is inscribed within the serekh.*

Finally, there were practical issues, especially those enhancing the tomb's security, or facilitating access to it for the provision of equipment and supplies, and then the deposition of the king's body. Such practical developments might also have been assigned symbolic value in terms of religion, ideology or both.

Fundamental continuities link the 1st Dynasty royal tombs to their precursors in cemeteries B and U. Like the earlier tombs, each 1st Dynasty tomb was built of mud-brick in a large open pit, its sides flush with the substructure, and then provided a flat wooden roof topped by layers of brick and sand and gravel fill. In both 1st Dynasty and later tombs the burial chamber was the principal one and, since at least Tomb U-j, was almost entirely filled by a large wooden shrine, its ceiling as high as, or identical with, the tomb's roof. The shrine contained the coffin, and much else besides.

The prehistoric and 1st Dynasty tombs of Umm el Qa'ab often had additional storage chambers, for supplies of food, drink, cloth and equipment. Tombs anterior to U-j sometimes had two or more; U-j had many; and if later tombs in Cemetery U usually had no cross-walling, a shrine in each would automatically have created a second compartment if sufficient space was left. This possibility is further indicated by the Dynasty o tombs, each of which has two separate chambers, one presumably for a shrine and its contents, the other for storage. First Dynasty tombs were provided with large scale and multi-chambered storage facilities, sometimes in or around the burial chamber, sometimes separate.

Continuities are therefore apparent but so are significant changes, the most obvious being periodic increases in scale which then flatten out along a plateau for a period. Thus, the more important tombs in Cemetery U are all similar, if variable in size over time (Tomb U-j excepted) but the largest occupy only about 22.5 sq. m (242 sq. ft), as compared to the average size of the Dynasty 0 double-chambered tombs, at a 45 sq. m (484 sq. ft) average. In its turn, Aha's tomb is about five times larger than these, at 304 sq. m (3,271 sq. ft) and thereafter the 1st Dynasty royal tombs maintain a similar average of about 307 sq. m (3,303 sq. ft), although individual tombs vary considerably in size, from about 211 sq. m or 2,270 sq. ft (King Semerkhet) to 475 sq. m or 5,111 sq. ft (King Den). Anedjib's substructure is exceptionally small (about 112 sq. m or 1,205 sq. ft), perhaps because he died early and the completion of an appropriately large tomb was thus precluded. (Oddly enough, tradition recorded an accidental royal death for this period, but for 'Menes', probably Narmer, not Anedjib: Menes was 'carried off by a hippopotamus and perished'.) What these successive expansions in scale mean is uncertain; they could be ideological or religious. The increasing massiveness of the architecture of the substructures was a result of the increase in scale, for the walls now had to support a much heavier weight of roofing and, above it, fill.

The subsidiary graves for kinsfolk, courtiers and others, mentioned above, seem to be an innovation of the 1st Dynasty, for they are first identifiable at Aha's tomb. However, it is possible that one or two sacrificial burials might have been placed within the larger tombs of cemeteries B and U, which in nearly all cases were almost completely plundered out. In any event, subsidiary graves as such were not unique ideological markers of royal status, for 1st Dynasty elite tombs at Saqqara, and others of lesser rank at Tarkhan and Abu Roash, also had them.

Within the 1st Dynasty itself, a significant innovation is the access stairway or ramp provided to all royal tombs after King Djet's reign. Here, practical issues were probably paramount. Before this time, each tomb could have been largely roofed prior to the royal burial, with a space or trapdoor left for the final interment, such as Bryan Emery inferred for the elite tombs at Saqqara. However, with the scale of tombs increasing it must have been awkward and, from the point of view of security, dangerous to first build substructures and construct the shrines within them, then to lay in large masses of often valuable materials, then to readmit the builders to the site to lay the roofs, and finally, after the burial was completed, to readmit them again for the remaining filling-in above the roof and the construction of any surface buildings that may have existed. With an access ramp or stairway provided, these processes became much more efficient: the tomb was built, roofed and filled in above, and any desired surface feature built, *then* it could be fully and more securely supplied and, finally, the royal burial could be performed more easily than before.

Even if the ramp or stairway was introduced for practical reasons, it might also have been assigned symbolic value. In later pyramids, such ramps were considered not only convenient for access, but also ascents to heaven for the deceased ruler's use. However, it is noteworthy that while most ramps or stairs were consistently placed on the 'east' side of the 1st Dynasty tombs, King Qa'a's was on the 'north', apparently because the tomb was located so close to an earlier one that an 'eastern' access was not possible. This circumstance suggests that the symbolic value of ramp or stairway, if it existed at all, was weak. It is also noteworthy that similar access was provided to contemporary tombs at Saqqara and many other places, presumably inspired by the royal model but primarily for the same practical reasons.

Once the burial was completed, the substructures of the 1st Dynasty royal tombs became invisible and inaccessible, covered over by an even, undisturbed sandy surface. Did features built upon that surface signal the presence of the tomb below, and if so, what might they have been? This is one of the great puzzles of Umm el Qa'ab, for except for the royal stelae mentioned above, no traces of such surface structures have survived; yet might they not be expected, since all contemporary tombs of importance did have superstructures – spectacularly so at Saqqara, but on ever-diminishing scales elsewhere, such as Helwan, Tarkhan and even near Thinis *itself*, at Nag el-Deir? In the 1st Dynasty at the latter site, even comparatively small substructures of 27.2 sq. m (293 sq. ft) and 34.5 sq. m (371 sq. ft) could have brick-walled, sand-filled superstructures of 83.9 sq. m (902 sq. ft) and 115.5 sq. m (1,242 sq. ft) respectively (in Cemetery 1500 at Nag el-Deir).

Certainly, the royal stelae of Umm el Qa'ab seem to have stood, embedded into the ground or some other support, at surface level – presumably above or near the relevant tomb, although emplacements for these stelae have not yet been located. The stelae themselves have never been found in situ, and are often broken into pieces. They are very similar in that each pair displayed, in relief, the royal name in a panel set above a representation of a niched façade, and itself surmounted by a falcon embodying the god Horus. This form of the royal name was widely used, not only in inscriptions, but also to indicate ownership on stone and even pottery vessels, and many kinds of objects.

A surprising variety in quality and size was tolerated. A stela of King Djet, for example, is beautifully carved; other stelae are less accomplished; and those of King Den – owner of the largest, implicitly richest tomb – are downright crude, even by the tolerant standards of Umm el Qa'ab. There is also a striking difference in heights, remembering that only part of the embedded stelae could be visible. King Djet's stela is 2.5 m (8 ft) high, of which perhaps 2 m (6.8 ft) was visible; queen mother Merneith's are 1.57 m (5 ft) and King Qa'a's 1.43 (4.7 ft), the visible parts being perhaps 1 m (3.3 ft) in each case.

What kinds of architectural settings, if any, might have been provided for these stelae? For a long time it was thought that each tomb once had a large surface mound, consisting of sand and gravel retained and capped by plastered and whitewashed mud-brick. The stelae, together with an altar or offering-table, were assumed to have stood at one side. However, Dreyer has shown that the mounds Petrie found evidence for but thought stood at the surface were themselves below ground level and thus buried and invisible.

Nevertheless, these hidden mounds are intriguing. Their proportions varied according to those of each burial chamber (the only part of the substructure covered by a mound); thus some were square in plan (e.g. those of Djer and Djet), others markedly rectangular (e.g. those of Den, Semerkhet and Qa'a). Traces of some, but not all mounds were recovered in the form of retaining walls along their edges. These walls survived to a sufficient height to show that the mounds were flat-topped or, at most, might have had a single shallow step.

Thus, the hidden mound was not a visible marker for the tomb but instead provided – like the substructure as a whole – some kind of service to the deceased. What this was is impossible to say. Analogies have been drawn with

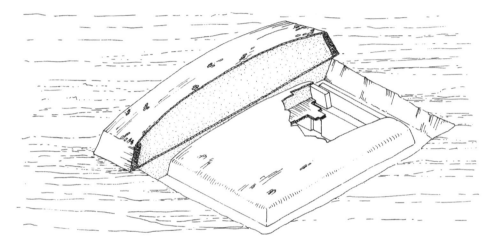

N

81 *Günter Dreyer's excavations have revealed that each 1st and 2nd Dynasty royal tomb at Umm el Qa'ab was capped with a carefully constructed mound; this was defined by brick walls filled with sand and gravel and entirely plastered and whitewashed. The mound was, however, below ground level, and hence a subterranean feature, completely invisible once the pit containing both tomb and mound was filled in. Dreyer surmises a larger, similarly constructed mound was built above, at ground level and hence visible, as shown in section here.*

82 *(left) The plan of King Qa'a's tomb as recorded by Petrie. Dreyer's subsequent excavation added many important details.*

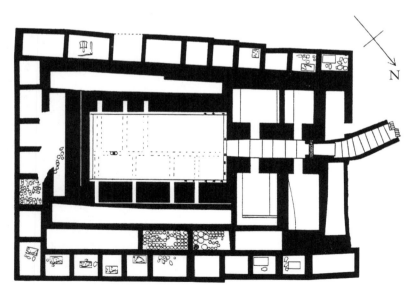

later Egyptian ideas about 'primeval mounds' which were places of creation and rebirth, but their relevance to the 1st Dynasty royal tombs is uncertain.

These concealed mounds seem to be an innovation introduced in the 1st Dynasty, under King Djer. Tombs in cemeteries U and B left no room for such mounds and whether they had surface mounds remains uncertain – no traces survive. It is surprisingly difficult to establish whether prehistoric Egyptian graves in general were capped by visible mounds. Apparently, alternative forms of tomb surface features existed, for Barbara Adams notes that a Naqada III tomb at Hierakonpolis 'had been surmounted by a wood and reed building and surrounded by a picket fence',[4] although no traces of such structures survived in cemeteries U and B. More recently, even more elaborate mortuary structures, at surface level, have been located by Renée Friedman at Hierakonpolis.

As for the 1st Dynasty royal graves, Dreyer believes that each in fact had a large surface mound, for a very pragmatic reason: the pit dug to house the substructure would generate a great deal of surplus sand and gravel, and to incorporate this into a mound would deal with it efficiently. The small subsidiary graves surrounding each royal tomb must have had (equally small) surface structures, perhaps in mound-like form. Numerous small stelae survive, identifying by name and title the owner of each subsidiary grave (owners who include some treasured hounds!). Their undressed backs show that each stela was set in a niche and, since no such emplacements occur in the substructures, the stelae imply that superstructures did exist, similar to actual examples found at Saqqara and Tarkhan. Some stelae were larger than others, and perhaps the size and height of surface structures varied in accordance with the rank and status of the tomb owner, just as subsidiary grave structures varied in size, presumably for the same reason.

As well as the surface mound suggested by Dreyer, the Abydos tombs may have had an additional surface feature, on the basis of a strange and seemingly

83 *The subsidiary tombs around the 1st Dynasty royal tombs at Abydos were often, perhaps always, supplied with a small limestone stela identifying the occupant of each. This particular example is for 'the dwarf [the top pictograph] Nofret [i.e. the beautiful one!]'. Most of the occupants of subsidiary graves were men and women of normal size, but the burials of a number of dwarves were also found. In later times, dwarves occur at royal courts, as personal attendants and entertainers, while dwarves also received significant administrative positions, at least in the Old Kingdom.*

unique structure associated with the tomb of King Den. This structure, first explored by Petrie, then re-excavated and restudied by Dreyer, is a subterranean building adjacent to the south corner of Den's burial chamber. Reached from the surface by a circuitously structured stairway, the building consisted of a single large room, with a wide and deep recess on its northwest side, a recess probably once containing a centrally placed statue of King Den. The stairway had been blocked, about two-thirds down its length, by a brick wall and Dreyer suggested that the structure was a kind of 'serdab' or inaccessible statue chamber intended to facilitate the dead king's departure from the tomb.

This subterranean chapel, however, is strikingly anomalous in that unlike most important features of the 1st Dynasty royal tombs it has neither antecedents nor successors. Features such as organized cemeteries of subsidiary burials (introduced under Aha) or access ramps or stairways (introduced under Den) continue on to the end of the dynasty, yet this is not the case for Den's relatively large and complex subterranean chapel. This suggests to me that this chapel *was* part of a series which otherwise did not survive, because normally such chapels were surface features. Den's chapel is a transposition of what was usually a surface feature to a subterranean locale, for reasons which escape us.

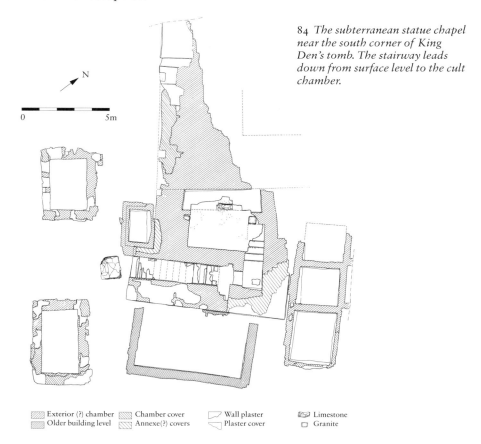

84 *The subterranean statue chapel near the south corner of King Den's tomb. The stairway leads down from surface level to the cult chamber.*

N

0   5m

▨ Exterior (?) chamber	▨ Chamber cover	◺ Wall plaster	▨ Limestone
▨ Older building level	▨ Annexe(?) covers	◺ Plaster cover	▢ Granite

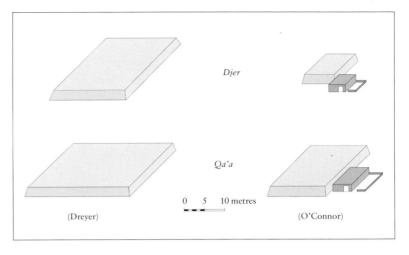

85 *Alternative reconstructions of the surface features above 1st and 2nd Dynasty royal tombs at Umm el Qa'ab.*

On this basis, one could suggest that each royal tomb was surmounted originally not only by a mound, but also by a relatively small brick chapel (reminiscent of the building apparently surmounting the contemporary or earlier tomb at Hierakonpolis) dedicated to a statue and offering cult for the relevant ruler. If we follow the model of Den's subterranean chapel, these surface chapels would have been relatively small (Den's is 9 × 9 m, or 81 sq. m, 871 sq. ft), with an entrance on the southwest. This entrance might have been flanked externally by the two royal stelae mentioned above – in fact, in front of the doorway into Den's chapel are two symmetrically placed, brick-walled rectangular features that might represent emplacements for the stelae. The stairway into Den's chapel would correspond in the surface chapels to an equally circuitous corridor leading to the cult room and its statue recess.

The surface chapels thus hypothesized for Umm el Qa'ab were likely to have been built over the tomb, and probably specifically over its southern quadrant, to judge from the location of Den's chapel, close to the south corner of the tomb. Such a location would relate to the gap left in the line of subsidiary tombs near the south corner of *all* the 1st Dynasty royal tombs at Umm el Qa'ab. Dreyer suggested that the gap permitted the dead king's spirit to move towards the valley, a kind of entrance to the netherworld, south of Umm el Qa'ab. However, I think instead that the gap might have provided mortuary priests access to a chapel located in this approximate area.

Naturally, these surface chapels – and the stelae emplacements near them – would collapse into the general debris of each tomb once the tomb roof had decayed, burnt, or been broken open by pillagers. Thus, no trace of them would ever be found at surface level.

The 2nd Dynasty at Umm el Qa'ab

Prior to kings Peribsen and Khasekhemwy, all 2nd Dynasty kings seem to have been buried at Saqqara – naturally enough, since nearby Memphis had probably been the royal residence since Aha's day. Two of their tombs have been inscriptionally identified, and the funerary stela of a third king recovered. Moreover, Kelly Simpson has shown that one of these kings – Ninetjer – is the first Egyptian ruler for whom a complete example of statuary has survived, although its provenance is unknown.[5]

The two tombs whose owners are known (kings Hetepsekhemwy and Ninetjer) are entirely rock-cut and subterranean; in each case an extensive complex of regularly laid out, uniformly sized storage galleries precedes the tomb itself. The scale of these tombs is impressive: Hetepsekhemwy's defines an area of almost 4,000 sq. m (43,055 sq. ft), whereas the largest Abydos substructure – King Den's tomb – occupied only 728 sq. m (7836 sq. ft), if one includes all likely storage areas. This difference in size is due almost entirely to the enormous number of storage galleries provided at Saqqara, for reasons we cannot know. However, increased storage may always have been inherently desirable (it is a trend evident in the 1st Dynasty substructures at Umm el Qa'ab) and may have been easier to provide on a lavish scale at Saqqara. There, the galleries were carved out of rock (a labourious process but perhaps less so than digging an appropriately gigantic pit at Abydos), and providing the many storage units was thus made feasible.

Unfortunately, all significant traces of any superstructures over the Saqqara tombs seem to have been removed by later building activities. However, one or two educated guesses are in order.

First, since mortuary cult enclosures were provided for Peribsen and Khasekhemwy at Abydos, the same was probably done for their predecessors buried at Saqqara. However, while the Abydos enclosures were separate and far away from the royal tombs, at Saqqara enclosures and tombs were close to the floodplain (some large, unexcavated enclosures west of 2nd Dynasty royal tombs at Saqqara have been attributed to them, but more likely belong to unfinished step pyramid complexes of the 3rd Dynasty). Thus, as Kemp suggested, at Saqqara the royal tomb and its enclosure may have been combined. The proximity of Hetepsekhemwy's tomb to Ninetjer's suggests that each could only have had an enclosure of roughly 125 × 45 m (410 × 147 ft), comparable in scale to the enclosures of Peribsen (101 × 54 m or 331 × 177 ft) and Khasekhemwy (120 × 61 m or 393 × 200 ft) at Abydos.

Secondly, we can assume that surface features stood within each enclosure at Saqqara. The tomb proper (as distinct from the storage galleries) lay at the south end of the enclosure and over it one might imagine a surface mound, as Dreyer suggests, and a cult-chapel, such as I have proposed for the Umm el Qa'ab tombs. Nearby were two royal stelae, to judge from the sole surviving one from Saqqara (of King Nebra) and the two provided to Peribsen's tomb at Abydos.

Kings Peribsen and Khasekhemwy chose to be buried at Abydos. It is too speculative to suggest, as some do, that this reflects a political split between northern and southern Egypt compelling Peribsen to be buried at Abydos; and that Khasekhemwy, having reunited the country from a southern base, continued to identify with the south, and hence also preferred burial at Abydos. Later kings chose to be buried at already existent royal cemeteries for reasons that, whatever they were, have no known connection to politics. Thus, while most kings of the 4th and 5th Dynasties were buried elsewhere, the 6th Dynasty returned to Saqqara, to be buried alongside royal tombs of the 2nd and 3rd Dynasties.

At first glance, the substructures of Peribsen's and Khasekhemwy's tombs at Umm el Qa'ab seem very different, both from each other and from the earlier 2nd Dynasty royal tombs at Saqqara, but in fact all share important and fundamental characteristics, even if there is also some variation. For example, the actual tombs of Hetepsekhemwy (at the rear of the many storage galleries), Peribsen and Khasekhemwy are quite similar in plan and scale. In Hetepsekhemwy's tomb, a long, narrow antechamber precedes the burial chamber, to one side of which is a complex of smaller rooms. The two Abydos tombs have a similar antechamber, but the burial chamber in each case is flanked by smaller rooms. The differences may be due to the possibility that tunnelling encouraged the sideways development at Saqqara, whereas at Abydos, using the open pit technique, it was easier to build the complementing rooms around the burial chamber. In any event, the resulting tomb complexes (always excluding storage facilities) were similar in size: 163 sq. m (1,754 sq. ft) for Hetepsekhemwy, 158.4 sq. m (1,704 sq. ft) for Peribsen, and 212.8 sq. m (2,289 sq. ft) for Khasekhemwy.

For Peribsen's tomb, the builders did not attempt to replicate the extensive storage galleries found at Saqqara, although four long gallery-like storage chambers are arranged around the tomb proper. However, Khasekhemwy's tomb is clearly an Abydos version of the already existing Saqqara type. First, although the 1st Dynasty tombs and Peribsen's lay close to the surface, Khasekhemwy's was built in an enormously deep pit (its floor 7 m or 23 ft below ground level), in order to emulate the great depth of the Saqqara tombs, even though the labour involved was probably much greater than at Saqqara. Secondly, like the Saqqara tombs, Khasekhemwy's was also provided with many gallery-like store rooms, similarly regular in plan and repetitive in proportions, although Dreyer has shown that these were built over time, in 'add-on' fashion. However, while at Saqqara the storage galleries preceded the tomb, at Abydos they were placed on either side of the tomb itself.

As earlier, one could assume that Peribsen's and Khasekhemwy's tombs were marked by a surface mound, as Dreyer suggests, and the surface chapel I have proposed. The latter notion, with the chapel over the tomb and near the south corner, perhaps receives some slight support from Peribsen's two stelae; they were not found in their original position, but nevertheless were found by Petrie 'lying under a few inches of sand to the S.W. of the tomb'.[6]

Overall then, the 1st and 2nd Dynasty royal tombs at Umm el Qa'ab and their predecessors of Dynasty 0 and in Cemetery U provide a wealth of fascinating information. However, they also illustrate forcefully my point made earlier about early Egyptian material: that the ambiguities of the evidence often require us to keep two or more equally possible interpretations in play, rather than choosing one in preference to the others. Otherwise, we may not follow up unresolved issues with further excavation and study which could show which one of the possibilities is the most likely.

CHAPTER TEN

THE MYSTERIOUS ENCLOSURES OF ABYDOS

Discovering the Enclosures

The once massive mud-brick enclosures of the 1st and 2nd Dynasties which stood about 1.5 km (0.93 miles) north of the royal tombs at Umm el Qa'ab have long intrigued archaeologists. It is clear that these enclosures were as important for the mortuary cults of the early kings as the royal tombs themselves, and yet the enclosures are much more mysterious. One enclosure was first excavated about 50 years before the royal tombs were discovered but, in general, their exploration has been sporadic and still remains incomplete.

The mysterious character of the enclosures is all the more surprising when we consider that one of them survives largely intact and is a striking feature of Abydos' archaeology today. Its dark brick mass looming over the otherwise largely featureless North Cemetery, this enclosure (called today the Shunet el Zebib, or 'Storehouse of Raisins' – another mystery!) rises about 11 m (36 ft) above ground level and measures 133.5 m (438 ft) in one direction, 77.7 m (255 ft) in the other.

Defining an area of 1.04 ha (2.56 acres), the Shunet el Zebib, or 'Shuneh' – built for King Khasekhemwy at the end of the 2nd Dynasty – is the largest of the two still-standing monuments of the Early Dynastic period. At Hierakonpolis, a better-preserved enclosure was also dedicated to King Khasekhem (Khasekhemwy's earlier name) but, at 5,195 sq. m (55,898 sq. ft), it is only about half the size of the Shuneh.

First mapped by Napoleon's savants, the Shuneh naturally attracts many visitors, but in entering it one immediately confronts a mystery, for its gigantic walls seemingly define and protect nothing. Various excavators have gradually removed much of the sand that once partially filled the Shuneh's interior, but the only structure discovered was a small brick building near the east corner. The Shuneh's desert location might suggest an empty and romantic tranquility, but in reality its wall-faces house hundreds of small birds. Not only do they steal string and reed-matting from excavators working there, but their

86 *The large interior of the enclosed space of the Shunet el Zebib is filled with old spoil heaps, early excavation pits and – in the south corner and along the northwest wall – towering sand dunes. Because of the loose, sandy nature of much of the overlying material, controlled excavation is difficult, but has revealed an extraordinary amount of new information about this enclosure, its functions and history.*

incessant chirping fills the air all day long. Only once, when we were excavating there, did they fall completely silent; looking up, we saw – as the birds had – a great hawk circling lazily above, looking for prey!

Well before other, nearby enclosures had been located, Mariette had speculated about the Shuneh's function. Perhaps it had been a 'sort of police station' guarding the surrounding cemetery from robbers; or had held vast masses of living animals, periodically sacrificed to the dead; or had been an embalming area, producing hundreds of mummies at a time. He even suggested that the Shuneh might be the 'tomb of Osiris' often referred to in texts. Thus intrigued, Mariette made his agent Gabet excavate much of the Shuneh, but with disappointing results. It was, Mariette concluded, most likely to have been a fortified police post and, in any case, the Shuneh's interior 'keeps its secret … everything indicates the double-walled enclosure had never surrounded an edifice of any significance'.[1]

Subsequent discoveries provided no support for Mariette's interpretations, and led instead to new theories. In 1904, Edward Ayrton dated the Shuneh definitively to the reign of Khasekhemwy (Mariette was unsure of its date), discovered and explored an enclosure of King Peribsen next to it, and noted an apparently early enclosure associated with the nearby Coptic village. He concluded that all three were 'a series of royal forts … which served as residences for the kings when they came to worship at the temple of Abydos'.[2] Herbert Ricke, an eminent historian of Egyptian architecture, agreed with this notion and later Jean-Phillipe Lauer – who devoted much of his life to the excavation and restoration of Djoser's step pyramid at Saqqara – proposed a variation on it. Lauer argued that each enclosure (including others discovered after Ayrton's work) was a repository for mortuary provisions supplied by the relevant king. They were not for him but rather for his subjects buried at Abydos, and the temple of Khentamentiu – the then god of Abydos – was responsible for distributing the provisions to the many private mortuary cults involved.

The theories outlined above, however, seem unlikely in view of further discoveries made by Flinders Petrie in 1921–22, close to the Shuneh. These included yet another, relatively small enclosure (Petrie was unsure of its date and function, noting that it could be a 'fort', i.e. an early enclosure, but opting to label it the 'Western Mastaba') and three impressive, seemingly hollow rectangles of subsidiary graves, similar to those surrounding the 1st Dynasty royal tombs at Umm el Qa'ab. All could be inscriptionally dated. The smallest rectangle (3,042 sq. m or 32,732 sq. ft; partially located by an earlier excavator) belonged to queen mother Merneith; much larger were those for kings Djer (9,215.4 sq. m or 99,157 sq. ft) and Djet (6,798 sq. m or 73,146 sq. ft).

Petrie thought that Merneith's graves had surrounded a mastaba or tomb superstructure, parts of which survived, but despite many test excavations he could find no monumental remains within the vast rectangular spaces defined by the subsidiary graves datable to Djer and Djet. He therefore suggested that while the 'intimate' associates of each king were buried around the royal tomb at Umm el Qa'ab, here – in what later became the North Cemetery – 'the court

87 *The best preserved of the Early Dynastic royal mortuary cult enclosures at Abydos, the Shunet el Zebib was built for King Khasekhemwy at the end of the 2nd Dynasty. The enclosure still stands about 11 m (36 ft) high. Here, it is viewed from the south.*

staff was buried at the edge of the desert, at a site open to all for royal worship: these two cemeteries developed later as the upper and lower temples of the kings'.[3] Thus, Petrie envisaged the early royal tomb and its environs as the ancestor of the later pyramids, each with its attached temple; and the grave rectangles in the North Cemetery (or 'the tombs of the courtiers', as he called them) as the prototype for the later valley temples which, set at the edge of the floodplain, were each linked to the relevant pyramid (set far back in the desert) by a causeway.

Thereafter, no important discoveries were to be made about the enclosures until our own excavations commenced in 1986, but 20 years earlier Barry Kemp restudied the then-available evidence and reached significant new conclusions. He persuasively argued that Merneith's mastaba and the Western Mastaba were in fact enclosures (he dated the latter tentatively to the late 1st Dynasty), and predicted that therefore the grave rectangles of Djer and Djet each probably surrounded a mud-brick enclosure also. Werner Kaiser thought that structures of wood and matting were more likely, but our excavations in 1988 proved that Kemp's prediction was correct.

As to their function, Kemp suggested that the enclosures' 'fortress-like character' indicated that they were 'funerary palaces' serving 'as dwelling places for the kings' spirits'.[4] German scholars, mostly agreeing with this idea, prefer to call the enclosures *Talbezirke* or 'valley places', with reference to an assumed connection with later valley temples.

Nevertheless, incomplete evidence about the enclosures leaves plenty of room for other interpretations. For example, Dieter Arnold has recently suggested that the Abydos enclosures were indeed intended for the use of deceased kings, but were modelled not on living kings' palaces but on what he calls 'fortresses of the gods'. Arnold surmises that at places like Hierakonpolis and Heliopolis there were enclosed areas at which the living king presided over an impressive annual ceremony. Divine images from all over Egypt sailed to the enclosure, alongside ships laden with the annual taxes. Not only were images and treasure assembled within the enclosure, in the king's presence, but such enclosures perhaps were also arenas for 'the delivery, display and ritual killing of prisoners of war and desert animals'.[5]

Whatever their precise functions, the Abydos enclosures helped to end a long debate as to whether the 1st and 2nd Dynasty royal tombs at Umm el Qa'ab were real ones, or cenotaphs. In the latter case, the supposedly elite tombs of Saqqara would actually be the real royal tombs. Some scholars, such as Jean-Phillipe Lauer and Rainier Stadelmann, still prefer this possibility. However, Kemp, Kaiser and others have more persuasively pointed out that the Abydos enclosures and tombs, taken together, render the early royal monuments there larger, more complex and higher in status than anything found at Saqqara or elsewhere.

Excavating the Enclosures

Renewed excavation of the enclosures began in 1986, in the form of the Abydos Early Dynastic Project, under the aegis of the Pennsylvania-Yale-Institute of Fine Arts, New York University Expedition; continuing up to the present, and planned to continue in the future, these excavations have revealed a great deal of new and exciting information about these structures and are bringing the enclosures into much clearer focus as regards their functions and significance. The Abydos Early Dynastic Project is directed by myself, and since 1999 in collaboration with Matthew Adams as Associate Director and since 2007 with Laurel Bestock as Assistant Director.

Our achievements are best appreciated by comparing the map of the enclosures as known in 1966 with the map as we have it today. By 1966 earlier excavators had identified two enclosures of the 1st Dynasty (Merneith's, and the anonymous Western Mastaba). Immediately to their northwest, the large grave enclosures of kings Djer and Djet were surmised to each surround a similarly large enclosure, but this remained to be proved. Northwest of Djet's grave rectangle, the modern Coptic village of Deir Sitt Damiana incorporated in its external wall the remains of an ancient brick enclosure, which most scholars guessed would also be 1st Dynasty in date. In all, since seven 1st Dynasty kings were buried at Umm el Qa'ab, along with queen mother Merneith, at least three and maybe four enclosures of that dynasty remained to be discovered. In addition, since his discovery of Tomb U-j at Umm el Qa'ab, Dreyer had suggested enclosures were built from this ruler onwards, a theory which implied that perhaps as many as 11 or more pre-1st Dynasty enclosures had been built, perhaps in the vicinity of the already known enclosures of North Abydos.

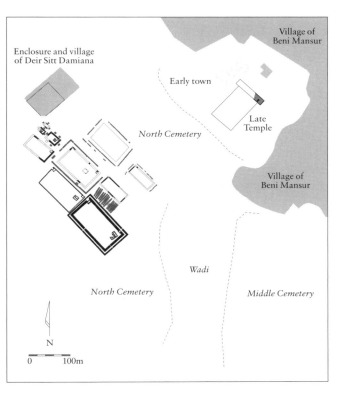

88 *(above left) Map of the Early Dynastic enclosures and their environs, including the boat graves discovered in 1991. About 250 m (820 ft) to the northeast are the remains of the Late Period temple of Osiris, in the vicinity of which was the Early Dynastic temple of the god Khentamentiu, itself associated with a town and, southwest of the latter, some elite graves of the period.*

89 *(above right) Map of the Early Dynastic enclosures at Abydos.*

Finally, to the southwest of the known or inferred 1st Dynasty enclosures were two large ones of kings Peribsen and Khasekhemwy of the 2nd Dynasty. Since no other kings of this dynasty were buried at Abydos, no further enclosures of that date were to be anticipated.

The picture today looks very different. Two (among many other) discoveries were especially exciting. First, 14 enormous boat graves were discovered next to Khasekhemwy's enclosure but actually contemporary with the earlier (1st Dynasty) Western Mastaba enclosure to the northeast. Secondly, over the period 2001–5, no fewer than three new enclosures, all built during the reign of King Aha at the beginning of the 1st Dynasty, were excavated. The largest of the three (labelled Aha I) was located by means of a sub-surface survey carried out by Tomasz Herbich of the Polish Academy of Sciences, and was excavated under Matthew Adams' direction in 2001–3. It was dated by inscribed jar sealings and pottery vessels from the five of its six subsidiary graves we were able to excavate, and it was possibly dedicated to the cult of King Aha himself.

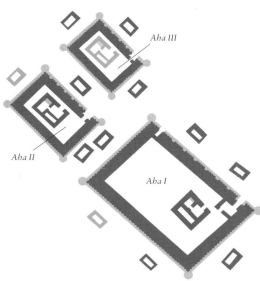

Aha III

Aha II

Aha I

90 *(above left) One of the subsidiary graves associated with the enclosure labelled Aha III.*

91 *(above right) Plan of the three enclosures from the reign of Aha.*

92 *(below) View of the enclosure labelled Aha I.*

Immediately northeast of this enclosure were two smaller ones (Aha II and III) – placed side by side and each provided with its own subsidiary burials, as with the larger example. Traces of one were located in 2002–3, but the other was discovered in 2004–5 by Laurel Bestock, of the Institute of Fine Arts of New York University, who also excavated as much of the two enclosures as survived or was accessible (a modern Coptic cemetery had unwittingly destroyed some of the structures, and also prevented the excavation of other parts of them). The discovery of these two smaller enclosures was revolutionary in that until then only a single enclosure was known for individual 1st and 2nd Dynasty kings. Bestock has proposed the plausible theory that the two smaller enclosures were dedicated to the cults of the two elite individuals (queens?) buried in separate tombs immediately adjacent to Aha's own three-chambered tomb at Umm el Qa'ab.

Even the larger of the three Aha enclosures was much smaller than subsequent ones. For example, the area defined by the enlcosure of Djer (Aha's immediate successor) was about 0.52 ha (1.28 acres), whereas Aha I defined only 0.07 ha (0.18 acres). However, their very smallness enabled the Aha enclosures to be excavated virtually in their entirety, which has not as yet been possible for any other known enclosures. The largest enclosure of Aha contained a cult chapel in its eastern quadrant, but was otherwise empty of structures. Aha III was largely destroyed by later tomb building and no cult chapel was found there. But Aha II had a cult chapel and a carefully stacked collection of wooden poles which likely came from a disassembled structure of a temporary nature which may have stood in the now seemingly empty part of that enclosure.

As for Djer's enclosure, our excavations in 1988, with subsequent ones in 2000–1, showed that it existed, making it virtually certain that Djet had an enclosure of very similar size. We have also found the remains of Djer's chapel, in the enclosure's east quadrant; it is similar in scale to Aha's chapel, but whereas the ground plan of the latter was fully recoverable, that of Djer's was destroyed by later tomb and chapel building in the same area.

In 1997 we explored the remains of the Western Mastaba enclosure, and the discovery of the blocked gateway near its north corner proved it too had been an enclosure, for similar gateways were found by us near the north corner of the enclosures of Aha and Djer. Full recovery of the excavated ceramic showed it dated to the 1st Dynasty, but the name of its royal owner remains as yet unknown.

More surprisingly, we found Petrie, who discovered the Western Mastaba enclosure, had not mapped its location correctly – it was much closer to Djer's enclosure than his plan indicated. Petrie's surveying has usually proved to be accurate, but here his usually adequate survey methods had let him down. Some idea of these methods is gained from his observation that he had mapped in (accurately) the grave rectangles of Djer, Djet and Merneith by 'setting up a scale of markers along the west, and another along the south, and reading off the positions by sighting a distant hill peak over each one of the scales'. Petrie added: 'This is the quickest method for a mass of detail where no great accuracy is required'.[6]

The boat graves, which are discussed in detail in the next chapter, were discovered in 1991. At the time, it was already clear from stratigraphic evidence that they were earlier than Khasekhemwy's enclosure. Remapping the Western Mastaba enclosure showed that it and the boat graves lined up neatly with each other, and in 2002–3 we recovered a stratigraphic link between the two, indicating the boat graves and the Western Mastaba enclosure were contemporary with each other.

In 2002–3 another important discovery was made when a further sub-surface survey by Tomasz Herbich located yet another enclosure, immediately southwest of Aha's. Adams was able to excavate its entire southeastern wall. Subsequently, Bestock excavated a portion of the northeast wall and was able to survey the line of the northwest wall, showing that the dimensions of the enclosure were 66.9 × 37.4 m, thus covering an area of 2,502 sq. m (26,931 sq. ft) or 0.25 ha (0.61 acres). The unexcavated parts of the enclosure are inaccessible beneath a modern Coptic cemetery. On the southeast were three subsidiary graves, containing not humans like the subsidiary graves of Djer's and Djet's enclosures, but instead no fewer than ten donkeys! Although the owner of the enclosure is as yet unknown, both associated ceramics and inscribed door sealings show it likely dates to the early 1st Dynasty or possibly even earlier.

Finally, as regards 1st Dynasty enclosures, we have discovered something important about the ancient enclosure still visible in part around the Coptic village of Deir Sitt Damiana. Although thought by some to be a 1st Dynasty enclosure, it is very different in proportions from the other known 1st Dynasty enclosures. The Coptic village enclosure walls have a ratio of about 1:1.2, i.e. it is almost square in plan. The other enclosures average 1:1.8, except for Merneith's, which is extremely elongated at 1:2.6. Recently, close examination of the exposed ancient brickwork around the Coptic village has shown these bricks are quite different in size, proportion and quality from the Early Dynastic brickwork, found consistently throughout the enclosures. The brickwork in question is identical to that of a structure located to the southwest of the Coptic village, a part of which was excavated in 2002–3 and proved to be associated with Ptolemaic pottery. The Coptic village enclosure remains an intriguing structure, and of major significance for the history of this part of North Abydos, but it may have nothing to do with the Early Dynastic period.

Thus, for the 1st Dynasty, we now have eight enclosures, three of which belong to one reign. There are at least two enclosures yet to be found. Of the eight identified, four can be assigned royal owners – Aha, Djer, Djet and queen-mother Merneith. Of course, as noted above, even earlier enclosures might exist, perhaps in the vicinity of Aha's; and we are not yet completely sure whether the most recently discovered enclosure, next to his, is 1st Dynasty or earlier.

As we have seen, the enclosures of Peribsen and Khasekhemwy were explored relatively early in the excavational history of Abydos. These excavations, however, were very partial, and we have added much further information about both, and expect to add even more in the future. In addition, with the support of a grant of United States International Agency for Development funds via the Egyptian Antiquities Project of the American Research Center in Egypt, we have begun a programme of conserving and stabilizing Khasekhemwy's enclosure, which is by far the largest monument to survive from Early Dynastic Egypt.

In 1904 Ayrton had traced three of the four walls of Peribsen's enclosure, located an entrance near its southeast corner (and another smaller one in the southeast wall), and found and excavated its chapel. He noted the northwest wall of the enclosure was not excavated because a modern cemetery was present, but in 1988 we found this wall unencumbered, and visible on the surface. Subsequent excavation revealed an elaborately planned gateway near the north corner, similar to that of Khasekhemwy's enclosure.

Khasekhemwy's enclosure was explored initially by Mariette's men, and later by Ayrton, who discovered a chapel in its eastern quadrant. However, much was left unexcavated, and even areas excavated by Ayrton were not recorded in the detail desirable today. Since 1986, we have studied various aspects and features of Khasekhemwy's enclosure, and are now in the process of completely exposing the bases of its main and perimeter walls, for the purposes of documentation and conservation mentioned above.

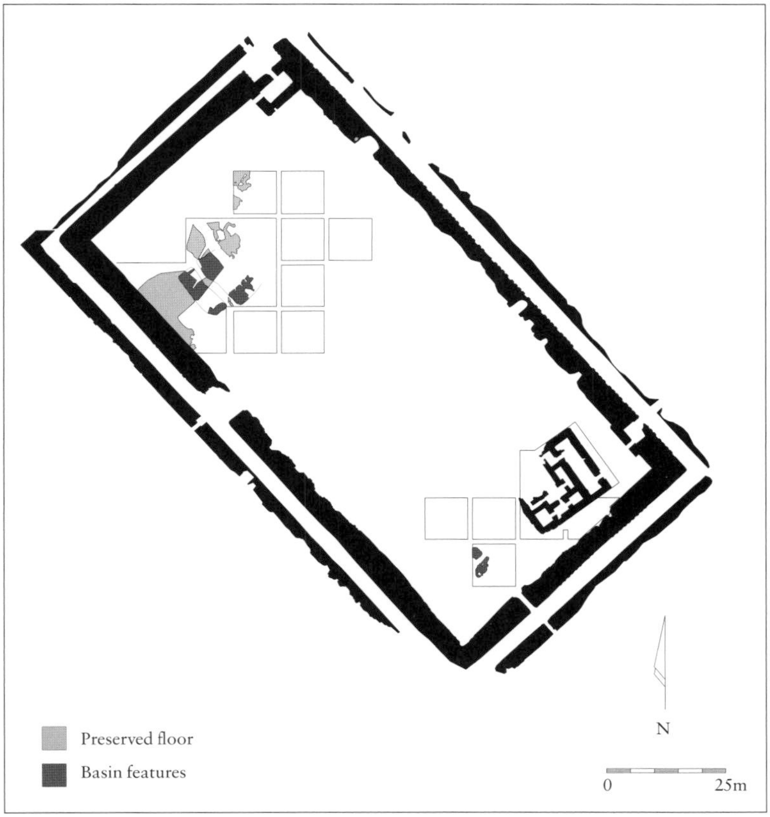

93 The plan of King Khasekhemwy's enclosure, the Shunet el Zebib. Note that the presence of gateways (in less elaborate form) in its southwest and southeast walls has been confirmed by our excavations. In the west quadrant a large exposure of original Early Dynastic remains indicates that much of the enclosed space consists of large basins and work surfaces generated by the actual building process, and left open and uncovered once the enclosure was completed. Similar areas have been located at various points external to the periphery wall as well.

Preserved floor

Basin features

N

0   25m

These activities have led to some surprises. One was the discovery, in 1986, that the area in front (i.e. northeast) of Khasekhemwy's chapel was filled with stratified debris (the product of offering ceremonies) that had been left largely undisturbed by earlier excavators. Seemingly more significant, but in the end unfortunately more misleading, was the discovery of fragments of a so-called 'proto-pyramid' in the western quadrant of the enclosure. I interpreted these as the remains of a surface mound of sand and gravel covered by a thin brick skin and discussed its possible significance in several articles. However, in 2000, when increased funding made expanded excavation possible in the Shunet el Zebib, the architectural fragments in question turned out to be the edge of a large, brick-lined basin and the notion of a 'proto-pyramid' here had to be abandoned!

As for the future of the Shunet el Zebib, two expert consultants (William Remsen of International Preservation Associates, Inc. and Tony Crosby) have carried out intensive studies of the monument. Although a great deal has survived to almost its original height for almost 5,000 years, much also collapsed in antiquity, and that surviving is in imminent danger of collapse. A primary problem is extremely large and deep recesses cut into the faces of the Shuneh's walls to accommodate cells for a religious community during the Coptic period, but there are also other major conservation issues that need to be addressed. Fortunately, the solutions are relatively straightforward, and require to a large extent the filling-in of recesses with new mud-brick, and the building of buttresses to support other parts of the enclosure walls. Nevertheless, these activities require making sure that the new brickwork is not only visually unobtrusive but also technically compatible with the old brickwork. Otherwise, the infilling could generate further stress, rather than ensure stability in the future. In connection with this stabilization work, an almost complete photogrammatic survey has been carried out on the Shunet el Zebib, and will be completed in the future. While necessary for planning conservation and stabilization activities, this survey also provides uniquely detailed documentation of this extraordinary early monument.

However, we are not planning to restore or reconstruct Khasekhemwy's enclosure, but only to stabilize and conserve it as it is. Walls that have collapsed are not being rebuilt, and the regular recessing that decorates its external faces is not being restored, although in a few places it still survives. The rugged and still massive remains of the enclosure attest to a long experience of re-use, intrusion and collapse that is as much a part of its history as its original pristine form.

The Archaeology of the Enclosures

As we have seen earlier in this chapter, there has been, and still is, much speculation about the functions and meanings of the enclosures, or of structures which might have inspired them – from Mariette's police station through royal forts or residences, a site for royal worship, a dwelling place or palace for deceased kings, to copies of 'fortresses of the gods'. Some of these suggestions are valuable and intriguing, but depend upon a high degree of extrapolation. Here

I shall focus primarily on the archaeology of these enclosures, as we know it today, and then move on to what we might infer about the enclosures' functions and meanings from this.

Obviously, the data are incomplete, but reasonable extrapolation can now be made from the much increased evidence available; only two, or maybe three 1st Dynasty enclosures are missing, although our information about some others is not complete, because of damage and denudation, or the need for further excavation. I believe the following observations, however, can reasonably be applied to all the enclosures, including the two or three not yet located.

Aha's enclosures – the earliest yet known – set a model the essentials of which are followed by all subsequent enclosures at Abydos to the end of the 2nd Dynasty. In this model, each enclosure is rectangular in plan, relatively massive in construction (actual wall widths vary), and has within it a small chapel. Most of the enclosures are similar in proportion, averaging 1:2.1 (Aha's large enclosure is closer to a square, at 1:1.45), and in all known cases the chapel is located partly or entirely within the east quadrant of each enclosure. The chapels are relatively small, except for Khasekhemwy's – its larger size (about 2.5 times greater than those of Djer and Peribsen) conforms to the larger size of his enclosure in general. All known enclosures are very similar in orientation, the long axis always being northwest to southeast, but in virtually none are all the corners true right angles, and in some cases, such as Aha's enclosure, the shape is noticeably trapezoidal. Each individual chapel varies in orientation, and sometimes does not closely conform to that of its enclosure.

Externally, the enclosures display a number of visually significant features. All of them were apparently quite high: the Shunet el Zebib, probably the tallest, still stands in part close to its original height of perhaps 11 m (36 ft), and others, to judge from their relatively thick walls, must have been of similar height. Even the Aha enclosure, while much smaller than the others, has walls so thick that a height of 5–8 m (16.4–26.2 ft) can reasonably be extrapolated. Both the inner and outer faces of the enclosures were covered with a thick mud plaster, dark grey in colour, although Khasekhemwy's alone had an additional coating of light coloured clay, very light brown in tone.

In all the known enclosures, the external faces had regularly placed and closely set recesses; these began at ground level and probably rose to a considerable height before being topped by, probably, wooden lintels. Along the northwest, southwest and southeast faces the shallow recesses were all the same in size and in their simple plan, but along the northeast face ('local east') each set of three (in one case, four) simple recesses alternated with single ones that were deeper, wider and more complex in plan. Visually, this recessing created an ever-changing pattern of light and shadow that would have relieved the blankness of the high walls, but we cannot know if this was the intention of the Egyptians, or whether the recessing conveyed some explicit symbolic meaning. In any event, this recessing is much simpler in plan than the elaborate,

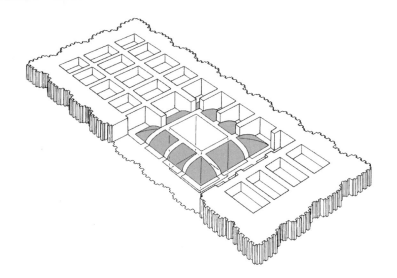

repetitive niching that makes up the complex so-called 'palace façade' exteriors of the 1st Dynasty elite grave superstructures at Saqqara.

From the external foot of each wall a mud-plaster surface extended outwards, sometimes for a considerable distance. Built on it, along the foot of each wall face, was – in all 1st Dynasty enclosures – a low brick bench, covered in mud plaster. So far, no traces of any emplacements have been found on these benches, although comparable benches around the tomb superstructures at Saqqara sometimes supported hundreds of bull's heads, modelled in clay but with real horns.

A new discovery, made in 2002–3, was that throughout the 1st Dynasty at least each enclosure had a circular, bastion-like feature built around each external corner. They occur both with Aha's enclosures and the (later 1st Dynasty?) enclosure southwest of it, so they were probably provided to all enclosures of this dynasty. The buttresses are quite low in elevation, rising not much higher than the bench and have no structural significance, so are 'symbolic' rather than functional.

Every enclosure – both 1st and 2nd Dynasty – had entrances near the north and east corners. Given the size of the enclosures, these were relatively modest features, doorways rather than gateways. The east entrance was always in the northeast face of the enclosure, the north corner one typically in the north-western, except in the case of Aha's enclosure, where both entrances were in the northeast face. The east corner entrance was stable in plan and proportions throughout the Early Dynastic period. It led into a small chamber, from which – via a change in axial position – another doorway gave access to the enclosure interior. In Khasekhemwy's enclosure, the room was actually set *within* the enclosure wall, probably because the latter was more massive than the walls of earlier enclosures. The east corner entrance in probably every enclosure had a door, which was regularly opened, then shut and re-sealed, because a consider-able number of discarded door sealings were recovered in the east corner chamber of the enclosure southwest of Aha's.

So far, there is no evidence that the north corner entrance had a door. In fact, although a finished entrance that must have been put to some use, the north corner entrance in every 1st Dynasty enclosure, where it survived, was blocked up with laid brickwork early in its history. This brickwork's external face was plastered, so the door was in effect transformed into a deep recess or niche. The 1st Dynasty north corner entrance was simple in plan, but in the 2nd Dynasty enclosure the entrance – itself modest in size – was set within a deep, wide recess and now led into a room in turn providing access to the enclosure interior, like the east corner entrance. So far, there is no indication that the north corner entrances in the 2nd Dynasty enclosures were blocked up, so a change in their function, as well as their plan, is indicated.

Second Dynasty enclosures had additional entrances: Khasekhemwy's had an entrance in the southwest and southeast walls, and Peribsen's in the latter and perhaps the former as well. In plan, these entrances were simple, with no attached rooms internal to the enclosure. However, they complemented the other two entrances, and all four were placed so as to ensure that each quadrant of the enclosed space had its own, non-centrally placed entrance, although the four quadrants were not, so far as we know, walled off from each other. First Dynasty enclosures probably did not have these additional two entrances; this seems certain for Aha's largely excavated enclosure, and for the southeast wall of the enclosure southwest of his.

The interior space within each enclosure was normally quite extensive and, since so far no indications of structures other than the chapel have been found, provided an impressive, open background to the chapel for those entering the enclosure via the east corner entrance. Aha's enclosure, however, is an exception: its walls are relatively high, but its interior space is so small it must have seemed more like a courtyard for the chapel, rather than providing an area so large it seems functionally independent of the chapel, as is the case in the other enclosures.

The chapel may well have been very similar in scale and plan throughout the 1st Dynasty, and even as late as Peribsen's reign. Similarity in scale is suggested by the closely related sizes of Djer's and Peribsen's chapels, respectively 104.5 sq. m (1,124.4 sq. ft) and 108 sq. m (1,162 sq. ft); and in plan by the very similar, almost identical layout of the two chapels of Aha and the Peribsen chapel. In these cases, an east corner entrance led into a long, narrow room (oriented northwest to southeast) and from there into a much smaller chamber. In both Aha's well-preserved chapels, the latter room had a bench filling its northeast side, a bench with extensive traces of libation and incense burning. This then seems to be a 'cult chamber', although whether a statue or stele provided a ritual focus is unknown. In the Aha and Peribsen chapels, the entire southwest side is occupied by a long, northwest to southeast oriented room. In the Aha I and possibly the Aha II chapels it seems completely enclosed and inaccessible, and reminiscent of the sealed-off 'serdabs' or statue rooms in Old Kingdom elite tomb chapels and, sometimes, royal mortuary complexes. However, in Peribsen's chapel this room is accessible, and given its position – furthest from the entrance – may have become the space in which cult was performed.

Khasekhemwy's chapel was much larger, and more complex in plan. Entered by an east corner doorway, the northeast half was reminiscent of the earlier chapel plan, but the southwest half (only partially preserved) consisted of a labyrinthine complex of chambers. Set in the south corner was a small room, furthest from the entrance and for this reason possibly the cult chamber, and, in fact, traces of incense burning and libations were recovered here during our recent re-excavation of the structure. In any event, the increased complexity of Khasekhemwy's chapel implies a more complicated ritual programme than the preceding chapel type.

As for the external appearance of these chapels, their approximately square plans (Peribsen's is an exception), presumably relatively low heights (probably about 3 m or 9.8 ft) and flat roofs (evidence for which was found in Aha's chapel), would have given them a cube-like appearance. Like the enclosures, they are covered inside and out with a thick, dark grey mud plaster. Aha's chapel had no articulation along its external wall faces, but Peribsen's had relatively complex niching extending along its northeastern façade, and simple niches along part of the exterior of its southeastern wall. Khasekhemwy's chapel had a complex niche at the exact centre point of its northeast façade, flanked symmetrically by smaller niches, indicating that the façade was the focus for ritual activity, as well as the interior. The other three walls had a simpler pattern of external niching.

As noted earlier, Aha's almost completely excavated enclosure (and partial excavation in Peribsen's and Khasekhemwy's enclosures) indicates that, aside from the chapel, each enclosure's interior space was empty of any substantial brick structures, and no post holes or other evidence suggestive of buildings in lighter materials were observed, although Aha II may be an exception. The remains of large basins were found in the west and south quadrants of Khasekhemwy's enclosure, but these were apparently related to the construction and plastering of the enclosure, and were subsequently filled in, or perhaps even left exposed. Yet specific access was provided to these empty spaces (see the discussion about entrances above), so they presumably were used for some function and were not simply the accidental or inevitable by-product of the construction of large, i.e. 'prestigious', enclosures.

Finally, we should turn to the other important feature of the enclosures, the subsidiary graves (and, in one case, boat graves) provided to at least some of them in the 1st Dynasty.

Subsidiary graves, external to the royal monument itself, are associated with the 1st Dynasty royal tombs at Umm el Qa'ab and their complementary enclosures in North Abydos. Each subsidiary tomb was small, and usually contained one individual, who was likely sacrificed at the time of the king's burial. The status of these subsidiary burials has long been debated: were the occupants killed, i.e. sacrificed, or did they die natural deaths and were buried at widely dispersed intervals? Our recent work has revealed archaeological evidence strongly supporting the sacrificial notion: both the subsidiary graves at Aha's enclosure, and some we re-excavated at Djer's, had been roofed all at one time, making 'all at once' sacrificial burials likely.

The occupants of the subsidiary graves at the royal tombs were not exclusively human – hunting dogs were buried near some of the royal tombs (and each supplied with an individual, identifying stela) and at Umm el Qa'ab King Aha's pet lions (buried together in an unusually long grave) accompanied him into the afterlife. The occupants of the subsidiary graves alongside the enclosures, however, seemed to provide a more elemental level of service to the dead pharaoh than the perhaps higher status individuals given burial alongside their kings at Umm el Qa'ab. For example, the subsidiary graves around Djer's and Djet's enclosures were badly plundered, but still yielded a surprising amount (not paralleled in Umm el Qa'ab subsidiary graves) of copper tools – knives, adzes, chisels, needles and even axes. These likely belonged to artisans who would continue to produce artifacts and even structures of wood, leather and cloth for the deceased ruler in the afterlife. Moreover, the needs for transportation and supply were also provided for in ways not found at Umm el Qa'ab – specifically, the ten donkeys buried next to the enclosure southwest of Aha's, and, for the owner of the Western Mastaba enclosure, the 14 boat burials, which are also a type of subsidiary grave.

As at Umm el Qa'ab, the subsidiary graves around or adjacent to enclosures were laid out in regular patterns, some more strictly than others. They also increase, then diminish over time, as is the case at Umm el Qa'ab as well. Thus Aha's enclosure has only six subsidiary graves, and his tomb 36, but Djer's and Djet's enclosures have 269 and 154, and their tombs 326 and 174. Merneith had only 80 (enclosure) and 41 (tomb), while at Umm el Qa'ab thereafter subsidiary graves drop steadily – 121 (Den), 63 (Anedjib), 69 (Semerkhet) and 26 (Qa'a). No subsidiary graves occur at either the 2nd Dynasty tombs or enclosures, although the practice of sacrificial burials may have continued; Khasekhemwy's tomb contained three human skeletons close to the king's burial chamber which are hard to explain as other than sacrificial.

At Umm el Qa'ab and around the enclosures serious denudation makes it difficult to say whether surface features were associated with subsidiary graves. So far as Aha's grave enclosure is concerned, however, we have good evidence that its large and well-built subsidiary graves did not have superstructures; the space above the roof was filled in, and then covered over by the mud-plaster surface extending outwards from the foot of the enclosure walls. Whether this was true of later subsidiary graves at the enclosures is uncertain. However, many subsidiary graves around all 1st Dynasty royal tombs after Aha, and around Djer's, Djet's and Merneith's enclosures had small limestone stelae, inscribed with the name and sometimes the title or occupation of the owner. Petrie persuasively argued, on the basis of the weathering patterns still preserved on some, that these stelae had been inserted upright into the ground above the relevant grave. Given the existence of at least these surface features (the stelae), it is possible they were actually each set in the niche of a low superstructure similar to those found with some subsidiary graves around elite tombs of the 1st Dynasty at Saqqara and elsewhere.

In this, and in other ways, the spatial disposition of subsidiary graves around or next to enclosures is also suggestive. Those around the enclosures of Djer, Djet and Merneith all leave a particularly conspicuous gap in the vicinity of the east corner entrance; in addition, the largest and hence implicitly most prestigious subsidiary graves are also found in this area. This circumstance suggests two things. First, it reflects the fact that the east corner entrance was used repeatedly for a period (as the door sealings from the enclosure southwest of Aha's indicate) and so easy access was desired. Second, this inference in turn indicates the subsidiary graves of these three enclosures had some kind of surface feature that impeded such access, or at least was considered inappropriate to it. The features could have simply been the low-rising, but still inconvenient surface stelae mentioned above, or actual super-structures, which would have been a more substantial impediment. A relevant analogy here is the gap in subsidiary graves found regularly near the south corner of each royal tomb. As I suggested in Chapter 9, this gap may have facilitated repeated access to an offering place, or even a small chapel, placed over the tomb itself.

Other variations in the spatial patterning around the enclosures are more irregular, and less susceptible to explanation. For example, the subsidiary graves of Djet and Merneith have a gap near the east corner of their enclosures, where there was an entrance; but Djer's enclosure had a similarly located entrance, yet has a continuous line of subsidiary graves in its vicinity. All three enclosures also have a gap in their subsidiary graves near the west corner, but as far as we know no entrance existed in this area. Further complexities are created by a partial doubling of some lines of subsidiary graves (Djet, south-west side) or their complete absence, southwest of Merneith's, an area Petrie specifically explored without result. As yet, we do not know if the Western Mastaba has subsidiary graves other than the boat graves along its southwest side. The boat graves, it should be noted, did have superstructures, rising to about 50 cm (19 in) above the then ground level.

Finally, Petrie discovered a small Early Dynastic chapel set above the southwest line of the graves at Djer's enclosure. The chapel was central to its own enclosure, the entrance of which had been bricked up. Chapel and enclosure appeared to have been built soon after the subsidiary graves had been roofed over.

The Enclosures and the Abydos Landscape

Having surveyed the archaeology of the royal enclosures, this is a good point to consider how they might have related to the larger landscape of Abydos in Early Dynastic times. Did the royal tombs of Umm el Qa'ab and the enclosures about 1.5 km (0.93 miles) to the north have a visual presence, and what might we guess was conveyed by that presence? The answer to these questions is perhaps a surprising one.

Each tomb at Umm el Qaʻab was probably capped by a substantial mound (see Chapter 9), but this would have been relatively low in elevation – maybe 2 to 3 m (6.5 to 10 ft) high. Khasekhemwy's may have been substantially higher, for mounds were essentially composed of the material generated by the pit excavated to hold the tomb, and Khasekhemwy's tomb was particularly deep and long. Assuming each mound had been left undisturbed, by the end of the 2nd Dynasty a bird's eye view would have revealed widely scattered mounds in the northeast part of the Early Dynastic cemetery (where the subsidiary graves next to or around the tombs covered a wide area), and a denser concentration in the south. In the extreme south, and some distance away, Khasekhemwy's mound would be perhaps the biggest and highest.

However, from the perspective of North Abydos, or from the floodplain, the mounds of Umm el Qaʻab, while visible, would not be particularly striking. They were far away, scattered in location, low in elevation, and must have seemed quite small against the background of the towering cliffs behind them.

The visual impression conveyed by the enclosures, should they all have survived as standing monuments to the end of the 2nd Dynasty, would probably have been much more impressive, even dramatic. The enclosures stood close to the inhabited floodplain, and would dominate the visual field of any observer at floodplain edge. Moreover, each enclosure was quite large, for the most part certainly much more so than the mound over the contemporary tomb, which in any case was far away in the distance. Enclosures had a crisp geometric shape and were quite high, ranging from perhaps 5 m (16.4 ft) to 11 m (36 ft). Finally, the enclosures were not scattered over the landscape, but tightly clustered together, a factor further reinforcing their visual impact.

Thus, as compared to the tomb mounds, the Abydos enclosures could be thought of as the more powerful statement about the presence of deceased kings at Abydos and of the unique status of these kings in Egyptian society. However, if we suggest instead that at any given time only one enclosure was visible, and North Abydos was otherwise seemingly empty, then the visual impression conveyed would have been quite different, and our ideas about the meaning or symbolism of the enclosures would have to be revised. Yet, it is this second possibility – a sole enclosure occupying the visual field at any time – that is the more likely.

During our excavations in North Abydos I[7] and Matthew Adams independently reached the conclusion that each of the known enclosures (and thus presumably all except Khasekhemwy's) had been deliberately razed very early in its history, probably about the time that the next enclosure in the series was being built. This impression was conveyed by the very uniform heights to which enclosure walls had been reduced, and by the absence of large amounts of brick collapse or erosional debris. Subsequently, Adams' excavation of Aha's enclosure and of the one southwest of it has provided strong additional evidence for this theory.

Thus, in Khasekhemwy's time his enclosure would have stood alone in North Abydos; even that of his immediate predecessor, Peribsen, would have disappeared from view. Moreover, this practice of the solitary enclosure can be projected backwards, for every reign of the 1st Dynasty. Of course, each enclosure would have stood in a different location, since the Egyptians were careful not to build one enclosure on the remains of another, however early the latter might have been, but these shifts in location would not have been recognized by most viewers.

What are we to infer from this, to us strange practice of building a large monument and then, almost immediately, destroying it? There is a utilitarian factor involved. The bricks from the demolished enclosure could be used for the large amounts of mortar, plaster and even new bricks needed for the next enclosure, often conveniently located next to the one being demolished. This may well have happened, but the Early Dynastic Egyptians certainly had the resources to fully provide for the next enclosure with new material, and leave earlier enclosures standing, if they wished. Some other motivation seems to be at work here.

Adams and I would suggest that each enclosure was deliberately destroyed, soon after the royal owner's death and subsequent burial at Umm el Qa'ab, so that the enclosure too could be considered buried, and hence fully transferred into the afterlife. After all, around both the tombs and the enclosures sacrificed retainers and others were buried so they could immediately enter the netherworld and be instantly available to serve the deceased king, and this logic was extended even further to cover transportation services – the donkeys and boats also buried near some enclosures. Apparently, the enclosure and its chapel, and whatever activities were carried out within them, were considered to be perpetual necessities for the dead king, and this burial process made them fully available to him. There is even an analogous situation at Umm el Qa'ab. Here, the royal tomb was already underground, hence fully entered into the netherworld, but the surface mound above the tomb, a mound serving as a focus for ritual, was apparently also considered a perpetual necessity. This is suggested by the second, fully subterranean mound placed above the tomb, an 'entombed' version of the surface mound which, thus symbolically buried, would exist forever in the afterlife as well.

Therefore, the message conveyed by the enclosures apparently focused on the unique status of the latest king to be buried at Umm el Qa'ab, and not on creating – over time – an impressive material manifestation or embodiment of the entire dynasty. Instead, earlier enclosures, having served their immediate ritual purposes (discussed below) had been ritually buried, transferred to the afterlife so they were fully available to the dead king, and the services they represented guaranteed eternal repetition.

As noted earlier, Khasekhemwy's enclosure is the exception: clearly, it was never razed and indeed has to a large degree survived into our own day. There are two possible reasons for it not being ritually buried like the earlier enclosures. First, it is the last royal enclosure built at Abydos. Khasekhemwy's successor, Djoser, ensured that Khasekhemwy's burial rites, and the rituals in the enclosure, were carried out, as we know from seal-impressions of Djoser found both at the tomb and near the chapel in the enclosure. However, with a vast new building project begun for Djoser's own mortuary complex at

Saqqara, far away to the north, it may have been decided not to expend time and labour on the removal of Khasekhemwy's enclosure.

A second possible explanation, however, seems a more satisfactory one. It may be that by Khasekhemwy's time the idea of how to ensure the survival and continued accessibility of the surface features of a royal mortuary monument had changed. These were now guaranteed not by a form of burial, but by increasing the durability of the monument itself, in Khasekhemwy's case by making the brickwork of the enclosure much more massive than had been the case before. Indeed, this massiveness in itself suggests that from the outset there was no intention to raze the monument, even though this had been done for its immediate predecessor, Peribsen's enclosure. Immediately after Khasekhemwy, durability was ensured even more effectively, for from Djoser's reign on through the entire Old Kingdom the core structures of royal mortuary complexes were normally built entirely of stone, an even better guarantee of eternal availability.

The Functions of the Abydos Enclosures

So far I have discussed the possible meanings of the enclosures as visible signifiers of individual kings and as ritual structures conveyed to the afterlife for the benefit of those kings. What, however, can we infer *about* those rituals from the archaeological evidence that we now have?

Their very existence – one for each ruler buried at Abydos – shows the enclosures were considered to be as important as the tomb itself in ensuring an eternal and successful afterlife for the dead king. This raises the possibility that the rituals performed at tomb and enclosure were connected to each other, though not necessarily fully identical in content; some rituals might be similar at both locales, others might be different yet complement each other. It may even be that tomb and enclosure, while physically separate from each other, were a conceptual unity in the minds of the Egyptians. Barry Kemp long ago pointed out that their separation might be particular to the circumstances at Abydos. For traditional reasons (the existence of an earlier, prestigious and in part royal cemetery), the Early Dynastic kings were buried far out in the desert. The topography of the site might have made the building of an enclosure around each tomb difficult, especially if the growth of the cemetery was anticipated. Or, a location for tombs closer to the floodplain might have been in more normal circumstances preferred, and the enclosures – standing in for the tomb – were thus sited in deference to this. In any event, the implication is that the preferred royal mortuary monument at this time would have consisted of an enclosure, set within which was the tomb, its position marked by a surface mound, the latter perhaps with a chapel to its southeast. This would still imply that much of the enclosed space remained empty of other structures.

Keeping this possible conceptual unity of tomb and enclosure in mind, but recognizing their physical separation at Abydos, what can we infer about the rituals associated with each from the extant archaeology? For each tomb, we can be sure of a one-time ritual, the king's burial, while the surface stelae associated with each tomb suggest a permanent offering place at which ritual activity would be repeated for a period. How long is hard to say; at Saqqara, the mortuary cult of a 2nd Dynasty king buried there lasted over a century (into the 4th Dynasty), but no inscriptional or archaeological evidence later than the reign of Djoser, Khasekhemwy's successor, has been identified at Umm el Qa'ab.

What about ritual activity at the enclosures? The very existence of the enclosure chapel shows ritual was performed there, a supposition reinforced by traces of libations and incense burning in at least three of these chapels (Khasekhemwy's and two from Aha's enclosures). Moreover, ritual in the chapel was likely repeated over an extended (but apparently not very long) period, for the east corner enclosure entrance which provided access to the chapel in the enclosure southwest of Aha's had been repeatedly opened, then re-sealed, as discarded door sealings showed. There is, however, no indication of cult continuing in the enclosures after Djoser's reign, and in fact, as noted above, each (apart from Khasekhemwy's) seems to have been razed, along with its chapel, during the reign of its owner's successor.

The enclosures did not contain actual royal tombs, so a one-time burial ceremony as such was not involved in their ritual life. However, in 1st Dynasty enclosures the north corner entrance was fully finished, and hence used, and yet carefully blocked up some time before the enclosure was razed. This circumstance raises the possibility the entrance was used only once, perhaps to allow some kind of one-time ritual to be performed in the enclosure. This could well have taken place in the northwest half of the enclosure, the area immediately accessed by the north corner entrance; if so, the rituals took place in the open, or in temporary structures which were then dismantled. That the enclosure chapel was involved in ritual involving entry through the north corner entrance seems less likely: this would be conceivable in Aha's relatively small enclosure, but less so in the much larger internal space defined by the enclosures of Djer and Djet.

As we have seen, important changes apparently occurred in Peribsen's and Khasekhemwy's enclosures which indicate possible changes in their ritual use, although the basic ritual processes may have been similar to those in the 1st Dynasty enclosures. First, the north corner entrance in these last two enclosures became more architecturally grandiose than before, and was not apparently blocked off. Thus, a ritual requiring access via the north corner entrance seems to have increased in status, and could have been repeated over a period. Second, additional entrances provided access to the west (Khasekhemwy's only?) and south (Peribsen and Khasekhemwy) quadrants of the enclosures. If these were for ritual purposes (and no other purpose is obvious from the archaeology) then this indicates ritual activity in and around the enclosures had become more complex than before.

It is possible the enclosure walls themselves were the focus for some of the rituals occurring within or around them. Later sources refer to ritual or ceremonial circumambulations by the king around city walls or temple enclosures, e.g. in connection with coronation rituals and *sed*-festival celebrations.

Although a deceased rather than a living king was involved, such rituals could have taken place around the inner or outer faces (or both) of the enclosures. This impression is reinforced by the admittedly unique peripheral wall around Khasekhemwy's enclosure, which created what looks like a processional route around the entire monument.

To what degree were ritual processes (rather than specific rituals) similar at the royal tomb and enclosure? At the tombs, two points seem to have been of special ritual significance. As noted in Chapter 9 and above, there may have been an offering place or chapel southeast of each tomb's surface mound. Its very existence, and the gap always left – at 1st Dynasty tombs – in the subsidiary tombs to facilitate access from the southwest, suggests that ritual was regularly performed here, on repeated occasions, although over how long a period is impossible to say. The other point of significance was the direction from which the tomb was approached during the one-time burial ceremonies so that the royal body could be deposited therein. In the four later 1st Dynasty tombs the entry points into the tomb (via a ramp or stairway) are on the northwest or in one instance the northeast. This suggests that earlier, when the body was simply lowered into the tomb, the preferred approach may have been from the northeast or northwest. Later, Khasekhemwy's tomb at least seems to have an entrance on the northwest.

The situation concerning ritual performance at the tombs finds significant, if generalized, parallels at the enclosures. Here, in the southwestern half of each enclosure, repeated rituals were performed in a chapel; while the north corner entrance may have been for a one-time ritual entry akin in location to the one-time burial rituals performed at the royal tomb.

Royal tomb and enclosure may also relate to each other in meaningful ways when we consider their symbolic functions or meanings. The tomb presumably symbolized the contemporary concept of the afterworld and the supernatural features and beings relevant to that. However, it was evidently also a buried and otherworldly residence for the dead king. This is indicated not so much by its plan, which does not evoke a palatial residence in any specific way, as by the large amounts of artifacts, materials, drink and foodstuffs deposited in the tomb, all identical to those required by the living king. Moreover, the subsidiary graves also placed in the other world a whole cohort of beings who would utilize these resources to meet the deceased king's needs and pleasures. He expected to be fed, clothed and entertained, and even – to judge from the dog burials (mentioned above) – to engage in the ceremonialized hunts that later were such a feature of royal life in ancient Egypt. Thus, the tomb evokes the 'private life' of the king, such as was experienced in the residential quarters of the royal palace, and in hunting and recreational areas set aside for his use. Yet the tomb does not seem to replicate in any specific way such a palace, or the open-air settings involved; it is the *concept*, not the materialization of the king's private life, transferred into the other world, that is represented.

The richly provided subsidiary tombs around the larger enclosure of Aha seem to be for elite individuals of varied status (including one small child, with its own large grave). Thereafter, however, the subsidiary tombs adjacent to the enclosures seem to represent a level of service different from that represented by the individuals buried around the tombs. The latter seem to relate to the king's direct personal needs, whereas the former relate to the economic infrastructure which provided for both living and dead king the artifacts, materials and supplies needed to satisfy those needs. Those buried around the enclosures were not likely to directly service the king, but operated at one or more removes from him. The surviving artifacts reveal a substantial number were male and female artisans who produced items made of wood, cloth or leather, and probably metal and stone as well. One group of six contiguous graves each contained gaming pieces, suggesting these individuals were the specialized craftsmen who produced such items. A significant number of enclosure subsidiary graves also contained miniature granaries. If these were for the personal (if symbolic) use of the grave owner, one would expect such granaries in many more of the subsidiary graves. Since they are not, the individuals involved were likely granary officials, responsible for supplying the royal court. The 'service' aspect of the enclosures' subsidiary graves is even further emphasized by those relating specifically to the provision of transportation, i.e. the donkey burials and boat graves, neither of which are represented near the royal tombs.

The enclosure itself, and the open spaces and chapel within it, should also relate to the activities and needs of the living king, and their transference into the other world. The enclosure is capable of being read or interpreted in two different, but complementary and co-existing ways. First, the large open area each enclosure defines may correspond to the areas in which the king participated in especially elaborate and semi-public ceremonies. Representations even earlier than the 1st Dynasty show that even by then the Egyptian kings experienced formal enthronements and led ceremonies involving substantial numbers of participants. Some of these, at least, are indicated as taking place in the open.

However, the presence of the subsidiary graves, together with the relationship of the owners to the economic infrastructure of palatial complexes, suggests that the enclosure also signifies, without actually representing in plan, the entirety of such complexes. This involved not only the actual royal residence (equivalent to the tomb which, it must be remembered, in circumstances other than those prevailing at Abydos, might literally have been set within the enclosure) and the arenas of royal display. Such palatial complexes, in their larger extent, included residences for support and service staff; workshops and processing units, such as bakeries and butcheries; storerooms and granaries; animal pens, donkey yards and mooring places. Without actually representing these multiple structures in material form, the enclosure can be envisaged as conceptually containing them, and standing for them.

These possibilities leave the significance of the enclosure walls themselves ambiguous. Do they represent the walls around royal residences and arenas of display, or around the entire palatial complex, with its living areas, workshops and storerooms, or around the entire royal city, with its temples, residential and other zones – the royal support system in its most extended form? The enclosure walls may have all of these meanings, and yet not represent literally the form that palace, palatial complex or city enclosure walls may have had. At one level, and the one exercised in reality, enclosures, like tombs, were for rituals intended to express the idea that the once-living king had moved from this world into the other world, and had become a being much more akin to a divine entity. The model for the enclosure then might have been a specific type used to surround early temples, rather than palaces or royal cities.

A partially excavated Early Dynastic enclosure at Hierakonpolis has been identified as that of a palace. It has recessed external niching (more elaborate than that of the Abydos enclosures) and a deeply recessed entrance near its north corner. Much of the adjacent interior is densely crowded with residences and workshops, and thus it seems to correspond to the more extended idea of a palace referred to above, with the actual palace itself further off, set deeper in the as yet unexcavated area. However, the Hierakonpolis complex may equally well be a temple enclosure, since temples too were likely surrounded by the houses and workshops of their priests and service populations.

In summary then, tomb, enclosure and subsidiary graves, despite their scattered locations at Abydos, form in the case of each king a conceptual whole. Taken together, they have function and meaning at different levels. At one, they represent the ritual features needed to transfer the king into the afterlife and successfully maintain him there. At another, they probably symbolize those aspects of the other world of significance to the deceased, now fully divinized king. Finally, tomb, enclosure and subsidiary graves also signify (without necessarily representing in any specific way) the aspects of the royal palace directly relevant to the king, i.e. his residence and arenas for royal display, the palatial complex and even the royal city in its broadest sense, encompassing the materiality of those who meet the king's personal needs, and those who provide the economic infrastructure required for the operations of the palace.

These interrelated yet parallel levels of meaning are also framed in a meaningful temporal sequence according to the events reconstructed in this chapter. First, the deceased king is ceremonially buried, and he and his subterranean residence are thus transferred into the afterlife. At about this time, his retainers are dispatched and buried, i.e. they move on into the afterlife, together with other necessary beings and items – dogs for hunting, donkeys and boats for transportation. At both royal tomb and enclosure ritual continues for a period, but soon ceases at the latter. The enclosure is duly razed and buried, becoming fully available to the dead king in the afterlife and representing the transformation of the totality of palace and palatial complex into an other-world entity. From this point on, the only continuing ritual activity has narrowed down to the offering place or chapel southeast of the tomb's surface mound, the only surviving visual signifier of a deceased ruler who now – fully equipped, serviced and housed – flourishes in the afterlife.

CHAPTER ELEVEN

BOAT GRAVES AND PYRAMID ORIGINS

Sailing Through Eternity

In 1991 the Pennsylvania-Yale-Institute of Fine Arts, New York University Expedition to Abydos made one of its most spectacular discoveries: 12 enormous boat graves immediately northeast of King Khasekhemwy's enclosure, the Shunet el Zebib. Further excavations in 2000 have increased the number to 14, while in 2002–3 it was shown that they most likely date to the 1st Dynasty. The boat graves are unique for their period. Each consists of a boat-shaped, mud-brick superstructure – very long, but narrow – enclosing an actual wooden hull of comparable proportions. Similar ones have been found with elite tombs of the 1st Dynasty (and possibly later) at Saqqara and Helwan, but these occur individually – one per tomb – not grouped into a virtual fleet as at Abydos. The Abydos boat graves are also substantially larger and more elaborate in form than contemporary ones elsewhere, and each contains a relatively well preserved wooden boat, while the boats at Saqqara and Helwan had nearly all crumbled to dust.

Most importantly, the Abydos boat graves are the first to be associated with early royal mortuary monuments, thus linking these with the later pyramid complexes of the Old and Middle Kingdoms, which sporadically incorporated boat pits and burials similar to the Abydos examples. More generally, these early boat burials at Abydos and elsewhere relate to the very long-lived and strong association of boats, ships and floats with Egyptian concepts of the afterlife, and with the burial and cult practices generated by these.

Verbal and visual imagery in Egyptian mortuary contexts often involves boats and ships, which *in toto* comprise a vast flotilla in which deities, long-dead kings and deceased Egyptians sail through eternity. In particular, the sun-god travels by boat through sky and netherworld in order to carry out his endless cycles of regeneration, as do deities and the dead, who use boats and canoes for other afterlife purposes. And when divinity penetrated into the world of the living Egyptians, it often did so on a boat – boat-shaped palanquins carried divine images in public processions, and actual boats ferried such images from one temple or cult centre to another.

95 *The reconstructed boat of King Khufu, in its museum adjacent to the Great Pyramid at Giza. Fourteen boats beside a 1st Dynasty enclosure at Abydos anticipate this later custom.*

This imagery was natural in Egypt, where boats frequently crossed or travelled up and down the bridgeless Nile, and canoes and floats traversed the extensive marshes. But boat imagery had tremendous symbolic weight as well. Boats typified virtually unlimited mobility, desired by deities and the dead who sailed vast distances in the other world in order to achieve and maintain endless regenerations. Moreover, boats symbolized the overcoming of danger. Living Egyptians feared drowning or other aquatic fatalities; crocodiles and hippopotami teemed in the Nile and the unrecovered bodies of Egyptians drowned or consumed in the river required special attention from the gods to ensure immortality. Boats thus protected the living, but also deities and the dead who – by using them – evaded or repelled the monstrous beings believed to lurk throughout the other world.

The mortuary significance of boats was a very ancient one in Egypt. Prehistoric decorated pottery found in graves sometimes bears depictions of boats and one early tomb (at Hierakonpolis, of Naqada II date) is famous for the fleet of ships depicted on one of its walls. Sometimes the dead in prehistoric times were provided with actual boat models, perhaps the modest origin for the spectacular, full-scale boat burials of Abydos.

Subsequently, while boat models are found in elite tombs of the Old and Middle Kingdoms, only the tombs of kings and queens were provided with boat pits or burials, and then only occasionally. Few actual boats survive: two were found – disassembled – in pits next to Khufu's pyramid at Giza (one, reconstructed, is 43.4 m or 142 ft long) and six hastily constructed boats had been placed in pits near the pyramid of Senwosret III (12th Dynasty) at Dahshur. The rarity of royal boat burials suggests that kings' burials might more often have included boat models – magically empowered substitutes for the real thing.

Unfortunately, royal tombs have usually been completely plundered, but boat models did survive in the tomb of a queen of Pepi II (6th Dynasty) and in a few New Kingdom pharaohs' tombs. The most complete surviving group of models is in Tutankhamun's tomb (18th Dynasty) and displays a complexity in typology, functions and spatial arrangement that corresponds to the equal complexity of Egyptian ideas about the role of boats in the afterlife. Of Tutankhamun's 35 boat models, 17 were in his tomb's annexe which, along with the adjacent antechamber, contained many items such as chariots, clothing, food and drink, indicating that in some ways the afterlife needs of a deceased pharaoh were similar to those of a living king. Appropriately, the boat models in question nearly all represented vessels actually used on the Nile by, or on behalf of, the pharaoh. In contrast, the treasury, a secluded room accessible only from the burial chamber, was filled mainly with religious and funerary objects. It contained 18 boat models, which were either of types useful to a pharaoh only in the afterlife (such as solar barques) or of actual vessels like state barges used by a living king but which held quasi-religious significance even then.

The Abydos Boat Graves

The discovery of the Abydos boat graves was surprising and unexpected. Since elite boat burials of similar date were always closely associated with tombs, boat graves seemed more likely to be placed at Umm el Qaʻab, not near the enclosures, which were far away from the actual royal tombs. Indeed, when the end of one boat grave was incidentally exposed in 1988, I speculated that it might be the buttressed corner of a new type of enclosure. In 1991, however, their true character became clear; each grave contains an actual wooden boat, one of which has been partially excavated (in 2000). In the future, one entire boat, and perhaps two, will be fully excavated and conserved. The remaining boat graves will be reburied and available to other archaeologists in the future.

Elite boat graves are each associated with a single tomb, so it is likely that the Abydos boat graves – built all at once, in a long row – were intended to service a specific early ruler, whose mortuary cult was celebrated in an adjacent enclosure. In fact, in 2002 it was shown they are contemporary with the 'Western Mastaba' enclosure, of the later 1st Dynasty. These boats may actually have been built at Abydos itself, or at least not far away. Kelly Simpson has pointed out inscriptional evidence for a royal dockyard at Abydos or Thinis in the 2nd Dynasty,[1] and this may of course have been active earlier as well.

The boat graves – lying on an ancient desert surface – are arranged in a long row about 60 m (196.8 ft) long, and closely packed together; most are either, on average, 60 cm (23 in) or 1.60 m (5.2 ft) apart. Parallel to each other, the boat graves are oriented northeast to southwest, like the enclosures themselves. Some experienced severe erosion because of a gully crossing their location, but

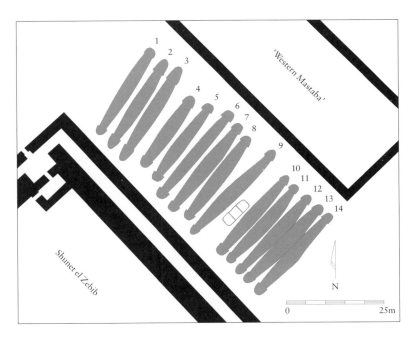

96 *Map of the boat graves of Abydos. Their proximity, and the regularity of their layout, suggests they were all constructed at one time and were dedicated to the afterlife service of a specific king, whose identity is as yet unknown. They appear to be contemporary with the 1st Dynasty Western Mastaba. The feature between boat graves 9 and 10 is a low-walled structure of uncertain function; it may comprise basins used for preparing materials needed for the boat graves.*

others are well preserved and very exciting in several ways. Not only are the Abydos boat graves unique in comparison to contemporary ones at Saqqara and Helwan, and thus able to provide dramatic new insights into early royal mortuary beliefs and practices; they also each contain a large wooden vessel, some seemingly very well preserved, and these will greatly enrich our knowledge of ancient Egyptian ships and boats in general. Our consulting expert on ancient boats, Cheryl Ward, characterizes the Abydos boats as wonderful in terms of preservation and information, and notes that they more than double the number of ancient Egyptian watercraft known to exist.

The unique character of the Abydos boat graves soon becomes apparent when they are compared to the elite examples from Saqqara (three) and Helwan (19; most not published in detail). At all three sites each boat grave consisted of a long, relatively shallow trench (sometimes omitted) supporting the bottom or sometimes enclosing most of a wooden boat, and a mud-brick superstructure built around the boat once it was in place. The superstructures were quite low in height (about 50 cm or 19.5 in at Abydos, once about 80 cm or 31 in high at Saqqara) and, because they followed the contours of the boat within, were themselves boat-like in form. The interiors of the hollow super-structures were normally filled with sand and gravel, in which the boat was buried, but at Abydos mud-brick masonry filled some, maybe all of the boats.

These general similarities aside, however, the Abydos boat graves differ markedly from the others. First, the Abydos boat graves occur not singly, as was the case elsewhere, but as a fleet-like group; and second, they are larger (usually, much larger) and more elaborate in form than the elite boat graves.

On average, the superstructures of the Abydos graves are 26.23 m or 86 ft long (the longest, 28.42 m or about 93 ft long), whereas the Saqqara superstructures average 19.7 m or 64.6 ft (the longest, 22.15 m or 75.6 ft) and those at Helwan about 12.3 m or 40.3 ft. The Abydos superstructures (and one at Saqqara, near Tomb 3357 and dating to Aha) were all flat-topped; those at Saqqara and Helwan had their sand or rubble fill kept in place by a curving shell of mud-brick and thus resemble – in Zaki Saad's evocative words – 'the backs of surfacing whales'.[2]

In addition, the 'prows' and 'sterns' of the boat-shaped superstructures were treated differently at Abydos. In every case they were modelled as boldly defined and large buttress-like forms, whereas at Saqqara this modelling was much less emphatic and usually confined to one end of the boat, although the boat grave belonging to Tomb 3506 has some modelling of both prow and stern. At Helwan the superstructures were especially poorly preserved, but only one of the surviving trench outlines published indicates a modelled prow or stern.

Boat graves at Abydos and elsewhere had their superstructures coated with smoothly applied, thick mud plaster, which was then washed or stuccoed white or cream. Thus, they would have conveyed the impression of large, schemati-cally defined white vessels, moored near the relevant tomb or (at Abydos) enclosure. To reinforce this impression, some Abydos boat graves were

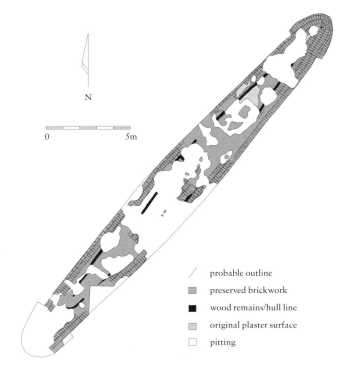

97 Plan of boat grave 10, displaying all the characteristic features of the boat graves. The brick shell in which the actual boat rests is clearly visible, as are the 'prow' and 'stern', filled solid with brickwork. Each grave, once the boat was in place, had been filled with bricks and sand, but erosion of the shallow capping meant that the actual outline of each boat was visible in the top of the grave, as seen here. Again, the damage caused by later intrusive pits is obvious.

N

0   5m

/   probable outline

   preserved brickwork

   wood remains/hull line

   original plaster surface

   pitting

provided with a large, irregularly shaped rock that may have represented an anchor or a mooring stone. Thus, while we can archaeologically distinguish between the superstructure and the actual boat of each grave, conceptually it is the vessel within *and* the superstructure that comprises the 'boat' available to the deceased. In this sense, the boat graves are similar, but certainly not identical to a boat next to a solar temple built near a 5th Dynasty pyramid at Abusir. This Abusir boat was described by I. E. S. Edwards as 'a hundred-foot-long model of the boat in which the sun-god made his daily journey across the sky. The hull, built of brick, had been covered with a layer of plaster and painted. All the other parts of the boat were made of wood'.[3]

Limited excavations in 1991 and 2000 have already told us much about how the Abydos boat graves were constructed and about the status of the large wooden vessel within each one. These excavations, and the associated conservation work, were funded in part by a grant of United States Agency for International Development funds provided by the Egyptian Antiquities Project of the American Research Center in Egypt. The conservation of the fragile timbers was carried out by Lawrence Becker and Deborah Schorsch, both now at the Metropolitan Museum of Art, New York. Recently, Sanchita Balachandran has been added to our conservation team, with responsibilities for a wide range of artifacts and materials. These vessels, the top outline revealed in the eroded upper surface of each superstructure, seem to average about 18 or 19 m (about 60 ft) in length. To construct each grave, a shallow trench was dug to support the relatively flat bottom of each boat. The Saqqara and Helwan graves usually (although not always at Saqqara) had similar trenches, but deeper; at Helwan they average about 80 cm (31 in) in depth, while

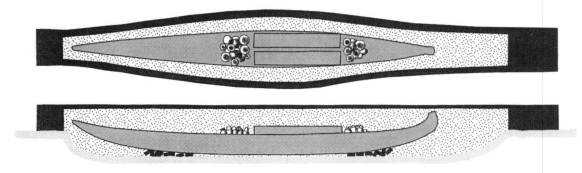

98 *A 1st Dynasty boat grave was excavated by W. B. Emery at Saqqara, in the vicinity of the elite tomb No. 3506. This is the only boat grave outside of Abydos where the boat was sufficiently well preserved to enable a reconstruction drawing. What was actually found is not recorded, and apparently none of the wood could be retained.*

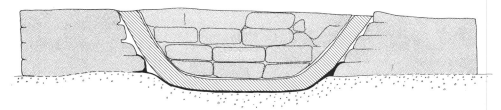

99 *Cross-section of a typical boat grave (No. 10), illustrating the sequence of events involved. A shallow trench was cut in the desert surface and the wooden hull placed in it. Then the walls of the boat grave were built in brick around the hull. Finally, in this case, the hull itself was filled with loosely laid bricks, and the whole grave capped in some way, perhaps with a thick layer of mud plaster. This capping was often eroded away, and the top of the hull visible as here.*

at Saqqara Tomb 3506 the trench was deep enough (at 1.19 m or 3.9 ft) to accommodate the entire boat. Saqqara and Helwan also reveal that the long axis of each trench had a concave profile, to fit the convex profile of the boat it supported or contained, and this is likely to prove true at Abydos also.

At Abydos, the superstructure walls built around each boat were sturdy (about 65 cm or 25.6 in thick), whereas (except at Saqqara Tomb 3357 where the boat grave superstructure walls were about 58 cm (22.6 in) wide) superstructure walls elsewhere were much thinner and shell-like. At Abydos, once the walls reached the same height as the boats, the latter were filled solid with brick masonry, sometimes resting on a bed of sand or layers of reed matting. Offering pottery could be placed near or, at Saqqara Tomb 3506, on the boat.

VII *(opposite) King Khasekhemwy's unusually large, deeply set and architecturally complex tomb at Umm el Qa'ab during Dreyer's re-excavations.*

VIII *(overleaf) A reconstruction of the boat graves being built. To the left is the wall of the Western Mastaba. In the rear, a boat is being dragged to the site. In the foreground the various stages involved in constructing a boat grave are shown.*

IX *(overleaf) Exposed planking in an Early Dynastic boat grave (Boat Grave 10) at Abydos.*

X *(overleaf) Early Dynastic boat graves at Abydos. At the rear is Khasekhemwy's enclosure.*

VII

VIII

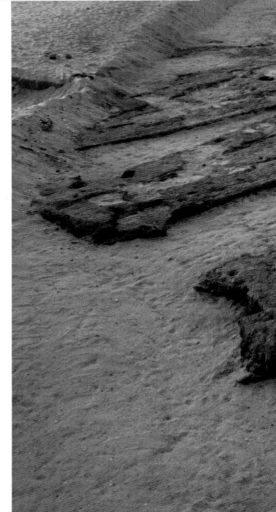

IX

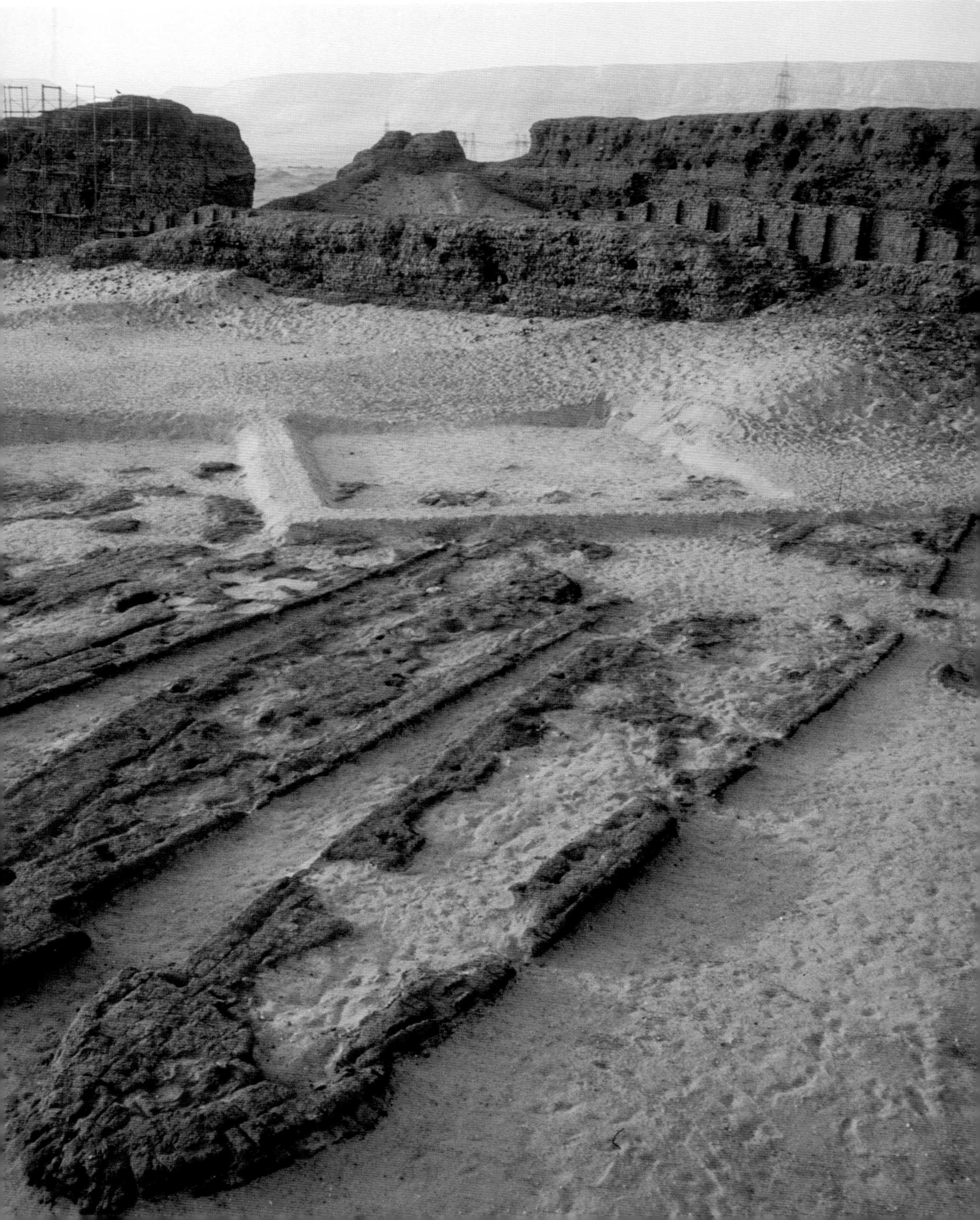

100 Deborah Schorsch, one of the project's conservators, carrying out conservation and stabilization procedures on the in-situ planks.

As for the Abydos boats themselves, the only one so far partially exposed (in boat grave 10) is a relatively shallow but sturdily built wooden shell using, according to Cheryl Ward, a style of construction previously undocumented in Egypt: the boat's timbers were lashed together with leather straps fed through lashing channels.[4] The boat in grave 10, and one other, were both painted yellow on the outside. So far, no decking has been observed at Abydos, but the boat at Saqqara Tomb 3506 was sufficiently well preserved to show that it had a hull, deck and dismantled cabin 'laid flat on the deck', although none of these materials apparently survived their removal from the grave. Perhaps similar features may be encountered at Abydos. Ward believes the Abydos boats were likely to have been fully functional, rather than models. They did not make use of sails, but were powered by up to 30 rowers. Interestingly, Kelly Simpson has published a much later (Middle Kingdom) reference from Thinis to the 30 men needed to man an *imw*-boat,[5] but this may refer to a crew or to merchantmen rather than oarsmen as such, for *imw*-boats then were cargo boats.

Finally, what can we guess about the functions of the Abydos boats? In the previous chapter I emphasized two points: first, since Early Dynastic boat graves at sites other than Abydos are always associated with tombs, the association of

XI *(opposite) A vast pile of offering pottery deposited for ritual purposes in front of the entrance to King Peribsen's enclosure; the high wall at the rear belongs to Khasekhemwy's enclosure.*

boat graves with an enclosure indicates, as do other features, that the enclosures had a mortuary function. Second, the boats were provided (like the donkey burials associated with another enclosure) to meet the general needs of the deceased king with regard to riverine transportation. This said, however, we can reasonably speculate a little further about the possibility that these needs varied to some degree. Some of the boats may represent supply ships, but others might have been more ceremonial in function. These could relate to ceremonies involving the living king, his afterworld needs as a deceased king, or both.

There are two reasons for making these suggestions. First, at the elite tomb Saqqara 3357, dating to King Aha's reign, the boat grave was physically integrated with an extraordinary and so far unique group of miniaturized courts and buildings, 'formed of rubble with a thick mud casing in which the architectural detail has been modelled',[6] and then faced with white gypsum plaster. If this architectural complex represented granaries and storerooms (and it included three miniaturized granaries of circular type), the attached boat (the composite structure in wood and brick) might symbolize the supply ship intended to deliver new foodstuffs on a regular basis in the afterlife. However, if the architectural complex incorporates replicas of cult buildings, then the boat may represent a type to be found only in the other world. Finally, if the complex represents the royal palace, then the boat may be the king's state barge. As is often the case, the archaeological evidence provides several options, but no easy means to choose one over the other!

The second point involves the Abydos boat graves themselves. Most of the boat graves have relatively short and stubby prows and sterns, which comprise on average 8.5 per cent of each superstructure's total length. However, graves 2 and 3, placed side by side, have distinctly longer and more elegantly proportioned prows and sterns, which average about 13.3 per cent of the two superstructures' total lengths. Thus, graves 2 and 3 comprise a pair of boats conceptually different from the others, and remind us that in later belief the sun-god made successive use of two boats, identical in form to each other, to carry out his cyclical circuit of the cosmos. Moreover, such solar boats had already been visualized by 1st Dynasty Egyptians, for one appears in art as early as Djet's reign.[7]

Evidently, much remains to be discovered about the fascinating royal boat graves of Abydos, but it already seems reasonable to suggest that they indicate a significant degree of continuity between early royal monuments at Abydos and the later royal pyramidal complexes. The occasional boat pits found with the latter are rock-cut, not brick-built like the Abydos boat graves, but they did sometimes (maybe usually) contain an actual wooden vessel and were nearly always boat-shaped in outline as at Abydos.

Nevertheless, boat graves and boat pits are discontinuously used features that are also somewhat peripheral to the core monument itself. But there is other, even stronger evidence indicating that the early royal monuments of Abydos (and Saqqara, in the 2nd Dynasty) are indeed ancestors of the pyramid complexes.

Mound and Pyramid

At first glance, the transition from the Early Dynastic royal mortuary monuments at Abydos to Egypt's first pyramid – Djoser's step pyramid at Saqqara – seems straightforward and even obvious. Djoser's step pyramid stands over the king's tomb and is likely derived from the surface mound which probably stood above each of the 1st and 2nd Dynasty royal tombs at Abydos. In addition, it stands within a large, stone-built enclosure which is similar in important ways to the royal enclosures of Abydos, discussed in the previous chapter. It would seem that Djoser simply combined what had been kept separate at Abydos, i.e. the mound-capped tomb and, some distance away, the enclosure. Djoser's other innovations were to build entirely in stone, not the mud-brick employed in the Early Dynastic monuments, and to build on a much larger scale than had been the case earlier.

In reality, the situation is more complicated than the simple scenario sketched above would suggest, for this scenario does not adequately take into account two things: first, the complicated building history of Djoser's monument and second, the relationship between Djoser's monument and the 2nd Dynasty royal tombs at Saqqara, rather than Abydos, where only the last two kings of that dynasty were buried. Here, I should like to explore these two issues.

The step pyramid complex of King Djoser underwent several building phases. In the first, the king's entirely subterranean, rock-cut tomb had a surface mound (not a pyramid) built over it. The mound, or 'mastaba' as some call it, occupied about 0.39 ha (0.96 acres) and was square in plan. It was 8 m (26 ft) high, and its external faces were carefully dressed – in other words, the mound or mastaba was a finished monument, not simply a masonry core prepared for some subsequent larger structure. Moreover, the tomb and the mound above lay (mostly) in the northwest quadrant of a large, stone-walled enclosure. This enclosure (occupying about 8.47 ha or almost 21 acres) was, like the Abydos Early Dynastic enclosures, rectangular in plan and had entrances near its northeast and southeast corners. Although the details are different, the external southern and eastern faces of Djoser's enclosure were

101 *Cut-away view of the Step Pyramid showing stages of construction including the mound-like mastaba originally built over the tomb.*

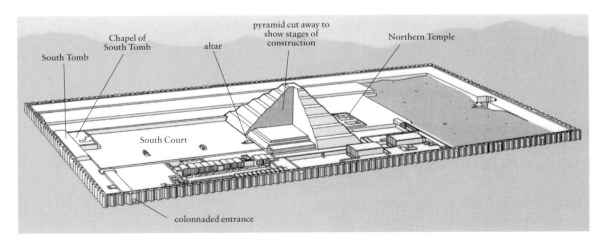

deeply and regularly recessed, in a fashion reminiscent of the recessed façades of the Abydos enclosures.

Later, Djoser's builders made substantial changes to the original plan of his mortuary complex. The initial surface mound of stone was overlaid by a four-stepped pyramid which, in a third stage of development, was transformed into a six-stepped one, that which we see today towering some 62 m (204 ft) high. In addition, the enclosure itself was enlarged (to about 15.9 ha or 39.2 acres), and the pyramid surrounded by buildings of various kinds, as well as open courts.

Thus, the transition from an Early Dynastic tradition as regards royal mortuary monuments to a new form – the pyramid complex – basically takes place over the course of Djoser's reign. However, as I noted above, it may not have been directly inspired by the royal tombs of Abydos and their separate enclosures. Instead, the mortuary monuments of the 2nd Dynasty kings buried at Saqqara, and in close proximity to the site of the future step pyramid complex, may have been the most influential factor as regards the original plan of Djoser's monument-tomb, surface mound and surrounding enclosure.

As I noted in Chapter 9, the subterranean components of some of these 2nd Dynasty royal tombs at Saqqara have been identified; and, as Kemp pointed out, at Saqqara there would be no reason to keep the tomb and its assumed surface mound separate from the enclosure. Thus, we could reconstruct the typical 2nd Dynasty royal tomb complex at Saqqara as consisting of a large, brick-walled enclosure of rectangular plan, with an entrance near the northeast and southeast corners respectively. In the case of King Hetepsekhemwy's tomb, its extensive size would indicate an enclosure of about 131.3 × 50.5 m (430 × 165 ft) occupying 0.66 ha (1.6 acres), and hence similar in scale to the enclosure of Peribsen at Abydos (0.57 ha or 1.4 acres). The entrance to the tomb would lie in the extreme north of the enclosed space, and is separated from the burial chamber by an enormous mass of storage chambers. As a result, the actual burial chamber, with presumably a surface mound above it, would lie in the southern part of the enclosure, relatively close to the assumed southeast corner entrance. The mound may have had a chapel to its south, similar to those I hypothesize stood south or southwest of the tomb surface mounds at Umm el Qa'ab.

Obviously, this suggested reconstruction of the surface features associated with the 2nd Dynasty royal tombs at Saqqara needs to be proved, and no confirmative data are yet recovered. Moreover, the areas above these tombs are filled with later tombs and much intrusive pitting, so the discovery of such data will be difficult. For the moment, however, this reconstruction is a good working hypothesis. Some scholars suggest that the 2nd Dynasty royal tombs at Saqqara did have enclosures, but separate from them and some distance to the west. However, the archaeological remains in question (which are partially visible) may instead be those of incomplete or demolished step pyramid complexes built by 3rd Dynasty kings who came after Djoser.

The hypothesis outlined above therefore suggests that the 2nd Dynasty royal mortuary monuments combined tomb, surface mound (and perhaps chapel) and enclosure, and provided a model followed fairly closely in the first phase of Djoser's mortuary complex which had, as we have seen, a tomb, surface mound and enclosure. The main difference would be that in the 2nd Dynasty the tomb and surface mound is near the south end of the enclosure, whereas in Djoser's case they have been moved into the northwest quadrant of the enclosed space. Why the radical change was made is difficult to say, but it may be related to the fact that in Djoser's tomb the access shaft is not separated from the tomb chamber by an extensive set of magazines.

In any event, the final phase of Djoser's complex may have continued to have a significant relationship to its hypothetical 2nd Dynasty prototype, but in a 'fossilized' or symbolic form. Apparently belonging to the first phase is the so-called 'South Tomb' – a symbolic tomb too small to contain a real body, and placed next to the southern wall of the enclosure. Above the South Tomb is a surface feature, a rectangular mastaba largely concealed within the south wall of the enclosure and, some distance to the east, is a separate chapel which is largely solid, and hence also emblematic. Perhaps the dummy tomb and chapel symbolically represent the actual tomb, surface mound and chapel located approximately in this area in the 2nd Dynasty mortuary complexes discussed above.

Even in its final form, the Djoser step pyramid complex is reminiscent of Early Dynastic traditions in another way. Most of its buildings are filled almost solid, and hence are symbolic rather than 'real'. They are intended to be fully functional only in the afterlife, where the dead king will use them. This concept is akin to that which led to the razing of the enclosures and their chapels at Abydos, so that these structures would become fully available for the dead king.

The step pyramid complex raises an especially intriguing question: why was the initial surface mound, which stood above the tomb, transformed into a step pyramid, first (with four steps) 41.7 m or 136.7 ft high, then (with six steps) 62 m or 204 ft high? Günter Dreyer has suggested that, since Djoser's enclosure wall was 10 m (about 33 ft) high and the original surface mound only 8 m (26 ft) high, the latter would not be visible to viewers located externally to the enclosure. This result, he suggests, was unanticipated (since tomb, surface mound and enclosure had not been combined before, in his view) and the discomfited builders therefore devised the much higher pyramid so as to make the superstructure above the king's tomb visible to all. This idea, however, is problematical. First, the Egyptians, as skilful builders, could surely have predicted the masking of the surface mound by the enclosure and, if they had wished to avoid this situation, built a pyramid from the outset. Second, if my suggestion about the inspirational effect of pre-existing 2nd Dynasty royal mortuary monuments at Saqqara is correct, then Djoser's builders would have been used to the idea that the mortuary enclosure hid the surface mound above the tomb from view.

In these circumstances, there would have been other reasons why Djoser's builders transformed the initial surface mound into a pyramid. It may not so much have been due to a desire to make the tomb's superstructure more visible as to make it much larger, in accord with the great enlargement of Djoser's monument in general. In this case, making the mound much larger in extent, and higher in elevation, would almost lead to the pyramidal form as an accidental by-product. An extremely large mound, especially built of stone masonry, would have been very unstable if its sides were vertical, or very steeply angled. Only by providing the mound with a pyramidal form could the destructive stresses that would otherwise occur be avoided.

Primeval Hill or Celestial Stairway?

Since the preceding discussion has demonstrated a very close connection between the early royal mortuary monuments of Abydos and Saqqara on the one hand, and the step pyramid and its descendant the true pyramid on the other, it is legitimate to ask if the symbolic meaning of the latter helps us understand the possible symbolic meaning of the mounds – both surface and subterranean – that are such a feature of the earlier royal tombs. To answer the question requires extensive reference to materials later than the 1st and 2nd Dynasties, and indeed later than the 5th Dynasty as well, a procedure usually best avoided. However, this is a traditional source of information about pyramid symbolism and about the only one available, so I will use it here nonetheless.

Most Egyptologists believe that pyramids had multiple, co-existent symbolic meanings, of which two are particularly emphasized. The first is that the pyramid represents the 'primeval hill', a mound on which the creator manifested itself, or used as a support, when it initiated the process involved in the creation of the cosmos; the second, that the pyramid is a stairway enabling the deceased pharaoh to ascend into the sky and reach the celestial locales in which his eternal regeneration and well-being can be assured. Some scholars suggest that the latter idea was more important, particularly since the earliest pyramids are actually stepped, as if they are gigantic stairways rising up to the sky.

However, we cannot know if this was the Egyptians' intention when creating the step pyramid form and if we turn to the Pyramid Texts, displayed on royal burial chamber walls through the late 5th Dynasty as well as the 6th and our chief source of information, we find a more subtle picture of the concepts of primeval hill and celestial stairway than is usually recognized.

First, one can conclude that the concept of pyramid as celestial stairway is not very likely. The need for the deceased king to ascend into the sky is certainly an omnipresent theme through the Pyramid Texts, which are made up of over 700 individual spell-like 'utterances', but this idea is rarely related to the use of constructed means of ascent, and those that are referred to are not easily related to the pyramid form. Most typically, the king is lifted into the sky by various deities, or they literally extend a hand down to him from the sky. Quite commonly, the king ascends skyward as a star, or flies upwards in bird form – stars and birds being entities with an inherent upward mobility, not dependent on any artificial support. Similarly, the king can also ascend via a whirlwind or storm, or even on a cloud.

Two principal kinds of structures enabling the king to ascend are referred to in the Pyramid Texts. The commonest form is the ladder, an image not easily reconcilable with the shape of the pyramid, especially when it turns out that the ladder is sometimes, perhaps often, a rope ladder let down from heaven by the gods for the king's use. More rarely (in only about five of over 700 utterances) a stairway is the image used; however, this is never specifically associated with the pyramid, and the notion that the single reference to a stairway as 'the sunshine of Re' (Utterance 508) relates to the idea of the pyramid as representing downward shining rays seems far-fetched, and in any case not applicable to the more stairway-like step pyramids. Thus there seems little reason to regard the pyramid as a stairway or similar form of constructed ascent. Rather, the stairway seems but one, and not the most popular, of a plethora of images in the Pyramid Texts which provide metaphors to describe the king's ascent into heaven. The stairway is a verbal image, not an identification of the pyramid and its meaning.

In fact, specific constituents of the pyramid complex are rarely referred to in the Pyramid Texts, and when they are, the very rarity of the practice suggests that a particularly important point is being made about the specific entity – sarcophagus, coffin, tomb, pyramid and temple – involved. The coffin, sarcophagus and tomb are identified as the goddess Nut, within whom the deceased king gestates prior to his rebirth (Utterance 364) and appropriately the coffin and tomb doors are abjured to 'open' so that the king can leave them and continue the process of regeneration and maintenance (Utterances 553, 665A and 676; see also 223). The pyramid and its temple, or the larger entity of 'construction', can be also cited, for example as a gift from the gods Geb and Atum to the king, a gift magically protected from profanation (Utterance 534), or described as 'fair and enduring' (599).

However, the rarity of references to the constituents of the pyramid complex highlights the significance of the only two (identically worded) utterances that come closest to linking the pyramid specifically to a symbolic meaning, which is that of the primeval hill. Utterances 600 and 601 open with a description of creation initiated by Atum 'high on the height', i.e. the supporting primeval mound or hill, and continue on to state that Atum will set his arms about the king, the 'construction' and the pyramid 'as the arms of a *ka*-symbol, that the king's essence may be in it, enduring forever'. Thus, the tremendous powers associated with creation and the primeval hill are seen as infusing the king and his pyramid complex with life-giving and eternal force, suggesting that if pyramids have any specific meaning at all, it is most likely as symbolizing the primeval hill.

This notion also seems to fit with the development of the pyramid outlined in the previous section, for the process I describe requires the pyramid – stepped or true – to be seen primarily as a gigantic version of the more simply shaped, and smaller, mounds associated with the 1st and 2nd Dynasty royal monuments. These may have been seen as symbolizing ascent, but visually seem to conform more closely to the image of the primeval mound or hill.

The stepped, then true, form of pyramid is essentially the technical response to the problem of representing the mound on a gigantic scale, for an actual stone mound of this size would be structurally unsound. However, the pyramid form, combined with skilful structural elements within the pyramid, dealt efficiently with the enormous pressures and strains inevitably experienced by such massive and elevated stone structures.

Conclusion

Boat graves, mounds and pyramids might initially seem an unrelated group of features, but as I have tried to show in this chapter they are more closely connected than might first appear to be the case. Surface mounds above royal tombs, and pyramids in the same position are not unrelated to each other, and the former do not simply precede the latter. The Early Dynastic evidence and that of Djoser's step pyramid complex indicate that the surface mound and the pyramid are inextricably linked, and that the pyramid may simply be the mound much enlarged in size, and hence given a pyramidal form largely in the interests of structural stability. However, it is also likely the Early Dynastic royal tomb mound had symbolic significance as well, a significance that the pyramid shared. As my analysis of relevant data from the later Pyramid Texts suggests, both represented the primeval hill, the site of creation, and neither may have had much to do with the concept of the deceased king ascending into the sky. The king *did* make such ascensions, by a variety of means, but none seem to have involved the pyramid or its ancestor, the surface mound.

The Early Dynastic boat graves of Abydos are also important in the processes that link the later pyramid complexes with the royal mortuary monuments of Early Dynastic times. Initially, the boat graves, although of great interest in themselves, might seem almost incidental to the primary functions of those early monuments. After all, so far they have been found only in connection with one Early Dynastic king, not all of them, and they occur, also sporadically, with elite tombs of the same period as well.

However, these observations underrate the Abydos boat graves' significance for future developments. Most importantly, they are the first boat graves associated with a royal monument of Early Dynastic times, and hence can reasonably be considered a prototype for the boat graves and boat-shaped pits associated with later pyramid complexes. It is true the latter practice is also sporadic, yet if anything this increases the similarity between Early Dynastic and later practices in this regard. Even if they were not a regular feature of royal mortuary monuments, boat graves and boat pits evidently gave material form to a conception of a dead king's needs which must have applied to all such kings, even if they were only provided in actuality to a minority of these rulers. Thus, boat graves, surface mounds and pyramids are among the most important evidence for a coherent and evolutionary process of development as far as Egypt's royal mortuary monuments are concerned, rather than a seemingly unrelated and somewhat arbitrary set of events.

CHAPTER TWELVE

ABYDOS: SUMMING-UP

Abydos is one of the most exciting sites in Egypt currently being excavated. Its complexity and multi-layered significance are becoming clearer every year, yet apart from a few important conclusions, definitive understanding is still far away. The available, if ever increasing, evidence is in flux and can be interpreted in different ways; proposing, criticizing and testing new theories about this challenging site will continue long into the future.

This conclusion is based on some 35 years of exploring and thinking about Abydos. During that time I and William Kelly Simpson have also made it possible for younger generations of scholars to become engaged in their own, spectacularly successful, fieldwork at Abydos. Their discoveries and new ideas, along with those of Günter Dreyer, are greatly expanding the already important achievements of the earlier Egyptologists active at Abydos between the 1860s and 1920s.

Abydos and its sacred landscape were shaped by two powerful, interactive forces. Local or regional dynamics specifically related to activities unfolding at Abydos itself, and were ascribed symbolic and social meanings by the Egyptians. More external in origin were influences from the changing circumstances shaping and altering Egyptian society and culture as a whole from one period to another, each period having a distinctive *Zeitgeist*, or 'spirit of the age', which found expression at Abydos, as at other important centres.

Two other things about Abydos are also certain. The first is that since the great Seti I temple was cleared and documented by Auguste Mariette, the testimony of Egyptian, Greek and Latin sources that Abydos was the centre of the god Osiris' cult has been confirmed. Moreover, the approximate site of the temple of Osiris has been located, although much of its long (from *c.* 2000 BC into late Roman times) and complex history remains debatable. Indeed, Michelle Marlar of the Institute of Fine Arts, New York University has only just started on a systematic sampling and study of the last Osiris temple built at Abydos. She has already shown that this temple, reduced to rubble in antiquity, was definitely built by kings Nectanebo I (381–362 BC) and, probably, Nectanebo II (358–341 BC), and it appears to have been preceded by at least one other temple.

The second major conclusion is that Abydos was the Giza of the Early Dynastic period, in that the kings of the 1st Dynasty and (partially) the 2nd Dynasty were buried there. Textual sources to this effect (e.g. Manetho's history of Egypt, 300 BC) were ambiguous. So Amélineau's, then Petrie's, work at these tombs was very much an archaeological triumph. Dreyer's identification of even earlier, nearby tombs as 'royal' has expanded the significance of these former discoveries even further.

Yet some aspects of both conclusions remain mysterious. For example, why – and exactly when – did Osiris become established at Abydos? He was, after all, preceded as Abydos' god by Khentamentiu throughout the Early Dynastic and Old Kingdom periods, even though during the latter Osiris was already textually associated with Abydos. Some scholars suggest Osiris was a product of the rituals and beliefs associated with Egyptian kings from the Early Dynastic period onwards. However, one could alternatively argue that Osiris' myth responded to community-wide needs for reassurance about the impact of death upon the individual. He might then have already been a significant mortuary deity before he became incorporated into royal burial rituals.

Ambiguity also exists about the significance of Abydos' early royal tombs for later generations over the millennia. These tombs, as sources for early civilization, certainly seem very important to us today, but it is striking that so far no archaeological evidence has been found for Old Kingdom ritual activity in the vicinity of the tombs. From the Middle Kingdom (when the tombs were actually excavated and, in some cases, renovated) onwards, direct Egyptian interest in the Umm el Qa'ab cemetery is obvious. But to what degree did this relate to the earliest kings themselves? After all, in the Middle Kingdom, the Egyptians reached a quite unhistorical conclusion, namely that one of the tombs belonged to Osiris himself. All subsequent activity seems focused on this aspect, not on the early kings themselves.

Sacred Landscape and Local Dynamics

Local factors are a better basis than national ones for theorizing about the development of Abydos' distinctive attributes and the landscape in which they found expression. The latter, by the end of the New Kingdom, displayed three interrelated patterns.

First was a not unusual one: the distribution of not only cemeteries, but also temples and associated towns along the low desert adjacent to the floodplain. More often in Egypt, important temples and towns were close to the river, the main administrative and economic artery, but desert-edge towns have also been found. They had convenient access to water and farmland, and were linked by track, road and canal to the Nile. In fact, an ancient if minor branch of the latter may have run immediately alongside Abydos.

The second pattern is more unusual, and found only at a few Egyptian sites. It is characteristic of royal cemetery fields in the 3rd and 2nd millennia BC such as those of Giza, Saqqara, Dahshur and Lisht. Here we find valley temples at the desert edge, linked by causeways to royal tombs under pyramids set further out in the desert. In contrast, at Thebes in the New Kingdom, mortuary temples lay along the junction between floodplain and desert, with rock-cut tombs located much further away in a steep-sided desert valley. Abydos is similar to such sites in that a series of mortuary temples and chapels extended from the Osiris temple (itself a kind of mortuary temple for the distant tomb of Osiris himself) along the floodplain edge to the southeast. These included the temples of Senwosret III, Ahmose and Seti I, but we have reason to think that, in the future, further royal temples or at least chapels will be found amongst these known ones.

However, the analogy is not complete. The exact physical linkages between the Senwosret III and Ahmose temples and their respective royal tombs are as yet unknown, and – more importantly – these tombs are quite possibly ceno-taphs or dummy tombs, the kings in question being buried elsewhere. The 'tomb' set immediately behind Seti's temple is unquestionably a cenotaph, and another may lie behind the temple of Ramesses II.

The third distributional pattern characteristic of Abydos is unique to it, namely these symbolic rather than actual royal tombs dispersed across its surface. Various explanations have been offered for this. Some suggest the layout of temple and distant tomb were inspired by the Old and Middle Kingdom pyramid complexes, although only one Abydos monument, that of Ahmose, actually includes a pyramid. Here the pyramid is next to the 'valley temple', and far away from the tomb, the reverse of normal practice. It has also been argued that Senwosret and Ahmose *were* actually buried at Abydos, but the certain or probable existence of tombs for them elsewhere makes this suggestion less likely. Most theories also recognize the possible influence of Osiris' own desert tomb, and distant temple, at Abydos, but I think underestimate the power of these factors in the shaping of Abydos' built landscape. The similarities in each case – desert-edge temple and an empty tomb – seem to me overwhelming, and reinforced by the reluctance to provide either Osiris' tomb or the royal ones at Abydos with any substantial surface features. In other words, the royal mortuary monuments of Abydos seem to be intentional, if varied, replicas of Osiris' own monuments there.

This leads us, however, to another, more fundamental question. Osiris' tomb is set far out in the desert because the Early Dynastic royal cemetery, and its predecessors, were so located. Why was this the case? Recent commentators such as Diana Patch and Günter Dreyer suggest a deep desert valley about 1 km (0.62 miles) due south of Umm el Qa'ab was seen by the Egyptians as an entrance to the netherworld, and Umm el Qa'ab, relatively close by, was there-fore considered an appropriate location for an especially prestigious cemetery. However, no text from Abydos or elsewhere supports the idea that the valley in question was so regarded, and in fact Umm el Qa'ab was already the location of elite graves as early as Naqada I and II, long before any are recognizably or arguably 'royal'. Other as yet unknown factors, then, might have influenced the development of the Umm el Qa'ab cemetery and ultimately the location of Osiris' supposed tomb.

Abydos and Egypt

Egypt as a whole influenced in many ways the history of Abydos and the form its sacred landscape took. In some instances, the impact of external factors is easy enough to evaluate, but in other ways suggestions are more speculative and involve lively debate. In particular, one senses the interaction between external factors and local ones was especially subtle and complicated.

For example, the decision to bury all 1st Dynasty and two 2nd Dynasty kings at Abydos was made far away, at the new political and royal centre of Memphis. In this sense, an external factor profoundly affected the Abydos landscape then and far into its future. Yet local or regional factors were also involved, for presumably the long anterior history of Umm el Qa'ab as an elite, then royal, burial ground influenced that decision.

Similarly, the earliest town at Abydos – adjacent to what became the Khentamentiu and later the Osiris temple – seems to go back to no earlier than Dynasty 0 (the kings preceding the 1st Dynasty). Since the town apparently serviced the tombs of Dynasty 0 at Umm el Qa'ab, was its founding due to a decision made externally at this time? If so, where are the settlements presumably related to the earlier, elite burials of Naqada I and II at Umm el Qa'ab?

The earliest temple – of Dynasty 0 and the 1st and 2nd Dynasties – built in the town of North Abydos has not yet been archaeologically defined. However, as Simpson and John Cooney (1976) have shown, one of its cult objects may well have survived, an impressively large (15.6 cm or 6.1 in high) stone statue of the goddess Heqat embodied as a frog. In later times, Heqat was prominent at Abydos, and in the Middle Kingdom was believed to assist in the resurrection of deceased Egyptians. Another important object associated with the early temple is an elaborately decorated cult stand.[1] Given the early royal burials at Abydos, the state may well have taken a keen interest in the temples located there as well.

It has been suggested that external factors were less important for the Old Kingdom temple of Khentamentiu at Abydos and that, like other provincial temples, it was essentially locally funded, maintained and staffed. However, even if this debatable suggestion is correct, the kings of the period at least built ka-chapels for themselves near the temple, and exempted it from some of the services and payments due to the state. Although it has been surmised that the Osiris temple complex remained surprisingly informal well into the New Kingdom, this supposition is made less likely by a high level of state investment in the temple, as well as other monuments, during the Middle Kingdom and later. Only further excavation will reveal which of these various theories are correct.

The impact of other externally generated initiatives is also evident in the larger landscape of Abydos. Most obvious here are the four royal temples referred to above, and the settlements and economic arrangements that were provided for their benefit. But local dynamics were also at play, if in fact the layout of these royal complexes is basically inspired by the spatial and ritual relationships between the Osiris temple and his distant tomb in the desert.

As we have seen, not only royalty was involved in the external factors affecting Abydos over the millennia. The important Old Kingdom officials in the Middle Cemetery, now being re-investigated by Janet Richards, may or may not have resided at Abydos, but the income that made their large and well-decorated tombs possible was in part external and derived from the state. Some of the tombs even incorporated actual royal gifts, such as the stone sarcophagus, false door and other items provided by King Pepi I of the 6th Dynasty to Weni, the 'Overseer of Upper Egypt'. Later, from the Middle Kingdom onwards, many elite and even lower-order cult structures were built near the Osiris temple to link their owners eternally to the offerings and festival of the god, while at various periods great numbers of graves much expanded the size of the several cemeteries of Abydos. Many of the individuals, families or groups thus commemorated or buried were probably inhabitants of Abydos and its region, but others were probably buried elsewhere or brought to Abydos from other centres for burial. For example, no fewer than four royal women of the 25th Dynasty were buried at Abydos. All of this activity over the millennia had ritual, constructional and other needs that must have brought great prosperity to the various communities of Abydos.

Other ideas about the influence of external factors upon Abydos are more speculative and debatable because the relevant evidence is more susceptible to different and contradictory interpretations. For example, Eberhard Otto, in a rare comprehensive discussion of Abydos, suggested that in prehistoric times it was a place where incoming nomadic pastoralists and already settled Nile Valley agriculturists interacted in a particularly intense way, in a process contributing significantly to the evolution of Egyptian civilization. Otto even suggested that at Abydos 'the plan was conceived to create a spacious kingdom including the whole of the Nile Valley'.[2] However, Otto's ideas about the pastoralist–agriculturist interaction are now seen as overly simplistic, while the fact that Abydos was already a 'royal' burial ground in Dynasty o does not automatically mean it was the political centre of Egypt at the time.

Generally, during the historic period, texts about Abydos focus on ritual and mortuary concerns (and some of the related administrative and economic arrangements) but rarely relate to more specifically political events. If they sometimes seem to, the implications nevertheless can remain ambiguous.

For example, the troops of King Khety of the 10th Dynasty supposedly sacked royal monuments and elite tombs at Abydos during the civil war between Herakleopolis (the seat of the 9th and 10th Dynasties) and Thebes (the seat of the 11th Dynasty) during the First Intermediate Period. Specific archaeological data, such as the plundering of the Early Dynastic royal tombs and the burning of the decorated burial chamber of Weni, have been linked to this seemingly historical event. However, the only evidence for the event itself comes from a literary work composed for the early 12th Dynasty royal court and hence a source of doubtful value for the erstwhile enemies of that dynasty's ancestors, the 11th Dynasty. Moreover, the text itself is ambiguous, referring to the 'destruction' of the province of Thinis, rather than specifically to Abydos itself.

Abydos was, however, at least once certainly affected by civil war. During the rule of the Ptolemaic dynasty, through the last three centuries BC, southern Egypt won independence for a period and was ruled by two native Egyptian pharaohs from 205 to 186 BC. Their names were Herwennefer and Ankhwennefer, names expressing a strong relationship to Abydos in their incorporation of 'Wennefer', a common epithet of Osiris. During the suppression of the revolt, Abydos itself was specifically besieged by Ptolemaic troops in 199 BC. Our excavations at the 'portal' temple of Ramesses II, just outside the precinct walls, revealed many scattered bronze arrowheads of Ptolemaic type, perhaps relics of the siege.

Scholars have also suggested that specific kings had political motives for building monuments for themselves at Abydos. Perhaps 12th Dynasty kings wanted to reassert the legitimacy of royal authority after the divided politics of the First Intermediate Period. Senwosret III may have been trying to strengthen the power and authority of his co-ruler and heir, Amenemhet III, by stressing their respective identifications with Osiris and *his* legitimate heir, the god Horus. Similarly, Ahmose has been seen as trying to celebrate and sanctify, via Osiris, a new era of unity after the conflict between Thebes and the Hyksos or Levantine overlords of northern Egypt. Finally, the enormous investment of Seti I in a temple celebrating not only Osiris' cult and his mortuary one, but also the great national deities of Amun-Re, Re-Horakhty and Ptah can be read as an assertive statement about the religious conservatism that returned to Egypt after the efforts of the 'heretic' pharaoh Akhenaten to impose monotheism on the traditionally polytheistic Egyptians.

All these ideas are stimulating and merit continuing discussion, but necessarily involve a high degree of speculation. From my perspective, the available evidence suggests that, while most kings maintained the cult of Osiris and sought some kind of a monument at Abydos, major initiatives – such as the four royal temples – are surprisingly sporadic. In the circumstances, such initiatives may have been due largely to personal and idiosyncratic reasons, including a desire on the part of each of the four kings to manifest their relationship to Osiris, and the personal immortality it promised, in a particularly impressive way.

Abydos will continue to intrigue and excite scholar and lay-person alike for many generations to come, and the ongoing recovery of new evidence will keep changing our ideas about the site. What will endure unchanged, however, is the powerful ambience of Abydos, conveyed by the strongly defined landscape that fills our vision as it did that of the ancients. A vivid green floodplain; the tawny expanse of low desert; the steep, dark cliffs rising abruptly over the site; and an overwhelming sense, supported by both visible and invisible archaeology, of the intense interest this mysterious place had for the ancient Egyptians throughout the entire span of their history.

Visiting Abydos

A visit to Abydos is highly recommended: the surrounding landscape is spectacular, while the temples of Seti I and Ramesses II – both accessible to tourists – are two of the most important New Kingdom temples to survive in Egypt. The Seti temple is exceptionally well preserved and provides the most authentic experience of a New Kingdom temple available in Egypt. Within the temple, its beautiful reliefs, often still vividly coloured, have experienced little damage, while the roof is, uniquely for New Kingdom temples, completely in place, conveying an authentic impression of the ways in which light and darkness were manipulated in such temples. Visitors should note that the rest of Abydos, described in this book, is not open to tourists unless they acquire specific permission in advance from the Supreme Council of Antiquities in Cairo – this is best done through a travel agency. With such permission, tourists could visit the early royal tombs at Umm el Qa'ab, the gigantic enclosure of King Khasekhemwy (local name: Shunet el Zebib) – both in North Abydos – and the picturesque ruins of Ahmose's pyramid in South Abydos.

Access

Until recently, tourists visiting Abydos, whether individually or with a package tour, were required to travel in escorted convoys. Due to the high level of security now enjoyed in Egypt these restrictions no longer apply.

Tourists may join a package tour from Cairo or Luxor, or freely travel on their own initiative. In the latter instance, tourists can travel by car from Cairo to Abydos, a long journey of several hours; travel by car from Luxor to Abydos, a journey of two and a half or three hours (Dendereh temple can be visited en route);

or take the train from Cairo or Luxor to Balliana, where taxis can be obtained for a trip to Abydos, about 20 minutes away.

On Site

An access road leads to the Seti I temple, while the nearby Ramesses II temple can be easily reached on foot or by car. If the visitor is not part of a packaged tour, tickets must be purchased at the kiosk in front of the Seti temple. Visitors should also request at the kiosk that the Ramesses II temple should be unlocked, if it happens to be closed. No official guides are available at Abydos. Visitors not on a package tour should prepare for their visit to the enormous Seti temple in particular by reference to a guidebook.

Other sites at Abydos, such as Umm el Qa'ab, the Khasekhemwy enclosure and the Ahmose pyramid are all accessible by unpaved roads, and drivers unfamiliar with Abydos will need to seek directions.

Unfortunately neither Abydos nor Balliana have hotels suitable for tourists, so overnight or longer stays are not feasible.

In front of the Seti temple is a parking lot and a recreational space, the 'Osiris Park'. At the latter, stands offer food, drink (non-alcoholic) and souvenirs. Toilet facilities are available in Osiris Park and in front of the Seti temple. Adjacent to the two temples is a large modern village, the inhabitants of which are friendly and accustomed to tourists' visits. In addition, there is a strong police presence, and tourists' movements are carefully monitored.

A visitor centre and a site museum are in the planning stage, but have not as yet been constructed.

Chronology

Includes rulers named in the text. Absolute dates cannot be calculated for any individual king prior to Nebhepetre Mentuhotep.

Period	Dynasty and Kings	Absolute Dates (estimated to 664 BC)
Prehistoric		*c.* 4000 – 3100 BC
Naqada I		*c.* 4000 – 3850 BC
Naqada II		*c.* 3850 – 3300 BC
Naqada III a-b	Dynasty 0	*c.* 3300 – 2950 BC
	Owner of tomb	
	U-j, Abydos	
	Narmer	
Early Dynastic	1st Dynasty	*c.* 2950 – 2775 BC
	Aha	
	Djer	
	Djet	
	Merneith	
	Den	
	Anedjib	
	Semerkhet	
	Qa'a	
	2nd Dynasty	*c.* 2775 – 2650 BC
	Hetepsekhemwy	
	Nebra	
	Ninetjer	
	Peribsen	
	Khasekhemwy	
Old Kingdom	3rd Dynasty	*c.* 2650 – 2575 BC
	Djoser	
	4th Dynasty	*c.* 2575 – 2450 BC
	Khufu	
	Menkaure	
	5th Dynasty	*c.* 2450 – 2325 BC
	6th Dynasty	*c.* 2325 – 2175 BC
	Pepi I	
	Merenre	
	Pepi II	
	7th/8th Dynasty	*c.* 2175 – 2130 BC
First Intermediate Period	9th Dynasty	*c.* 2130 – 2080 BC
	10th Dynasty	*c.* 2080 – 1980 BC
	Khety	
	11th Dynasty	*c.* 1980 – 1938 BC
	Nebhepetre Mentuhotep	*c.* 2010 – 1957 BC
	Sankhkare Mentuhotep	*c.* 1957 – 1945 BC
Middle Kingdom	12th Dynasty	*c.* 1938 – 1759 BC
	Amenemhet I	*c.* 1938 – 1909 BC
	Senwosret I	*c.* 1919 – 1875 BC
	Senwosret II	*c.* 1842 – 1837 BC
	Senwosret III	*c.* 1836 – 1818 BC
	Amenemhet III	*c.* 1818 – 1772 BC
	13th Dynasty	*c.* 1759 – 1630 BC
	Ugaf	
	Khendjer	
	Neferhotep I	
	Khaneferre	
	Sobekhotep IV	
	14th Dynasty	Dates not available
Second Intermediate Period	15th Dynasty (Hyksos)	*c.* 1630 – 1520 BC *c.* 1630 – 1520 BC
	16th Dynasty	Dates not available
	17th Dynasty	*c.* 1630 – 1540 BC
	Sekenenre Tao II	Dates not available
New Kingdom	18th Dynasty	*c.* 1539 – 1292 BC
	Ahmose	*c.* 1539 – 1514 BC
	Amenhotep I	*c.* 1514 – 1493 BC
	Thutmose I	*c.* 1493 – 1483 BC
	Thutmose III	*c.* 1479 – 1425 BC
	Hatshepsut	*c.* 1473 – 1458 BC
	Thutmose IV	*c.* 1400 – 1390 BC
	Amenhotep III	*c.* 1390 – 1353 BC
	Akhenaten	*c.* 1353 – 1336 BC
	Tutankhamun	*c.* 1332 – 1322 BC
	19th Dynasty	*c.* 1292 – 1190 BC
	Seti I	*c.* 1290 – 1279 BC
	Ramesses II	*c.* 1279 – 1213 BC
	Merenptah	*c.* 1213 – 1204 BC
	20th Dynasty	*c.* 1190 – 1075 BC
	Ramesses III	*c.* 1187 – 1156 BC
	Ramesses IV	*c.* 1156 – 1150 BC
Third Intermediate Period	21st Dynasty	*c.* 1075 – 945 BC
	Psussenes II	*c.* 960 – 945 BC
	22nd Dynasty	*c.* 945 – 712 BC
	Shoshenk I	*c.* 945 – 924 BC
	Osorkon I	*c.* 924 – 910 BC
	23rd Dynasty	*c.* 830 – 712 BC
	Osorkon III	*c.* 777 – 749 BC
	Takeloth III	*c.* 754 – 734 BC
	24th Dynasty	*c.* 730 – 712 BC
	25th Dynasty	*c.* 770 – 656 BC
Late Period	26th Dynasty	664 – 525 BC
	Apries	589 – 570 BC
	Amasis	570 – 526 BC
	27th Dynasty	525 – 404 BC
	Cambyses	525 – 522 BC
	28th Dynasty	404 – 399 BC
	29th Dynasty	399 – 381 BC
	30th Dynasty	381 – 341 BC
	Nectanebo I	381 – 362 BC
	Nectanebo II	358 – 341 BC
	2nd Persian Period	341 – 332 BC
Graeco-Roman Period	Macedonian Dynasty	332 – 305 BC
	Alexander the Great	
	Ptolemaic Dynasty	305 – 30 BC
	Ptolemy I	305 – 284 BC
	Herwennefer (rebel king)	205 – 199 BC
	Ankhwennefer (rebel king)	199 – 186 BC
	Roman emperors (including Eastern)	30 BC – 641 AD
	Theodosius I	379 – 395 AD

Notes to the text

Chapter 2
1. M. Lichtheim, 1976, pp.81–6.
2. J. Allen, 1988, p.9.
3. M. Lichtheim, 1976, pp.214–223.

Chapter 3
1. K. Kitchen, 1996, p.164.
2. P. Grandet, 1994, Vol. 1, p.306 (58,9 – 58,10).
3. K. Kitchen, 1996, p.165.
4. H. Frankfort, 1933, Vol. I, pp.12–13, 31–32; the 'surface mound' surmised by some (e.g. Barguet, 1962) to have stood above the cenotaph is unlikely to have existed.
5. A.R. David, 1981.

Chapter 4
1. W.K. Simpson, 1974a, 1995.
2. K.P. Kuhlmann, 1979, 1982.

Chapter 5
1. J. Richards, 1999.
2. R. Layton and P. Ucko, 1999, pp.1–2.
3. J. Allen, 1988, p.7.
4. A. Gardiner, 1961, p.53.
5. P. Grandet, 1994, Vol. I; compare pp.225–302 to 305–306.
6. D. Patch, 1991, p.362.
7. J. Richards, 2002, p.99.
8. B. Kemp, 1968.
9. D. Arnold, 1996, p.54.
10. B. Kemp, 1977.

Chapter 6
1. W.K. Simpson, 1963, 1965, 1969, 1986.
2. A. Leahy, 1984, p.49.
3. J. Richards, 1997, p.40.

Chapter 7
1. For the relevant text see Breasted 1906/2001, Vol. 2, p.39 (line 15 of text); the actual spelling used in the original hieroglyphic text is *mr*, 'pyramid', followed appropriately by a determinative representing a pyramid; see K. Sethe, 1927, IV.100.16.
2. S. Harvey, 2003, p.21, fig.7 and p.24; 2004, p.6.
3. See especially M.-A. Pouls Wegner, 2002, Ch. 4.
4. P. Grandet, 1994, p.306 (58,9–58,10).
5. M.-A. Pouls Wegner, 1997–98, p.57.
6. D. Silverman, 1989.
7. D. Silverman, 1989, pp.273–275.

Chapter 8
1. J. Černy, 1957, p.137.
2. D. Montserrat, 1996, p.165.
3. B. Kemp, 1975a, p.36.
4. K. Kitchen, 1973.
5. H.I. Bell, 1956, p.61.
6. On the last days of the Seti I temple, see D. Frankfurter, 1998, pp.128–131, 169–174.
7. B. Kemp, 1975a, p.38.
8. J. Breasted, 1906/2001, Vol. 4, pp.325–333; A. Blackman, 1941.
9. M. Lichtheim, 1980, pp.33–36.
10. M. Lichtheim, 1980, p.36.
11. M. Burchardt, 1907, p.57.
12. W.M.F. Petrie, 1901, p.8.
13. H. Jaquet-Gordon, 1967.
14. M. Smith, 1998, p.434.
15. E. Hornung, 1982, p.164.

Chapter 9
1. I.E.S. Edwards, 1971, p.44.
2. H. Nissen, 1988, p.89.
3. Since the preceding was written, see now F. Breyer, 2002.
4. B. Adams, 1999, p.373.
5. W.K. Simpson, 1956.
6. W.M.F. Petrie, 1901, p.12.

Chapter 10
1. A. Mariette, 1880, p.49; Author's translation.
2. E. Aryton, *et al.*, 1904, p.4.
3. W.M.F. Petrie, 1925, p.3.
4. B. Kemp, 1996, p.16.
5. D. Arnold, 1997, pp.32–39.
6. W.M.F. Petrie, 1925, p.2.
7. D. O'Connor, 1993, pp.328–329.

Chapter 11
1. W.K. Simpson, 1965, p.17, n.12.
2. Z. Saad, 1969, p.70.
3. I.E.S. Edwards, 1993, p.155.
4. C. Ward, 2001, p.45; 2003.
5. W.K. Simpson, 1965, p.38.
6. W.B. Emery, 1954, p.170.
7. W.M.F. Petrie, 1925, pl.XII.5.

Chapter 12
1. S. Harvey, 1996.
2. E. Otto, 1968, p.14.

Sources of Illustrations

All images courtesy of the Pennsylvania-Yale-Institute of Fine Arts, New York University (PYIFA) Expedition to Abydos, unless otherwise stated. Matthew Adams: 76; akg–images / François Guénet: III; akg–images / Andrea Jemolo: IV; E. Ayrton, C. Currelly and A. Weigall, *Abydos III* Egypt Exploration Fund, London, 1903: 54; Richard Barnes: 26; Günter Dreyer, German Archaeological Institute, Cairo: 77, 78, 79, 81, 84, *VII*; courtesy of the Egypt Exploration Society: 4, 11, 14; Stephen Harvey, Abydos Ahmose and Ahmose-Nefertary Project: 55, 56, 57 (drawings by William Schenk); photo Hirmer: 9, 21, 42; Charles Lane: II; P. der Manuelian: 23; W. M. F. Petrie, *Abydos I*, Egypt Exploration Fund, 1902: 82; W. M. F. Petrie, *Royal Tombs of the First Dynasty*, Part I, Egypt Exploration Fund, London, 1900: 82; Mary-Ann Pouls Wegner, North Abydos Cultic Zone Project: 62; PYIFA, drawing by David O'Connor and Laurel Bestock: 85; PYIFA, drawing by Laurel Bestock: 16, 18 (after S. Golvin et al et al., *L'Égypte Restituée*, Tome 1, Editions Errance, Paris 1997), 58 (after B. Kemp), 60 (based on a map provided by Mary-Ann Pouls Wegner, North Abydos Cultic Zone Project), 75 (incorporating data from Günter Dreyer German Archaeological Institute, Cairo), 98 (after W.B. Emery; *Great Tombs of the First Dynasty*, Egypt Exploration Society, London, 1958); PYIFA/University of Pennsylvania Museum: 64; Janet Richards, Abydos Middle Cemetery Project, University of Michigan: 27, 31, 32, 33, 34; Janet Richards, Abydos North Cemetery Project, PYIFA, Abydos Expedition: 50, 73; photo John Ross: 95; Richard Schlecht/National Geographic Image Collection: *VIII*; Drazen Tomic: 101; University of Pennsylvania Museum: frontispiece, I, 61, 80, 83; photo Sandro Vannini: XI; Josef Wegner, Abydos Senwosret III Project, University of Pennsylvania Museum: 48, 49, 51, 52; Philip Winton: 94; © Roger Wood/CORBIS: VI; Roger Wood: 5

Select Bibliography

The items cited here are arranged in part by topic, in part with reference to specific chapters.

Abydos: General
Kees, H. 'Abydos, a Sacred City', in *Ancient Egypt A Cultural Topography*, ed. H. Kees, translated by I. Morrow, Faber and Faber, London, 1961, Chapter IX.
Kemp, B. 'Abydos', in *Lexikon der Ägyptologie* I, ed. W. Helck and E. Otto, Otto Harrassowitz, Wiesbaden, 1975a, cols. 28–41.
Otto, E. *Ancient Egyptian Art and the Cults of Osiris and Amun*, translated by K. Bosse-Griffiths, Thames & Hudson, London, 1968.
Wegner, J. 'Abydos', in *The Oxford Encyclopedia of Ancient Egypt*, Vol. 1, edited by D. Redford, pp. 7–12, Oxford University Press, 2001.

Abydos: Excavation Reports
(additional reports are cited in the bibliography for specific chapters)
Amélineau, É. *Les nouvelles fouilles d'Abydos 1895/96, 1897/98*, A. Burdin, Angers, 1896–1898.
—— *Mission Amélineau. Les nouvelles fouilles d'Abydos: compte rendu in extenso des fouilles, description des monuments et objets découverts 1895–1896, 1896–1897, 1897–1898*, E. Leroux, Paris, 1899–1904.
Ayrton, E. R., C. T. Currelly and A. E. P. Weigall, *Abydos Part III, 1904*, Egypt Exploration Fund, London = Egypt Exploration Fund Memoir no.25, 1904.
Baker, B. 'Secrets in the Skeletons: Disease and deformity attest the hazards of daily life', *Archaeology* 54/3, 2001, p. 47.
Frankfort, H. 'Preliminary Report of the Expedition to Abydos 1925–6', *Journal of Egyptian Archaeology* 12, 1926, pp. 157–165.
—— 'The Cemeteries of Abydos: Work of the Season 1925–26', *Journal of Egyptian Archaeology* 14, 1928, p. 242.
Garstang, J. *El Arábah: A Cemetery of the Middle Kingdom; Survey of the Old Kingdom Temenos; Graffiti from the Temple of Sety*, with notes by P. Newberry on the hieroglyphic inscriptions and by J. Grafton Milne on the Greek graffiti, *Egyptian Research Accounts* 6th Memoir, B. Quaritch, London, 1900.
Ghazouli, E. 'The Palace and Magazines Attached to the Temple of Seti I at Abydos and the Façade of this Temple', *Annales du Service des Antiquités de l'Égypte* 58, Cairo, pp. 99–186.
James, T. G. H. 'The Archaeological Survey', in *Excavating in Egypt: The Egypt Exploration Society 1882–1982*, ed. T.G.H. James, University of Chicago Press, Chicago and London, pp. 141–160.
Kemp, B. 'Abydos', in *Excavating in Egypt: The Egypt Exploration Society 1882–1982*, edited by T.G.H. James, pp. 71–88, University of Chicago Press, Chicago and London, 1982.
Mariette, A. *Abydos, description des fouilles exécutés sur l'emplacement de cette ville*, Tome I: *Ville antique, Temple de Séti*, A. Franck, Paris, 1869, reprinted Georg Olms, Hildesheim, 1998.
—— *Abydos, description des fouilles exécutés sur l'emplacement de cette ville*, Tome II: *Temple de Séti, supplément; Temple de Ramsès, Temple d'Osiris, Petit temple de l'ouest Nécropole*, A. Franck, Paris, 1880, reprinted Georg Olms, Hildesheim, 1998.
—— *Abydos, description des fouilles exécutés sur l'emplacement de cette ville*, Tome III: *Catalogue général des Monuments d'Abydos découverts pendant des fouilles de cette ville*, Imprimerie nationale, Paris, 1880, reprinted Georg Olms, Hildesheim, 1998.
Naville, E. *The Cemeteries of Abydos Part 1, 1909-1910*, The mixed cemetery and Umm el Ga'ab by E. Naville, with chapters by T.E. Peet, H.R. Hall and K. Haddon, Egypt Exploration Fund, London = Egypt Exploration Fund Memoir no.33, 1913–1914.
O'Connor, D. 'Abydos: A Preliminary Report of the Pennsylvania-Yale Expedition', *Expedition: Magazine of the University of Pennsylvania Museum* 10/1, 1967, pp. 10–23.
—— 'Fieldwork in Egypt', *Expedition: Magazine of the University of Pennsylvania Museum* 11/1, 1968, pp. 27–30.
—— 'Abydos and the University Museum, 1898–1969', *Expedition: Magazine of the University of Pennsylvania Museum* 12/1, 1969, pp. 28–29.
—— 'Abydos: The University Museum-Yale University Expedition', *Expedition: Magazine of the University of Pennsylvania Museum* 21/2, 1979, pp. 46–49.
Peet, T. E. *The Cemeteries of Abydos Part 2, 1911–12*, Egypt Exploration Fund, London = Egypt Exploration Fund Memoir no.34, 1913/1914.
—— and W.L.S. Loat *The Cemeteries of Abydos Part 3, 1912–13*, Egypt Exploration Fund, London = Egypt Exploration Fund Memoir no. 35, 1913–1914.
Petrie, W. M. F. *Abydos Part 1, 1902*, with a chapter by A. Weigall, 2 volumes, Egypt Exploration Fund, London = Egypt Exploration Fund Memoir no. 22, 1902.
—— *Abydos Part II, 1903*, Egypt Exploration Fund, London = Egypt Exploration Fund Memoir no. 24, 1903.

Randall-Maciver, D. and A. C. Mace *El Amrah and Abydos, 1899–1900*, with a chapter by F.Ll. Griffith, Egypt Exploration Fund, London = Egypt Exploration Fund Memoir no.23, 1902.
Simpson, W.K. *Inscribed Material from the Pennsylvania-Yale Excavations at Abydos*, Publications of the Pennsylvania-Yale Expedition to Egypt no.6, Peabody Museum of Natural History, New Haven, 1995.

Chapter 1: The Discovery of Abydos
Drower, M. S. *Flinders Petrie: A Life in Archaeology*, Victor Gollancz Ltd, London, 1985.
Lambert, G. *Auguste Mariette, ou, l'Égypte ancienne sauvée des sables*, J.C. Lattès, Paris, 1997.
Strabo *Le voyage en Égypte: un regard romain*, translated by P. Charvet, commentary by J. Yoyotte and P. Charvet, Nil, Paris, 1997.
Le Tourner d'Ison, C. *Mariette Pacha*, Plon, Paris, 1999.

Chapter 2: Osiris – Eternal Lord Who Presides in Abydos
Allen, J. *Genesis in Egypt: The Philosophy of Ancient Egyptian Creation Accounts*, Yale Egyptological Studies 2, New Haven, Connecticut, 1988.
Griffiths, J. G. *Plutarch's De Iside et Osiride*, University of Wales Press, Cardiff, 1970.
—— *The Origins of Osiris and his Cult*, Studies in the History of Religions 40, E.J. Brill, Leiden, 1980.
Hornung, E. *Conceptions of God in Ancient Egypt: The One and the Many*, translated by J. Baines, Cornell University Press, Ithaca, New York, 1982.
Lichtheim, M. *Ancient Egyptian Literature*. Volume II: *The New Kingdom*, University of California Press, Berkeley, Los Angeles, London, 1976.
Plutarch *De Iside et Osiride*, see Griffiths, J.G., 1970.
Spiegel, J. *Die Götter von Abydos: Studien zum ägyptischen Synkretismus*, Göttingen Oreintforschungen, 4. Reihe, Ägypten, Bd 1, Harrasowitz, Wiesbaden, 1973.

Chapter 3: The Temple of Seti I
Baines, J. 'Abydos, Temple of Sethos I: Preliminary Report', *Journal of Egyptian Archaeology* 70, 1984, pp. 21–2.
—— 'Techniques of Decoration in the Hall of Barques in the Temple of King Sethos I at Abydos', *Journal of Egyptian Archaeology* 75, 1989, pp. 13–30.
—— 'Recording the Temple of King Sethos I at Abydos in Egypt', *Bulletin of the Ancient Orient Museum* XI, Tokyo, 1990, pp. 65–95.
Barguet, P. 'Note sur le complexe architectural de Séti Ier à Abydos', *Kêmi* 16 (1962): 21–28.
Brand, P. *The Monuments of Seti I: Epigraphic, Historical and Art Historical Analysis* = W. Helck, ed., *Probleme der Ägyptologie* 16. Bd, E.J. Brill, Leiden, Boston, 2000.
Calverley, A. and M. Broome. ed. A. Gardiner *The Temple of King Sethos I at Abydos*, Joint Publication of the Egypt Exploration Society (Archaeological Survey) and of the Oriental Institute of the University of Chicago, 4 volumes, Egypt Exploration Society, London, University of Chicago Press, Chicago, 1933–1959.
Capart, J. *Abydos, le temple de Séti Ier; étude général*, Rossignol and van den Bril, Bruxelles, 1912.
Caulfeild, A. *The Temple of the Kings at Abydos: Seti I*, with a chapter by W.M.F. Petrie, *Egyptian Research Accounts* 8th Memoir, B. Quaritch, London, 1902.
David, R. *A Guide to Religious Ritual at Abydos (c. 1300 B.C.)*, Aris & Phillips Ltd., Warminster, Wilts., England, 1981.
Eaton, K. 'The Ritual Functions of Processional Equipment in the Temple of Seti I at Abydos', Ph.D. Dissertation, New York University, 2003.
Frankfort, H., A. de Buck and B. Gunn *The Cenotaph of Seti I at Abydos*, vols. 1–2, Egypt Exploration Society, London = Egypt Exploration Society Memoir no. 39, 1933.
Grandet, P. *Le Papyrus Harris I (BM 9999)*, vols. I–II, Institut Français d'Archéologie Orientale, *Bibliothèque d'Étude* T.CIX/I and II, Cairo, 1994.
Griffith, F. Ll. 'The Abydos Decree of Seti I at Nauri', *Journal of Egyptian Archaeology* 13, 1937, pp. 193–208.
Kitchen, K. *Ramesside Inscriptions Translated and Annotated: Translations I. Ramesses II, Sethos I and Contemporaries*, Blackwell Publishers, Oxford, 1993.
—— *Ramesside Inscriptions Translated and Annotated. Translations Vol. II. Ramesses II, Royal Inscriptions*, Blackwell Publishers, Oxford, 1996.
Mekhitarian, A., M. Kunnen and R. Wulleman, *Abydos: Sacred Precinct of Abydos*, Mappamundi, Knokke, Belgium, 1998.
Murray, M. *The Osireion at Abydos*, with sections by J. Grafton Milne and W.E. Crum, *Egyptian Research Accounts* 9th Memoir, B. Quaritch, London, 1904.
Shubert, S. 'Abydos, Osiris Temple of Seti I', in ed. K. Bard *Encyclopedia of the Archaeology of Ancient Egypt*, Routledge, London and New York, 1999, pp. 103–104.

Chapter 4: The Rediscovery of Abydos

Cott, J. *The Search for Omm Sety: A Story of Eternal Love*, in collaboration with Hanny el Zeini, Doubleday, Garden City, NY, 1987.

Kuhlmann, K. 'Der Tempel Ramses II in Abydos: Vorbericht über eine Neuaufnahme', *MDAIK* 35 (1979): 189–193.

—— 'Der Tempel Ramses II in Abydos: Zweiter Bericht über eine Neuaufnahme', *MDAIK* 38 (1982): 355–362.

Omm Sety (Dorothy Louise Eady), *Omm Sety's Abydos*, edited by D. M. Kolos, Benben Publications, 1982.

O'Connor, D. and D. C. Patch 'Sacred Sands: Exploring the Tombs and Temples of Ancient Abydos', *Archaeology* 54/3 (2001): 43–49.

Simpson, W.K. *Terrace of the Great God: The Offering Chapels of Dynasties 12 and 13*, Publications of the Pennsylvania-Yale Expedition to Egypt no. 5, Peabody Museum of Anthropology, New Haven, 1974a.

—— *Inscribed Material from the Pennsylvania-Yale Excavations at Abydos*, Publications of the Pennsylvania-Yale Expedition to Egypt no. 6, Peabody Museum of Natural History, New Haven, 1995.

Chapter 5: The Evolution of a Sacred Landscape

Adams, M. 'Community and Societal Organization in Early Historic Egypt', *Newsletter of the American Research Center in Egypt* 158/159 (1992): 1–10.

—— 'The Abydos Settlement Site Project: Investigation of a Major Provincial Town in the Old Kingdom and the First Intermediate Period', in *Proceedings of the Seventh International Congress of Egyptologists Cambridge, 3–9 September 1995*, edited by C. Eyre, Orientalia Lovaniensia Analecta 82, pp. 19–30, Uitgeverij Peeters, Leuven, 1998.

—— 'Abydos, North', in *Encyclopedia of the Archaeology of Ancient Egypt*, edited by K. Bard, pp. 97–100, Routledge, London and New York, 1999.

—— 'Digging in the Ancient Town of Abydos', *Archaeology* 54/4 (2001): 55.

—— 'Community and Society in Egypt in the First Intermediate Period: An Archaeological Investigation of the Abydos Settlement Site,' Dissertation, University of Pennsylvania, Philadelphia, 2004.

Allen, J. *Genesis in Egypt: The Philosophy of Ancient Egyptian Creation Accounts*, Yale Egyptological Studies 2, New Haven, Connecticut, 1988.

Arnold, D. 'Hypostyle Halls of the Old and Middle Kingdom?' in *Studies in Honor of William Kelly Simpson*, vol. 1, edited by P. der Manuelian and R. Freed (supervisor), pp. 39–54, Dept of Ancient Egyptian, Nubian and Near Eastern Art, Boston Museum of Fine Arts, Boston, 1996.

Brovarski, E. 'Abydos in the Old Kingdom and First Intermediate Period Part I', in *Hommages à Jean Leclant*, C. Berger et al., pp. 99–121, Bibliothèque d'Étude Institut Français d'Archéologie Orientale 106/1, vol. I, Cairo, 1993.

—— 'Abydos in the Old Kingdom and First Intermediate Period Part II', in *For His Ka: Essays Offered in Memory of Klaus Baer*, edited by D. Silverman, pp. 15–44, Oriental Institute, University of Chicago, Chicago, 1994.

Faulkner, R. *The Ancient Egyptian Coffin Texts*, vols. 1–3, Aris & Phillips, Warminster, Wilts., England, 1973–1978.

Gardiner, A. *Egypt of the Pharaohs: An Introduction*, Clarendon Press, Oxford, 1961.

Kemp, B. 'The Osiris Temple at Abydos', *MDAIK* 23 (1968): 138–155.

—— 'The Osiris Temple at Abydos: A Postscript to *MDAIK* 23 (1968): 138–155', *Göttinger Miszellen* 8 (1973): 23–25.

—— 'How Religious were the Ancient Egyptians?' *Cambridge Archaeological Journal* 5/1 (1975b): 25–54.

—— 'The Early Development of Towns in Egypt', *Antiquity* 41 (1977): 22–32.

Layton, R. and P. Ucko 'Introduction: Gazing on the Landscape and Encountering the Environment', in *The Archaeology and Anthropology of Landscape: Shaping Your Landscape*, edited by P. Ucko and R. Layton, pp. 1–20, Routledge Press, One World Archaeology, vol. 30, 1999.

O'Connor, D. 'The Status of Early Egyptian Temples: An Alternative Theory', in *The Followers of Horus: Studies in Memory of Michael Allen Hoffman*, edited by B. Adams and R. Friedman, pp. 83–98, Oxbow Press, Oxford = Oxbow Monograph 20, 1992a.

Patch, D. *The Origin and Early Development of Urbanism in Ancient Egypt: A Regional Study*, Dissertation, University of Pennsylvania, UMI, Ann Arbor, Michigan, 1991.

Richards, J. 'Conceptual Landscapes in the Egyptian Nile Valley', in *Archaeologies of Landscape: Contemporary Perspectives*, edited by W. Ashmore and B. Knapp, pp. 83–100, Blackwell, London and Malden, MA, 1999.

—— 'Quest for Weni the Elder. An Old Kingdom cemetery yields the tomb of a "True Governor of Upper Egypt"', *Archaeology* 54/3 (2001): 48–49.

—— 'Time and Memory in Ancient Egyptian Cemeteries', *Expedition: Magazine of the University of Pennsylvania Museum* 44/3 (2002): 16–24.

—— 'The Abydos Cemeteries in the Late Old Kingdom', in *Egyptology at the Dawn of the Twenty-first Century: Proceedings of the Eighth International Congress of Egyptologists Cairo*, edited by Z. Hawass, pp. 400–407, American University in Cairo Press, Cairo, 2003.

—— 'Text and Context in late Old Kingdom Egypt: the Archaeology and Historiography of Weni the Elder', *Journal of the American Research Center in Egypt* 39 (2002): 75–102.

—— 'The Archaeology of Excavations and the Role of Context', in *The*

Archaeology and Art of Ancient Egypt: Essays in Honor of David B. O'Connor, vol. 2, edited by Z. Hawass and J. Richards, pp. 313–319, Annales du Service des Antiquités de l'Égypte, Cahier no. 36, Cairo, 2007.

—— 'Wonderful Things': The 2007 Abydos Middle Cemetery Project', in *Kelsey Museum Newsletter* (2007): 1–4.

Chapter 6: The Expanding Landscape of the Middle Kingdom

Amélineau, É. *Le tombeau d'Osiris; monographie de la découverte faite en 1897–1898*, E. Leroux, Paris, 1899.

Anthes, R. 'Die Berichte des Neferhotep und des Ichernofret über das Osirisfest in Abydos', in *Festschrift zum 150 jahrigen Bestehen des Berliner ägyptischen Museums*, edited by W. Müller, Mitteilungen aus der Ägyptische Sammlung (Staatlichen Museen, Berlin) Bd 8, pp. 15–50, Akademie, Berlin, 1974.

Arnold, D. 'Buried in Two Tombs? Remarks on "Cenotaphs" in the Middle Kingdom', in *The Archaeology and Art of Ancient Egypt: Essays in Honor of David B. O'Connor*, vol. 1, edited by Z. Hawass and J. Richards, pp. 55–61, Annales du Service des Antiquités de l'Égypte, Cahier no. 36, Cairo, 2007.

Dodson, A. 'The So-Called Tomb of Osiris at Abydos', *KMT* 8/4 (1997–1998): 37–47.

Freed, R. 'Stela Workshops of Early Dynasty 12', in *Studies in Honor of William Kelly Simpson*, vol. 1, edited by P. der Manuelian and R. Freed (supervisor), pp. 297–336, Dept of Ancient Egyptian, Nubian and Near Eastern Art, Boston Museum of Fine Arts, Boston, 1996.

Lavier, M.-C. 'Les mystères d'Osiris à Abydos d'après les stèles du Moyen Empire et du Nouvel Empire', in *Akten des vierten internationalen Ägyptologen Kongresses München 1985*, Bd 3, edited by S. Schoske, pp. 289–295, Studien zur altägyptischen Kultur, Beihefte, Bd 3, Helmut Buske Verlag, Hamburg, 1991.

Leahy, A. 'The Osiris "Bed" Reconsidered', *Orientalia* 46 (1977): 424–434.

—— 'A Protective Measure at Abydos in the Thirteenth Dynasty', *Journal of Egyptian Archaeology* 75 (1989): 41–60.

O'Connor, D. 'The Cenotaphs of the Middle Kingdom at Abydos', in *Mélanges Gamaleddin Mokhtar*, edited by P. Posener-Krieger (director), pp. 161–177, Bibliothèque d'Étude Institut Français d'Archéologie Orientale XCVII/2, Cairo, 1985.

—— 'Abydos, North, *Ka* Chapels and Cenotaphs', in *Encyclopedia of the Archaeology of Ancient Egypt*, edited by K. Bard, pp. 100–103, Routledge, London and New York, 1999a.

Richards, J. *Mortuary Variability and Social Differentiation in Middle Kingdom Egypt*, Dissertation, University of Pennsylvania, UMI, Ann Arbor, Michigan, 1992.

—— 'Abydos: Middle Kingdom', in *Encyclopedia of the Archaeology of Ancient Egypt*, edited by K. Bard, pp. 95–97, Routledge, London and New York, 1998.

—— 'Ancient Egyptian Mortuary Practice and the Study of Socio-economic Differentiation', in *Anthropology and Egyptology: A Developing Dialogue*, edited by J. Lustig, pp. 33–42, Monographs in Mediterranean Archaeology, Sheffield Press, 1998.

—— *Society and Death in Middle Kingdom Egypt*, Cambridge University Press, forthcoming.

Schäfer, H. *Die Mysterien des Osiris in Abydos unter Konig Sesostris III nach dem Denkstein des Oberschatzmeister I-Cher-Nofret im Berliner Museum*, Untersuchungen 4:2, J.C. Hinrichs, Leipzig, 1904.

Simpson, W. K. *Papyrus Reisner I: The Records of a Building Project in the Reign of Sesostris I*, Museum of Fine Arts, Boston, 1963.

—— *Papyrus Reisner II: Accounts of the Dockyard Workshop at This in the Reign of Sesostris I*, Museum of Fine Arts, Boston, 1965.

—— *Papyrus Reisner III: The Records of a Building Project in the Early Twelfth Dynasty*, Museum of Fine Arts, Boston, 1969.

—— *Terrace of the Great God: The Offering Chapels of Dynasties 12 and 13*, Publications of the Pennsylvania-Yale Expedition to Egypt no. 5, Peabody Museum of Anthropology, New Haven, 1974a.

—— 'Polygamy in Egypt in the Middle Kingdom?' *Journal of Egyptian Archaeology* 60 (1974b): 100–105.

—— 'Kenotaph', in *Lexikon der Ägyptologie*, Bd III, edited by W. Helck and W. Westendorf, cols. 387–391, Otto Harrassowitz, Wiesbaden, 1978.

—— *Papyrus Reisner IV: Personal Accounts of the Early Twelfth Dynasty*, Museum of Fine Arts, Boston, 1986.

—— 'A Landscape of Empty Tombs', *Archaeology* 54/3 (2001): 46.

Wegner, J. 'South Abydos: Burial Place of the Third Senwosret? Old and New Excavations at the Abydene Complex of Senwosret III', *KMT: A Modern Journal of Ancient Egypt* 6/2 (1995): 58–71.

—— *The Mortuary Complex of Senwosret III: A Study of Middle Kingdom State Activity and the Cult of Osiris at Abydos*, Dissertation, University of Pennsylvania, UMI, Ann Arbor, Michigan, 1996.

—— 'Excavations at the Town of *Enduring-are-the-places-of-Khakaure-maa-keru-in-Abydos*: A Preliminary Report on the 1994 and 1997 Seasons', *Journal of the American Research Center in Egypt* 35 (1998): 1–44.

—— 'South Abydos', in *Encyclopedia of the Archaeology of Ancient Egypt*, edited by K. Bard, pp. 106–109, Routledge, London and New York, 1999.

—— 'Excavating the Residence of an Ancient Egyptian Mayor', *Expedition* 41/3 (1999): 4–5.
—— 'Reconstructing the Temple of Pharaoh Senwosret III', *Expedition* 42/2 (2000): 9–18.
—— 'A Middle Kingdom Town at South Abydos', *Egyptian Archaeology* 17 (2000): 8–10.
—— 'The Organization of the Temple *Nfr-K3* of Senwosret III at Abydos', *Ägypten und Levante* 10 (2000): 83–125.
—— 'Seat of Eternity: Excavations at Abydos reveal an elaborate funerary complex linking a deceased Middle Kingdom pharaoh to the god Osiris', *Archaeology* 54/4 (2001): 56–60.
—— 'The Town of *Wah-sut* at South Abydos: 1999 Excavations', *Mitteilungen des Deutsches Archäologisches Institut Abteilung Kairo* 57 (2001): 281–308.
—— 'Institutions and Officials at Middle Kingdom South Abydos: An Overview of the Sygillographic Evidence', in *Cahiers de Recherches de l'Institut de Papyrologie et Egyptologie de Lille*, no. 24, pp. 23–57, Université Charles de Gaulle-Lille III, Villeneuve d'Ascq, 2001.
—— 'A Decorated Birth-Brick from South Abydos', *Egyptian Archaeology* 21 (2003): 3–5.
—— *The Mortuary Temple of Senwosret III at Abydos*, Peabody Museum of Natural History of Yale University: the University of Pennsylvania Museum of Archaeology and Anthropology, New Haven and Philadelphia, 2007.

Chapter 7: The Landscape Completed: Abydos in the New Kingdom
Dreyer, G., E.-M. Engel, U. Hartung, T. Hikade, E. C. Köhler and F. Pumpenmeier 'Umm el Qaab: Nachuntersuchungen im frühzeitlichen Königsfriedhof. 7/8 Vorbericht', *MDAIK* 52 (1996): 11–81.
——, U. Hartung, T. Hikade, E. C. Köhler, V. Müller and F. Pumpenmeier 'Umm el Qaab: Nachuntersuchungen im frühzeitlichen Königsfriedhof. 9/10 Vorbericht', *MDAIK* 54 (1998): 77–167.
Eaton, K. 'Memorial Temples in the Sacred Landscape of Nineteenth Dynasty Abydos: An Overview of Processional Routes and Equipment', in *The Archaeology and Art of Ancient Egypt: Essays in Honor of David B. O'Connor*, vol. 1, edited by Z. Hawass and J. Richards, pp. 231–250, Annales du Service des Antiquités de l'Égypte, Cahier no. 36, Cairo, 2007.
Harvey, S. 'Monuments of Ahmose at Abydos', *Egyptian Archaeology* 4 (1994): 3–5.
—— *The Cults of King Ahmose at Abydos*, Dissertation, University of Pennsylvania, UMI, Ann Arbor, Michigan, 1998.
—— 'Tribute to a Conquering King: Battle scenes at Abydos honor a pharaoh's triumph over Hyksos occupiers and his reunification of Egypt', *Archaeology* 54/4 (2001): 52–55.
—— 'Abydos', *The Oriental Institute 2002–2003 Annual Report* (2003):15–25.
—— 'New Evidence at Abydos for Ahmose's Funerary Cult', *Egyptian Archaeology* 24 (2004): 3–6.
—— 'King Heqatawy: Notes on a Forgotten Eighteenth Dynasty Royal Name', in *The Archaeology and Art of Ancient Egypt: Essays in Honor of David B. O'Connor*, vol. 1, edited by Z. Hawass and J. Richards, pp. 343–356, Annales du Service des Antiquités de l'Égypte, Cahier no. 36, Cairo, 2007.
Kitchen, K. *Ramesside Inscriptions Translated and Annotated. Translations* Vol. II: *Ramesses II, Royal Inscriptions*, Blackwell Publishers, Oxford, 1996.
Kuhlmann, K. 'Der Tempel Ramses II in Abydos: Vorbericht über eine Neuaufnahme', *MDAIK* 35 (1979): 189–193.
—— 'Der Tempel Ramses II in Abydos: Zweiter Bericht über eine Neuaufnahme', *MDAIK* 38 (1982): 355–362.
Legrain, G. 'Un miracle d'Ahmes I à Abydos sous le regne de Ramsès II', *Annales du Service des Antiquités de l'Égypte*, Cairo 16 (1917): 161–179.
Moret, A. 'Un jugement de dieu au cours d'un procès sous Ramsès II', *Comptes Rendus de l'Académie des Inscriptions et Belles-Lettres* (1917): 157–165.
Munro, I. 'Zum Kult des Ahmose in Abydos: ein weiterer Beleg aus der Ramessidenzeit', *Göttinger Miszellen* 101 (1988): 60–62.
O'Connor, D. 'Abydos: The Last Royal Pyramid?' in *The Seventy Great Mysteries of Ancient Egypt*, edited by W. Manley, pp. 77–79, Thames & Hudson, London and New York, 2003.
Polz, D. and A. Seiler *Die Pyramidanlage des Königs Nub-Cheper-Re Intef in Dra' Abu el-Naga: Ein Vorbericht*, Deutsches Archäologisches Institut Abteilung Kairo, Sonderschrift 24, Phillip von Zabern, Mainz am Rhein, 2003.
Pouls, M.-A. 'A Newly Discovered Temple of Thutmose III at Abydos', *KMT* 8/4 (1997–1998): 48–59.
Sethe, K. *Urkunden der 18. Dynastie I*, J.C. Hinrich'sche Buchhandlung, Leipzig, 1927.
Silverman, D. 'The So-called Portal Temple of Ramesses II at Abydos', in *Akten des vierten internationalen Ägyptologen Kongresses München 1985*, Bd 2, edited by S. Schoske, pp. 269–277, Helmut Buske Verlag, Hamburg, 1989.
Wegner, M.-A. Pouls 'The Chapel of Thutmose III: New Kingdom Pilgrims and Patrons at Abydos', *Archaeology* 54/4 (2001): 58–59.
—— *The Cult of Osiris at Abydos: An Archaeological Investigation of the Development of an Ancient Egyptian Sacred Center during the Eighteenth Dynasty*, Dissertation, University of Pennsylvania, UMI, Ann Arbor, Michigan, 2002.
Winlock, H. *Bas-Reliefs from the Temple of Ramesses I at Abydos*, Metropolitan Museum Papers no. 1, Metropolitan Museum of Art, New York, 1921.
—— *The Temple of Ramesses I at Abydos*, Metropolitan Museum Papers no. 5, Metropolitan Museum of Art, New York, 1937.

Chapter 8: The Climax of the Osiris Cult
Abdalla, A. *Graeco-Roman Funerary Stelae from Upper Egypt*, Liverpool University Press, Liverpool, 1992.
Bell, H. I. *Egypt from Alexander the Great to the Arab Conquest: A Study in the Diffusion and Decay of Hellenism*, Oxford at the Clarendon Press, Oxford, 1956.
Blackman, A. M. 'The Stela of Shoshenk, Great Chief of the Meshwesh', *Journal of Egyptian Archaeology* 27 (1941): 83–95.
Breasted, J. *Ancient Records of Egypt*, vols. 1-6, University of Chicago Press, Chicago; republished by University of Illinois Press, Urbana and Chicago, 1906/2001.
Burchardt, M. 'Ein Erlass des Königs Necht-har-ehbet', *Zeitschrift für ägyptische Sprache und Altertumskunde* 44 (1907): 55–58.
Černy, J. *Ancient Egyptian Religion*, Hutchinson's University Library, London, 1957.
Frankfurter, D. *Religion in Roman Egypt Assimilation and Resistance*, Princeton University Press, Princeton, NJ, 1998.
Griffiths, J.G. 'Osiris', in *Lexikon der Ägyptologie*, Bd IV, edited by W. Helck and W. Westendorf, cols. 623–633, Otto Harrassowitz, Wiesbaden, 1982.
—— 'Osiris', in *The Oxford Encyclopedia of Ancient Egypt*, vol. 2, edited by D. Redford, pp. 615–619, Oxford University Press, 2001.
Hölbl, G. *A History of the Ptolemaic Empire*, Routledge, London and New York, 2001.
Hornung, E. *Conceptions of God in Ancient Egypt: The One and the Many*, translated by J. Baines, Cornell University Press, Ithaca, New York, 1982.
Ikram, S. 'Animals in the Ritual Landscape at Abydos: A Synopsis', in *The Archaeology and Art of Ancient Egypt: Essays in Honor of David B. O'Connor*, vol. 1, edited by Z. Hawass and J. Richards, pp. 417–432, Annales du Service des Antiquités de l'Égypte, Cahier no. 36, Cairo, 2007.
Jaquet-Gordon, H. 'The Illusory Year 36 of Osorkon I', *Journal of Egyptian Archaeology* 53 (1967): 63–68.
Kemp, B. 'Abydos', in *Lexikon der Ägyptologie*, Bd I, ed. W. Helck and E. Otto, Otto Harrassowitz, Wiesbaden, 1975a, cols. 28–41.
Kitchen, K. *The Third Intermediate Period in Egypt (1100–650 BC)*, Aris and Phillips, Warminster, Wilts., England, 1973.
Leahy, A. 'Nespamedu, King of the Thinis', *Göttinger Miszellen* 35 (1979): 31–39.
—— 'The Date of Louvre A.93', *Göttinger Miszellen* 70 (1984): 45–58.
—— 'Abydos in the Libyan Period', in *Libya and Egypt, c. 1300–750 BC*, edited by A. Leahy, pp. 155–200, SOAS, Centre for Near and Middle Eastern Studies, Society for Libyan Studies, London, 1990.
—— 'Kushite Monuments at Abydos', in *The Unbroken Reed: Studies in the Culture and Heritage of Ancient Egypt in Honour of A.F. Shore*, edited by C. Eyre, A. Leahy and L. Leahy, pp. 171–192, Egypt Exploration Society, London, 1994.
Lichtheim, M. *Ancient Egyptian Literature*, Volume III: *The Late Period*, Berkeley, Los Angeles, London, University of California Press, 1980.
De Meulenaere, H. 'Le clergé abydénien d'Osiris à la Basse Époque', in *Miscellanea in honorem Josephi Vergote*, edited by P. Naster, H. De Meulenaere and J. Quaegebeur, pp. 133–151, Department Oriëntalistiek Leuven, Leuven = *Orientalia Lovaniensia Periodica* 6/7 (1975–1976), 1976.
—— 'Meskhénet à Abydos', in *Religion und Philosophie im Alten Ägypten*, Festgabe für Philippe Derchain, edited by U. Verhoeven and E. Graefe, pp. 243–251, Department Oriëntalistiek Leuven, Leuven, Uitgeverij Peeters = *Orientalia Lovaniensia Analecta* 39, 1991.
Montserrat, P. *Sex and Society in Graeco-Roman Egypt*, London and New York, Kegan Paul International, 1996 (reference is p.165).
Petrie, W.M.F. *The Royal Tombs of the Earliest Dynasties, 1901, Part II*, Egypt Exploration Fund, London = Egypt Exploration Fund Memoir no. 21, 1901.
Rutherford, I. 'Pilgrimage in Graeco-Roman Egypt: New Perspectives on Graffiti from the Memnonian at Abydos', in *Ancient Perspectives on Egypt = Encounters With Ancient Egypt*, edited by R. Matthews and C. Roemer, pp. 171–190, London, UCL Press and Institute of Archaeology, 2003.
Smith, M. 'A Demotic Coffin Inscription', *Egyptian Religion: The Last Thousand Years. Studies Dedicated to the Memory of Jan Quaegebeur*, edited by W. Clarysse, A. Schoors, and H. Willems, pp. 425–439, *Orientalia Lovaniensia Analecta* 84, Peeters, Leuven, 1998.

Chapter 9: The Royal Tombs of Abydos
Adams, B. 'Elite Tombs at Hierakonpolis', in *Aspects of Early Egypt*, edited by J. Spencer, pp. 1–15, British Museum Press, London, 1996.
—— 'Hierakonpolis', in *Encyclopedia of the Archaeology of Ancient Egypt*, edited by K. Bard, pp. 371–374, Routledge, London and New York, 1999.

Anderson, D. 'Abydos, Predynastic Sites', in *Encyclopedia of the Archaeology of Ancient Egypt*, edited by K. Bard, pp. 104–106, Routledge, London and New York, 1999.

Baines, J. 'Origins of Egyptian Kingship', in *Ancient Egyptian Kingship*, edited by D. O'Connor and D. Silverman, pp. 95–156, E.J. Brill, Leiden, 1995.

—— 'The Earliest Egyptian Writing: Development, Context, Purpose', in *The First Writing: Script Invention as History and Process*, edited by S. Houston, pp. 150–189, Cambridge University Press, Cambridge, 2004.

Bard, K. *From Farmers to Pharaohs. Mortuary Evidence for the Rise of Complex Society*, Sheffield Academic Press, Sheffield, 1994.

Bestock, L. *First Dynasty Subsidiary Burials at Abydos*, Research Paper, Institute of Fine Arts, New York University, 2000.

—— 'Finding the First Dynasty Royal Family', in *The Archaeology and Art of Ancient Egypt: Essays in Honor of David B. O'Connor*, vol. 1, edited by Z. Hawass and J. Richards, pp. 309–336, Annales du Service des Antiquités de l'Égypte, Cahier no. 36, Cairo, 2007.

—— 'The Development of Royal Funerary Cult at Abydos: Two New Funerary Enclosures from the Reign of King Aha', Ph.D. Dissertation, Institute of Fine Arts, New York University, 2007.

—— 'The Evolution of Royal Ideology: New Discoveries from the Reign of Aha', in *Egypt at its Origins 2. Proceedings of the International Conference 'Origin of the State. Predynastic and Early Dynastic Egypt', Toulouse, 5th–8th September 2005*, edited by Béatrix Midant-Reynes and Yann Tristant, *Orientalia Lovaniensia Analecta*, Peeters Publishers, Leuven, (in press).

—— 'The Funerary Enclosures of Abydos', in *Archéo-Nil 18: Naissance de l'architecture funéraire*, (in press).

Breyer, E. 'Die Schriftzeugnisses des Prädynastischen Königsgrabes U-j in Umm el-Qaab: Versuch einer neue Interpretation', *Journal of Egyptian Archaeology* 88 (2002): 53–65.

Brunton, G. and Caton-Thompson, G. *The Badarian Civilization and Predynastic Remains Near Badari*, British School of Archaeology in Egypt = British School of Archaeology in Egypt Publications, vol. 46, London, 1928.

Dreyer, G. 'Umm el Qaab: Nachuntersuchungen im frühzeitlichen Königsfriedhof. 3/4 Vorbericht', *MDAIK* 46 (1990): 53–90.

—— 'Zur Rekonstruktion der Oberbauten der Königsgraber der 1. Dynastie in Abydos', *MDAIK* 47 (1991): 93–104.

—— 'Recent Discoveries at Abydos Cemetery U', in *The Nile-Delta in Transition: 4th–3rd Millennium BC*, edited by E. van den Brink, pp. 293–299, van den Brink, Tel Aviv, 1992.

—— 'Umm el Qaab: Nachuntersuchungen im frühzeitlichen Königsfriedhof. 5/6 Vorbericht', *MDAIK* 49 (1993): 23–62.

—— *Umm el Qaab I: Das prädynastische Königsgrab U-j und seine frühen Schriftzeugnisse*, mit Beitragen von U. Hartung und F. Pumpenmeier und einem Anhang von M. Feindt und M. Fischer, Verlag Phillip von Zabern = Archäologische Veröffentlichungen, Deutsches Archäologisches Institut Abteilung Kairo 86, 1998.

—— 'Abydos, Umm el Qa'ab', in *Encyclopedia of the Archaeology of Ancient Egypt*, edited by K. Bard, pp. 109–114, Routledge, London and New York, 1999.

—— 'The Tombs of the First and Second Dynasties at Abydos and Saqqara', in *Treasures of the Pyramids*, edited by Z. Hawass, pp. 62–77, White Star S.r.l., Vercelli, Italy, 2003.

——, E.-M. Engel, U. Hartung, T. Hikade, E. C. Köhler and F. Pumpenmeier 'Umm el Qaab: Nachuntersuchungen im frühzeitlichen Königsfriedhof. 7/8 Vorbericht', *MDAIK* 52 (1996): 11–81.

——, U. Hartung, T. Hikade, E. C. Köhler, V. Müller and F. Pumpenmeier 'Umm el Qaab: Nachuntersuchungen im frühzeitlichen Königsfriedhof. 9/10 Vorbericht', *MDAIK* 54 (1998): 77–167.

——, A. von den Driesch, E.-M. Engel, R. Hartmann, U. Hartung, T. Hikade, V. Müller and J. Peters 'Umm el Qaab: Nachuntersuchungen im frühzeitlichen Königsfriedhof. 11/12 Vorbericht', *MDAIK* 56 (2000): 43–129.

——, R. Hartmann, U. Hartung, T. Hikade, H. Köpp, C. Lacher, V. Müller, A. Nerlich and A. Zink 'Umm el Qaab: Nachuntersuchungen im frühzeitlichen Königsfriedhof. 13/14/15 Vorbericht', *MDAIK* 59 (2003): 67–138.

——, A. Effland, U. Effland, E.-M. Engel, R. Hartmann, U. Hartung, C. Lacher, V. Müller and A. Pokorny, 'Umm el Qaab: Nachuntersuchungen im frühzeitlichen Königsfriedhof. 16/17/18 Vorbericht', *MDAIK* 62 (2006): 67–130.

Edwards, I. E. S. 'The Early Dynastic Period in Egypt', in *The Cambridge Ancient History*, Third Edition, Volume I, Part II: *Early History of the Middle East*, edited by I.E.S. Edwards, C.J. Gadd and N.G.L. Hammond, Chapter XI, Cambridge University Press, 1971.

Emery, W.B. *Excavations at Saqqara: The Tomb of Hemaka*, Government Press, Cairo, 1938.

—— *Excavations at Saqqara 1937–1938: Hor-Aha*, Government Press, Cairo, 1939.

—— *Great Tombs of the First Dynasty*, vol. I, Government Press, Cairo, 1949.

—— *Great Tombs of the First Dynasty*, vol. II, Egypt Exploration Society, London, 1954.

—— *Great Tombs of the First Dynasty*, vol. III, Egypt Exploration Society, London, 1958.

—— *Archaic Egypt*, Penguin, Harmondsworth, 1961.

Fischer, H. 'An Egyptian Royal Stela of the Second Dynasty', *Artibus Asiae* 24 (1961): 45–56.

Friedman, R. 'New Observations on the Fort at Hierakonpolis', in *The Archaeology and Art of Ancient Egypt: Essays in Honor of David B. O'Connor*, vol. 1, edited by Z. Hawass and J. Richards, pp. 309–336, Annales du Service des Antiquités de l'Égypte, Cahier no. 36, Cairo, 2007.

Hartung, U. 'Zur Entwicklung des Handels und zum Beginn wirtschaftlicher Adminstration im prädynastischen Ägypten', *Studien zur altägyptischen Kultur* 26 (1998): 35–50.

—— 'Prädynastische Siegelabrollungen aus dem Friedhof U in Abydos (Umm el-Qaab)', *Mitteilungen des Deutschen Instituts fCr Ägyptische Altertumskunde in Kairo* 54 (1998): 187–218.

—— *Umm el-Qaab II: Importkeramik aus dem Friedhof U in Abydos (Umm el-Qaab) und die Beziehungen Ägyptens zu Vorderasien im 4. Jahrtausend v. Chr.*, Archäologische Veröffentlichungen 92, Deutsches Archäologisches Institut Abteilung Kairo, 2001.

Hassan, F. 'Egypt in the Prehistory of Northeast Africa', in *Civilizations of the Ancient Near East* II, edited by J. Sasson, pp. 665–678, Charles Scribner's Sons et al., New York, 1995.

Kahl, J. 'Hieroglyphic Writing during the Fourth Millennium BC: An Analysis of Systems', *Archéo-Nil* 11 (2000), 103–125.

—— 'Die frühen Schriftzeugnisse aus dem Grab U-j in Umm el-Qaab', *Chronique d'Égypte* 78 (2003): 112–135.

Kaiser, W. 'Zur Enstehung der gesamtägyptischen Staates', *MDAIK* 46 (1990): 287–299.

—— and G. Dreyer 'Umm el Qaab: Nachuntersuchungen im frühzeitlichen Königsfriedhof. 2 Vorbericht', *MDAIK* 38 (1982): 211–269.

—— and P. Grossmann 'Umm el Qaab: Nachuntersuchungen im frühzeitlichen Königsfriedhof. 1 Vorbericht', *MDAIK* 35 (1979): 155–163.

Kemp, B. 'Abydos and the Royal Tombs of the First Dynasty', *Journal of Egyptian Archaeology* 52 (1966): 13–22.

—— 'The Egyptian Ist Dynasty Royal Cemetery', *Antiquity* 41 (1967): 22–32.

—— 'Architektur der Frühzeit', in *Das alte Ägypten*, edited by C. Vanderslayen, pp. 99–112, Propyläen Verlag, Berlin = *Propyläen Kuntsgeschichte* 15, 1975c.

—— *Ancient Egypt: Anatomy of a Civilization*, second edition, Routledge, London and New York, 2006.

—— 'The Colossi from the Early Shrine at Coptos in Egypt', *Cambridge Archaeological Journal* 10/2 (2000): 211–242.

Köhler, E. 'The State of Research on Late Predynastic Egypt: New Evidence for the Development of the Pharaonic State', *Göttinger Miszellen* 147 (1995): 1–11.

Mace, A. *The Early Dynastic Cemeteries of Naga-ed-Dêr* II, J.C. Hinrichs, Leipzig, 1909.

Midant-Reynes, B. *The Prehistory of Egypt from the First Egyptians to the First Pharaoh*, Blackwell Publishers, Oxford and Malden, MA, 2000.

Morenz, L. D., *Bild-Buchstaben und symbolische Zeichen: die Herausbildung der Schrift in der hohen Kultur Altägyptens*, Academic Press, Vandenhoeck and Ruprecht, Fribourg, Göttingen, 2004.

Nissen, H. *The Early History of the Ancient Near East 9000–2000 BC*, translated by E. Lutzeier, with K. Northcott, University of Chicago Press, Chicago and London, 1988.

O'Connor, D. 'The Earliest Pharaohs and the University Museum', *Expedition: Magazine of the University of Pennsylvania Museum* 29 (1987): 27–39.

Petrie, W. M. F. *The Royal Tombs of the First Dynasty, 1900 Part I*, with a chapter by F.Ll. Griffith, Egypt Exploration Fund, London = Egypt Exploration Fund, Memoir no. 18, 1900.

—— *The Royal Tombs of the Earliest Dynasties, 1901 Part II*, Egypt Exploration Fund, London = Egypt Exploration Fund Memoir no. 21, 1901.

Reisner, G. *The Early Dynastic Cemeteries of Naga-ed-Dêr* I, J.C. Hinrichs, Leipzig, 1908.

el-Sayed, A. 'A Prehistoric Cemetery in the Abydos Area', *MDAIK* 35 (1979): 249–301.

Simpson, W. K. 'A Statuette of King Nyneter', *Journal of Egyptian Archaeology* 42 (1956): 45–49.

Smith, H. S. 'The Making of Egypt: A Review of the Influence of Susa and Sumer on Upper Egypt and Lower Nubia in the 4th Millennium BC', in *The Followers of Horus: Studies in Memory of Michael Allen Hoffman*, edited by B. Adams and R. Friedman, pp. 235–246, Oxbow Press, Oxford = Oxbow Monograph 20, 1992.

Trumble, A. *The Royal Stelae at Abydos*, Research Paper, Institute of Fine Arts, New York University, 1995.

Wegner, J. 'From Elephant-Mountain to Anubis-Mountain? A Theory on the Origins and Development of the Name Abdju', in *The Archaeology and Art of Ancient Egypt: Essays in Honor of David B. O'Connor*, vol. 2, edited by Z. Hawass and J. Richards, pp. 459–476, Annales du Service des Antiquités de l'Égypte, Cahier no. 36, Cairo, 2007.

Wengrow, D. *The Archaeology of Early Egypt: Social Transformation in North-East Africa, 10,000 to 2650 BC*, Cambridge University Press, Cambridge, 2006.

Wilkinson, T. *Early Dynastic Egypt*, Routledge, London and New York, 1999.

Chapter 10: The Mysterious Enclosures of Abydos

Adams, M. and D. O'Connor 'The Royal Mortuary Enclosures of Abydos and Hierakonpolis', in *The Treasures of the Pyramids*, edited by Z. Hawass, pp. 78–85, White Star S.r.l., Vercelli, Italy, 2003.

Alexanian, N. 'Die Reliefdekoration des Chasechemui aus dem sogenannten *fort* in Hierakonpolis', in *Les critères de datation stylistiques à l'Ancien Empire*, edited by N. Grimal, pp. 1–21, Institut Français d'Archéologie Orientale = *Bibliothèque Étude* 120, Cairo, 1998.

—— 'The Relief Decoration of Khasekhemwy at the Fort', *Nekhen News* 11 (1999): 14–15.

Arnold, D. 'Royal Cult Complexes of the Old and Middle Kingdoms', in *Temples of Ancient Egypt*, edited by B. Shafer, pp. 31–85, Cornell University Press, Ithaca, New York, 1997.

Ayrton, E. R., C. T. Currelly and A. E. P. Weigall, *Abydos Part III, 1904*, Egypt Exploration Fund, London = Egypt Exploration Fund Memoir no. 25, 1904.

Boessneck, J., A. von den Driesch and A. Elissa, 'Eine Eselsbestattung der 1. Dynastie in Abusir', *MDAIK* 48 (1992): 1–10.

Crosby, A. and W. Remsen 'The Conservation of the Shunet el Zebib, an Egyptian Mud Brick Monument from 2700 BC', *US / Cosmos Newsletter* 4 (2002): 3–5.

Friedman, R. 'Investigations in the Fort of Khasekhemwy', *Nekhen News* 11 (1999): 9–12.

Hampson, N., N. Bennett and R. Friedman 'Mapping the Fort and More', *Nekhen News* 12 (2000): 20–21.

Herbich, T. 'Magnetic Survey at Hierakonpolis', *Nekhen News* 10 (1998): 17–18.

Kaiser, W. 'Zu den königlichen Talbezirken der 1. und 2. Dynastie in Abydos und zur Baugeschichte des Djoser-Grabmals', *MDAIK* 25 (1969): 1–21.

Kemp, B. 'Abydos and the Royal Tombs of the First Dynasty', *Journal of Egyptian Archaeology* 52 (1966): 13–22.

Lauer, J.-P. 'Le développement des complexes funéraires royaux en Égypte depuis les temp prédynastiques jusqu'à la fin de l'Ancien Empire', *Bulletin de l'Institut Français d'Archéologie Orientale* 79 (1979): 355–394.

Mathieson, I. E. Bettles, J. Clarke, C. Duhig, S. Ikram, L. Maguire, S. Quie and A. Tavares 'The National Museum of Scotland Saqqara Survey Project 1993–1995', *Journal of Egyptian Archaeology* 83 (1997): 17–53.

O'Connor, D. 'New Funerary Enclosures (*Talbezirke*) of the Early Dynastic Period at Abydos', *Journal of the American Research Center in Egypt* 26 (1989): 51–86.

—— 'Social and Economic Organisation of Ancient Egyptian Temples', in *Civilizations of the Ancient Near East* III, edited by J. Sasson, pp. 319–329, Scribner's Sons et al., New York, 1993.

—— 'Abydos, Early Dynastic Funerary Enclosures', in *Encyclopedia of the Archaeology of Ancient Egypt*, edited by K. Bard, pp. 93–95, Routledge, London and New York, 1999b.

Petrie, W. M. F. *Tombs of the Courtiers and Oxyrhynkhos*, British School of Archaeology in Egypt and Bernard Quaritch = *British School of Archaeology in Egypt Publications*, vol. 37, London, 1925.

Ricke, H. *Bermerkungen zur ägyptischen Baukunst des Alten Reiches I*, Beiträge zur ägyptischen Bauforschung und Altertumskunde Heft 4, Verlegt im Borchardt-Institut für ägyptische Bauforschung und Altertumskunde in Kairo, Zurich, 1944.

Sharp, D. 'Funerary Enclosures. Early Dynastic "Forts" Reexamined', *KMT* 12 (2001): 60–72.

Stadelmann, R. 'Die Oberbauten der Königsgräber der 2. Dynastie in Saqqara', in *Mélanges Gamal Eddin Mokhtar*, edited by P. Posener-Krieger, pp. 295–308, *Bibliothèque Étude* XCVII/2, Institut Français d'Archéologie Orientale, Cairo, 1983.

—— 'Origins and Development of the Funerary Complex of Djoser', in *Studies in Honor of William Kelly Simpson*, vol. 2, edited by P. der Manuelian and R. Freed (supervisor), pp. 787–800, Dept of Ancient Egyptian, Nubian and Near Eastern Art, Museum of Fine Arts, Boston, 1996.

Swelim, N. 'The Dry Moat of the Netjerykhet Complex', in *Pyramid Studies and Other Essays Presented to I.E.S. Edwards*, edited by J. Baines, T.G.H. James, A. Leahy and A. Shore, Egypt Exploration Society, London, 1988.

Weeks, K. 'Preliminary Report on the First Two Seasons at Hierakonpolis, Part II: The Early Dynastic Palace', *Journal of the American Research Center in Egypt* 9 (1971–72): 29–33.

Wilford, J.N. 'With Escorts to the Afterlife, Pharaohs Proved their Power', *New York Times*, Science Times F3, Tuesday March 16, 2004.

Chapter 11: Boat Graves and Pyramid Origins

Adams, M. and D. O'Connor 'Les barques sacrées d'Abydos', *Le Monde de la Bible* 138 (2001): 54–57.

—— 'The Royal Boat Burials at Abydos', in *The Seventy Great Mysteries of Ancient Egypt*, edited by W. Manley, pp. 38–41, Thames & Hudson, London, 2003.

Edwards, I.E.S. *The Pyramids of Egypt*, revised edition with new material, Penguin Books, London and New York, 1993.

Faulkner, R. *The Ancient Egyptian Pyramid Texts*, Oxford, 1969.

Haldane, C. '"A Pharaoh's Fleet": Early Dynastic Hulls from Abydos', *The INA Quarterly* 19:2 (1992): 12–13.

Hawass, Z. (ed.) *The Treasures of the Pyramids*, White Star S.r.l., Vercelli, Italy, 2003.

Jones, D. *Model Boats from the Tomb of Tut'ankhamūn*, Tut'ankhamūn's Tomb Series IX, edited by J.R. Harris (general editor), Griffith Institute, Oxford, 1990.

Kaiser, W. 'Zur unterirdischen Anlage der Djoserpyramide und ihrer entwicklungsgeschichtlichen Einordnung', in *Gegengabe: Festschrift für Emma Brunner-Traut*, edited by I. Gamer-Wallert and W. Helck, pp. 167–190, Attempto Verlag, Tübingen, 1992.

O'Connor, D. 'Boat Graves and Pyramid Origins: New Discoveries at Abydos, Egypt', *Expedition: Magazine of the University of Pennsylvania Museum* 33/3 (1992b): 6–17.

—— 'The Earliest Royal Boat Graves', *Egyptian Archaeology* 6 (1995): 3–7.

—— 'Pyramid Origins: A New Theory', in *Leaving No Stones Unturned: Essays on the Ancient Near East and Egypt in Honor of Donald P. Hansen*, edited by E. Ehrenberg, pp. 168–182, Eisenbrauns, Winona Lake, Indiana, 2002.

—— 'Origins of the Pyramids', in *The Seventy Great Mysteries of Ancient Egypt*, edited by W. Manley, pp. 45–49, Thames & Hudson, London and New York, 2003.

—— and M. Adams 'Moored in the Desert: Digging an Ancient Armada', *Archaeology* 54/3 May/June (2001): 44–45.

Saad, Z.Y. *Royal Excavations at Saqqara and Helwan (1941–1945)*, Supplément aux Annales du Service des Antiquités d'Égypte, Cahier no. 3, Institut Français d'Archéologie Orientale, Cairo, 1947.

—— *Royal Excavations at Saqqara and Helwan (1945–1947)*, Supplément aux Annales du Service des Antiquités d'Égypte, Cahier no. 14, Institut Français d'Archéologie Orientale, Cairo, 1951.

—— *The Excavations at Helwan: Art and Civilization of the First and Second Egyptian Dynasties*, University of Oklahoma Press, Norman, 1969.

Simpson, W.K. *Papyrus Reisner II. Accounts of the Dockyard Workshop at This in the Reign of Sesostris I*, Museum of Fine Arts, Boston, 1965.

Ward, C. *Sacred and Secular: Ancient Egyptian Ships and Boats*, Archaeological Institute of America Monographs, New Series no. 5, University Museum, University of Pennsylvania Press, Philadelphia, 2000.

—— 'World's Oldest Planked Boats', *Archaeology* 54/3 (2001): 45.

—— 'Sewn Planked Boats from Early Dynastic Abydos, Egypt', in *Boats, Ships and Shipyards: Proceedings of the Ninth International Symposium on Boat and Ship Archaeology, Venice, 2000*, pp. 19–23, edited by C. Beltrame, ISBSA 9, Oxbow Books, Oxford, 2003.

Stadelmann, R. *Die ägyptische Pyramiden vom Ziegelbau zum Weltwunder*, Verlag Philipp von Zabern, Mainz am Rhein, 1985.

Wilford, J. 'Early Pharaoh's Ghostly Fleet', *New York Times*, Science Times F1 and F4, Tuesday October 31, 2000.

Chapter 12: Abydos: Summing-up

Harvey, S. 'A Decorated Protodynastic Cult Stand from Abydos', in *Studies in Honor of William Kelly Simpson*, vol. 1, edited by P. der Manuelian and R. Freed (supervisor), pp. 361–378, Dept of Ancient Egyptian, Nubian and Near Eastern Art, Museum of Fine Arts, Boston, 1996.

Otto, E. *Ancient Egyptian Art and the Cults of Osiris and Amun*, translated by K. Bosse-Griffiths, Thames & Hudson, London, 1968.

Simpson, W. K. and J. Cooney 'An Early Dynastic statue of the Goddess Heqat', *Bulletin of the Cleveland Museum of Art* 63 (1976): 201–209.

Index

Numerals in *italics* refer to illustration numbers

Dynasty 0
  tombs 140–1, 147, 149–50, 157; *75*
  town 28, 204–5
1st Dynasty *see also* Chs. 9–11
  history 138–9
  Abydos 15, 18–9, 28, 67, 89, 133, 147–8, 201, 204
2nd Dynasty *see also* Ch. 9–10
  history 140
  Abydos 15, 18–9, 28, 67, 89, 134, 155–7, 171, 185, 194–6, 198–9, 201, 204; *63*
3rd Dynasty 7, 141, 147, 156–7, 196
4th Dynasty 19, 76, 147, 157, 178; *32*
5th Dynasty 76, 88, 147, 157, 187, 198
6th Dynasty 28, 76, 88, 147, 157, 184, 205
9th Dynasty 205
10th Dynasty 205
11th Dynasty 87, 90, 205
12th Dynasty 28, 87–90, 98, 100–1, 184, 205–6
13th Dynasty 28, 87–91, 99–100
17th Dynasty 109–10
18th Dynasty 29, 35, 88, 109, 112–14, 184; *61*
19th Dynasty 131
20th Dynasty 73
21st Dynasty 122, 126, 128, 133
22nd Dynasty 122, 128, 133
23rd Dynasty 123, 128, 133
24th Dynasty 123
25th Dynasty 114, 123, 126–8, 133, 205; *69*
26th Dynasty 80, 123, 128; *69*
27th Dynasty 123
28th Dynasty 123
29th Dynasty 123
30th Dynasty 113, 123, 128, 131
31st Dynasty 135

Abu Roash 150
Abu Simbel 64
Abusir 187; *see also* Busiris
Abydos
  excavation history 15–16, 66–9, 79–80; *24, 35, 37*
  landscape 10, 15–16, 18, 24, 69, 74–5, 87, 90–6, 99–100, 103, 105, 109–110, 117, 123, 126, 130–1, 174–5, 201–6
  origin of name 144
  town development 15, 18, 23, 26, 28–9, 72, 82–5, 87, 96, 100, 103, 110–1, 116, 138, 204; *35, 36, 39, 60, 88*
Adams, Barbara 153
Adams, Matthew 14, 68, 82–4, 152–3, 166, 175–6; *26*
afterlife 73–4, 148, 173, 176–7, 181, 183–4, 194, 197
afterworld 50, 179, 194; *see also* netherworld, *Duat*
Aha 139–40, 147, 150, 154–5, 163–6, 169–74, 178–9, 186, 194; *75, 90, 91, 92*
Ahmose 14, 68, 29, 33, 68, 81, 87, 105–13, 116, 122, 203, 206; *3, 54, 55, 57, 59*
Ahmose-Nefertari 105; *56*
Akhenaten 54, 113, 118–9, 206; *65*
Allen, James 39, 71
Amasis 80–1, 128, 133; *66*
Amélineau, Emile 28, 90, 133–5, 140, 148, 202
Amenemhet I 72
Amenemhet III 89, 99, 206
Amenhotep I 108, 112–13; *58, 59*
Amenhotep III 29, 112–13, 128; *58*
Amenmose 35–7
American House 65; *24, 26*
American Research Center in Egypt (ARCE) 13, 20, 165, 187
Amun-Re 31, 45, 49, 73–4, 108–9, 126, 206
Anderson, David 9, 68, 26
Anedjib 134, 150, 173, 75
Ankhwennefer 206
Anubis 121
Apis Bull 124
Apries 128, 133
Assyria 73, 122–3, 126
Atum 39–40, 135, 199
Ayrton, Edward 160, 167
Avaris (*Hat Waret*) 108–9; *see also* Tell el-Da'aba

Baines, John 69
Baker, Brenda 79
bakeries 180

Balachandran, Sanchita 187
Becker, Lawrence 187
Bestock, Laurel 68, 162, 165–6
boats
  funerary 95
  gods' 128, 183
  imagery 40, 184
  imw 193
  models 184
  palanquin 45, 49–50, 75, 114, 183
  pits for 183–4, 194, 200
boat graves 15, 137, 163, 166, 172, 180–1; *88, 89, VIII, IX, X; see also* Ch. 11
Book of the Dead 114, 135
Bothmer, Bernard 14
Bubastis 126
Buhen 63
Busiris 31, 34–5, 41, 43, 72, 74

Calverly, Amice 69
Cambyses 73
Cambridge University 63–4
Cemetery B 139–41, 147–8; *75*
Cemetery D 131
Cemetery U 139–42, 146–51, 157; *75*
cenotaph 29, 33, 48, 99, 100, 109–10, 135, 140, 162, 203
  zone 68, 92–96, 110; 43, 44, 45, 46, 47, 60; *see also mahat,* memorial chapel
Černy, Jaroslav 121
coffin 101, 124, 130, 148–9, 199; *72*
Coffin Texts 73
Coptic 29, 47, 135, 160, 162, 165–6, 168
Coptos 21, 87
Cooney, John 204
cosmos 38–40, 71–2, 133, 194, 198
  temple 45, 61
chapels *see also* memorial chapel, *Ka*-chapel
  barque 45–51, 54–61
  divine 89, 114, 121
  private tomb 28, 34, 78
  royal cult 105, 108, 111–117, 128, 131, 154–6, 165–81, 196–7
  statue 95, 154–5, 171; *84*
  votive 77
Crosby, Tony 168
cult *see also* Osiris, cult of
  centre 9, 15, 18, 29, 38, 41, 43, 72–5, 80, 126, 183
  practices 10, 28, 52, 56, 64, 68, 77, 85, 88, 90, 98–9, 114, 116–7, 122, 124–6, 128–9, 131, 134–5, 148, 171–2, 183, 204–5
  private 87, 111, 116, 160, 165
  royal mortuary 19, 33, 87, 104, 108–10, 148, 155
  statue 54, 61, 126, 155, 163
  structures 19, 26, 67–8, 80–1, 89, 99–100, 107–9, 111, 113, 116–17, 128, 131, 194, 205; *36*
cylinder seals 146–7; *79*

Dahshur 23, 29, 98–100, 184, 202
David, Rosalie 53–6
delta 12, 122–3, 127, 138, 145
Den 114, 138, 150–2, 154–6, 173; *75, 84*
Dendereh 74, 124, 129
Deir Sitt Damiana 25, 162, 166
Dibble, Harold 69
Djedu 31
Djer 7, 19, 89–91, 96, 114, 133–4, 148, 152–3, 160–2, 165–6, 169, 171, 173–4, 178; *75*
Djet 135, 150–1, 160–2, 165–6, 173–4, 178, 194; *75*
Djoser 26, 141, 160, 176–8, 195–198, 200
dockyard (royal) 87, 185
donkey burials 166, 173, 176, 180–1, 194
Dreyer, Günter 9, 19, 20, 64, 138–57, 162, 197, 201–3; *78, 81, 82*
Duat 31–2, 73

Early Dynastic *see also* First Dynasty, Second Dynasty
  kings 19
  Abydos 75, 135, 137–8, 159, 162–81, 193, 200–4; *7, 74, 88, 89, 136*
  project 68, 162
Edie, Dorothy *see* Umm Seti
Edwards, I.E.S. 187
Elephantine 64, 68, 102, 144–7; *78*

elite 15, 28, 73, 87, 96, 100, 111, 114, 124, 126, 148
  houses 84, 102; *51*
  tombs 28, 76–7, 138–142, 147–8, 150, 162, 165, 170–1, 174, 179, 183–8, 194, 200, 203–5; *31, 32, 75, 85, 88, 89, 94, 98, 99*
Emery, Bryan 63, 150
Emery, Walter B. 137, 188
enclosures *see also* Ch. 10
  palace 181
  royal mortuary 12, 17, 19, 23, 25, 28, 67, 137–40, 156, 183, 185–6, 194–6; *28, X, XI*
  temple 29, 43, 85, 97–8, 111–2, 115, 128
Fayum 97
festival 33–4
  procession 45, 49, 56, 90, 95, 99, 108, 148, 179, 183; *62*
  temple 48; *see also* Osiris
figurines 68, 84, 114, 119; *67*
First Intermediate Period 84, 122
  Abydos 68, 73, 79–84, 88, 205–6; *25, 29, 30, 36, 37, 38, 39, 40*
fortress 63, 102, 109, 160–2, 168; *51*
Friedman, Renée 153

Gaballa, Ali Gaballa 11
Gardiner, Alan 73
Geb 35, 39, 73, 199
German Archaeological Institute, Cairo 8–9, 20, 68, 114
Giza 7, 10, 23, 26, 82, 137–8, 184, 201–2; *95*
Graeco-Roman Period 29, 135

Hansen, Donald 14
Hapetnebes 130
Harvey, Stephen 68, 105, 107–10; *26*
Hathor 74, 124
Hatshepsut 54, 88, 117; *61*
Hawass, Zahi 11–12
Hekreshu (Hill) 114, 131, 133
Heliopolis 38, 73–4, 162
Helwan 151, 183, 186–88
Heqat 204
Herakleopolis 73–4, 205
Herbich, Tomasz 105, 163, 166
Herwennefer 206
Hetepsekhemwy 156–7, 196
Hierakonpolis 154, 159, 162, 181, 184
Hornung, Eric 135
Horus 7, 36–40, 45, 49, 55, 74, 91, 114, 121, 126, 206; *9, 20, IV*
Hosni, Farouk 11
Hyksos 108, 206; *57*

Illahun 98
Institute of Fine Arts, New York University 9, 14, 20, 68, 113, 165, 201
Iry-Hor 147; *75*
Isis 7, 31, 36–41, 43, 45, 49, 55, 90, 114, 121, 126; *11, 16, 42, 50*
Iuput 126

James, T.G.H. 20

Ka 28, 98, 199
Ka-chapel 30
  royal 28, 32–3, 81, 85, 88–9, 99, 113, 204
Kahun 84, 102
Kaiser, Werner 9, 20, 140, 161–2
Kees, Herman 17
Kemp, Barry 17, 20, 64, 81, 84, 111, 121, 124, 140, 156, 161–2, 177, 196
Kenamun 114
Khaankhkhre Sobekhotep 99
Khaneferre Sobekhotep IV 89
Khasekhemwy
  tomb 141, 155–7, 173, 175, 179; *75, VII*
  mortuary enclosure 156, 159, 163, 166–72, 175–81, 183; *86, 87, 88, 89, 93, X, XI*
Khendjer 88–90
Khentamentiu 31, 202
  temple to 18–19, 25, 28, 31, 81, 84–5, 88, 124, 128, 134, 160, 204; *36, 88, 89; see also* Osiris Temple
Khety 205
Khufu 137, 184; *95*
king list 19; *see also* Seti Temple

Kom el Sultan *35, 36*
Kuhlmann, Peter 9, 69
Kushite 122, 126; *see also* Nubia, 25th Dynasty

Late Period 29, 43, 121–2, 130–1; *36, 66, 67, 69, 70, 88*
Lauer, Jean-Phillipe 160, 162
Leahy, Anthony 91
Libyan 123, 126, 134
Lintel *8, 10*
Luxor 12

Maadian culture 138
Mahasna 9, 68
mahat 96, 99, 110, 116; *see also* cenotaph, memorial chapel
Mainwaring, Bruce 14, 21, 69
Mariette, Auguste 20, 26–8, 76–7, 115, 160, 167–8, 201
Marlar, Michelle 68, 80–1, 113, 201
Mastaba 23, 78, 100, 160–1, 195, 197; *31, 32*
McCredie, Dr. 14
McPherrson, Shannon 69
memorial chapel; *see also* cenotaph, *mahat*
  private chapels 92–96, 99, 110, 116; *43, 44, 45, 46, 47*
  royal chapels 99
Memphis 23, 33, 64, 73–4, 78, 97, 109, 134, 140, 147–8, 155, 204
Menes 150
Menkaure 26
Merenptah 50, 108, 114
Merenre 77
Merneith 133–5, 140, 147, 151, 160–66, 173–4; *75, 89*
Mesopotamia 35, 138–9, 143–4, 146–7
Middle Cemetery 19, 28–9, 67, 76–8, 90, 124, 126, 130, 205; *3, 27, 30, 32*
Middle Kingdom 11, 81; *see also* Ch. 3
  Abydos 28–9, 110, 113, 116, 202–5; *41, 50*
mortuary
  cult practices 15, 33, 73, 75, 79, 140, 155, 160, 178, 185–6, 205–6
  monuments (royal) 17–19, 29, 33, 43, 45–49, 67, 82, 87, 96, 98–9, 105, 108, 137, 139, 142, 144, 148, 153, 156, 159, 171, 176–7, 183, 194–98, 200, 202–3; *87*
'Mother of Pots' *see* Umm el Qa'ab

Nag el-Deir 10, 34, 151
Narmer 141, 147, 150; *75*
Naqada periods 38, 153, 184
  at Abydos 138–42, 146, 203–4
Naqada 148
Nebhepetre Mentuhotep 88
Nebra 156
Nebwenenef 48
Nectanebo I 29, 80–1, 113, 125, 128–9, 131, 201; *70*
Nectanebo II 113, 130–1, 201
Neferhotep I 89, 91; *41*
Nefertem 50–1, 54; *16*
Nephthys 31, 36, 38–40
Neshmet barque 75, 89
netherworld 7, 15, 31–2, 35–6, 39–41, 51, 61, 71–4, 155, 176, 183, 203
New Kingdom 75, 121; *see also* Ch. 3 and Ch. 7
  Abydos 19, 29, 43, 81, 89, 122, 125, 202, 204; *8, 43, 58, 70*
  Thebes 17, 99, 137, 184, 202
Nimlot 126
Ninetjer 155–6
North Abydos 68, 79, 82, 162, 166, 172, 175, 204; *72, 73*
North Cemetery 28–9, 47, 67, 90, 100, 103, 110, 115, 118, 124, 126, 130, 159, 160–1; *3, 50, 61*
Nubia 63–4, 75, 102, 121–3, 128; *see also* Kushite
Nut 39, 131, 199

O'Connor, David 20, 65; *28*
Old Kingdom 37
  Abydos 18–19, 28, 68, 75–6, 80–3, 85, 88, 90; *27, 30, 36, 83*
  Giza 82, 171, 202
Olszewski, Deborah 69
Oriental Institute, University of Chicago 9, 68
Osiris *see also* Seti I Temple
  cult 9, 15, 24, 28, 31–41, 43, 45, 49–61, 72–7, 87–93, 98, 109–10, 119, 121, 124–9, 201–2, 206; *6, 10, 12*
  festival 19, 33, 43, 56, 74–5, 91, 95–6, 100, 114, 116–7, 130–1
  iconography 41, 91, 118; *42, 59*
  myth 16, 24, 31, 35–40, 43, 73, 91, 130; *9, 10*
  tomb 19, 43, 89, 90–1, 96, 99, 109–10, 114, 116, 118, 130–1, 148, 160, 203; *7, 43*

Osiris Temple 16, 25, 26, 28–9, 32, 34, 43, 45, 56, 68, 73, 81, *86*, 88–9, 92–3, 95–6, 99–100, 103, 109–17; *43, 111, 112, 115, 122, 124–128, 130, 135, 163, 201, 203–5; see also* Khentamentiu
Osireion 45, 48, 50–1, 110, 135; *16, 17, 18; see also* Seti Temple
Osorkon I 133–4
Osorkon II 133
Osorkon III 133
Otto, Eberhard 17, 205

palace
  ceremonial 48
  façade 170; *80, 94*
  funerary 161–2, 168
  royal 162, 179, 181, 194
Patch, Diana 67, 75, 203
Pennsylvania-Yale-Institute of Fine Arts, New York
  University Expedition 10, 12–13, 21, 69, 97, 103, 110, 137, 162, 183; *24*
Pepi I 28, 77–8, 205
Pepi II 77, 184
Peribsen 135, 141, 155–7, 160, 162, 166–7, 169, 172, 175, 177–8, 196; *75, 89, XI*
Persian Period 73; *128*
Petrie, William Flinders 21, 26–8, 65, 80–1, 89, 102, 110–15, 117, 128, 133–5, 140, 148, 152, 154, 157, 160–1, 165, 173–4, 202; *4, 35, 82*
piety 87–8
Poker 91, 95–6, 99; *41, 53*
'Portal' temple 14, 67, 93, 115–119, 125, 206; *3, 43, 53, 60, 63, 64, 65, 67, 69, I*
  stelae from *6, 8, 10, 12*
pottery 91, 114, 125, 133, 142–7, 151, 163, 166, 184, 188; *77, XI*
  pot marks 142
  potter's wheel 54
Pouls Wegner, Mary-Ann 68, 93, 111, 115–7, 125; *28*
Prehistoric 9, 15, 68–9, 75, 80, 138, 141, 144, 149, 153, 184, 205
Psusennes II 126, 133
Ptolemaic 74, 96, 113, 116, 121–2, 124–5, 135, 166, 206
Ptolemy I 124
pyramid 23, 26, 29, 68, 82, 84, 97–100, 105–8, 110, 134, 137, 139, 150–1, 161, 183–4, 187, 194, 196, 198–200, 203; *54, 55, 56; see also* Step Pyramid
  proto-pyramid 168
Pyramid Text 37–8, 40, 75, 199

Qa'a 114, 147–8, 151–2, 173; *75, 80, 82*
Quft 21; *see also* Coptos

Ramesses II 16, 55, 64, 108; *I; see also* Portal Temple
  Abydos temple 9, 16, 18, 25, 33, 69, 89, 107, 110, 203; *3, 15, 53*
  at Seti Temple 16, 45–6, 49, 53, 55; *21*
Ramesses III 43, 72, 126
Ramesses IV 43, 113–4; *58*
Re 31, 35, 73, 121; *60*
Re-Horakhty 39, 45, 49, 206
Reis 14, 21, 22
Remsen, William 168
Richards, Janet 28, 67, 71, 75, 76–9, 100–1, 205; *27*
ritual
  landscape 15, 74, 90–1, 96, 100, 103
  practices 7, 11, 15–17, 19, 31, 34–5, 37, 41, 43, 45, 49, 52–56, 61 (Seti Temple), 72, 74–5, 79, 90–1, 111, 114, 121–2, 125–6, 128, 148, 162, 171–2, 176–181, 202; *67, XI*
  structures 10, 68, 88, 100–1, 110, 116–7, 125, 162, 171–2, 176–7, 181
royal tombs 16, 18–20, 28–9, 43, 50–1, 75, 89, 97, 99, 107, 114, 134, 159–62, 172–81, 184–5, 195–6, 198, 200, 202–3, 205; *7; see also* Ch. 9

sacred landscape 7, 18, 71–5, 90–1, 122, 130, 201–3
Sankhkare Mentuhotep 88, 90
Saqqara 7–8, 19, 26–7, 82, 139–41, 147, 150–1, 153, 155–7, 160, 162, 170, 174, 177–8, 183, 186–8, 193–98, 202; *94, 98*
Schorsch, Deborah 187; *100*
Second Intermediate Period 108, 122
Sed-festival 178
Seidlmayer, Stephen 101
Sekenenre Tao II 108
Semerkhet 148, 150, 152, 173; *75*
Senwosret I 28, 88, 89–90, 99

Senwosret II 89, 98, 102
Senwosret III 17, 28–9, 33, 68, 81, 87, 89, 96–103, 105, 107, 109–10, 116, 122, 184, 203, 206; *3, 48, 49, 51, 52*
Serapis 121, 124–5, 135
Seshat 54
Seth 7, 16, 35–40, 130
Seti I 33, 114, 117; *14*
Seti Temple 15–6, 18–20, 25, 29, 65, 69, 81, 87, 99, 110, 122, 124–5, 135, 201, 203, 206; *5, 9, 11, 13, 14, II, III, IV, V, VI; see also* Ch. 3
  'Gallery of Lists' 49, 54–5; *16*
  Osiris complex 45, 49, 51, 55–6, 61, 81; *16, V*
Shoshenk I 126–7
Shu 35, 39–40
Shunet el Zebib 25, 28–9, 159, 168–9, 183; *3, 63, 86, 87, 93, 96*
Silverman, David 13–14, 67, 118–19
Simpson, William Kelly 10–11, 13, 20, 63–4, 67, 87, 92, 96, 99, 118, 155, 185, 193, 201, 204; *23*
Sitepehu 61
Smith, Harry 63–4
Smith, Mark 135
Snape, Steven 69
Snefru 19
Sohag 12, 69
Sokar 50–1, 54; *16*
Stadelmann, Rainier 162
Stela 1, 14, 34, 35, 37, 88, 92–3, 95–6, 116, 124, 126, 153; *6, 8, 12, 44, 68, 71, 83*
  royal 90–1, 105, 133–5, 148, 151, 155–7, 173–4, 177–8; *54, 57, 80*
Step Pyramid 26, 141, 156, 160, 195–200; *101*
subsidiary graves 28, 148, 150, 153–5, 160, 163–6, 172–5, 179–81; *83, 90*
Supreme Council of Antiquities 11–13, 21, 64–5

tags 142–7; *78*
Takeloth III 126
Talbezirke 140, 161; *see also* enclosures
Tanis 128, 139
Tefnut 39–40
Tell el-Amarna 64, 118–9
Tell el-Da'aba 68, 102
'Terrace of the Great God' 47, 96, 105, 114–19; *60*
Tetisheri 105, 108; *53, 54*
Thebes 17, 19, 23, 29, 33, 43, 45, 48, 50, 64, 72, 74, 99–100, 108–10, 117–19, 123, 126, 128, 133–4, 202, 205–6
Theodosius I 129, 131
Thinis 10, 75, 77, 87, 99, 126, 141, 145, 147, 151, 185, 193, 206
Third Intermediate Period 11, 29, 80, 116; *68*
  at Abydos 121–34; *73*
Thoth 114, 121
Thutmose I 105, 113
Thutmose III 19, 112–118, 125, 128; *58, 60, 61, 62*
Thutmose IV 113–14
Tiberius 129
Tomb U-j 138, 141–7, 149–50, 162; *75, 76, 77, 78, 79*
tourism 124, 207
Turah 78
Turin Canon 19
Tutankhamun 137, 139, 184

Ugaf 90
Umm el Qa'ab 20, 28, 43, 56, 64, 87, 89–91, 95–6, 99, 110, 114, 116, 118, 122, 124, 130–5, 159–160, 162, 165, 172–6, 178, 185, 196, 202–4; *3, 42, 43, VII; see also* Poker, Ch. 9
Umm Seti 46–7, 65
University of Pennsylvania 9–10, 12–14, 67–9, 92, 97; *64, I*

votive offerings 84, 114, 134

Ward, Cheryl 186, 193
Wegner, Josef 68, 97–103; *26*
Wengrow, David 137
Weni 28, 77–9, 205; *31, 32, 33, 34*
Wennefer 35, 43, 45, 206
Wepwawet 91, 95, 114, 121
Western Mastaba 69, 160–66, 173–4, 185; *28, 88, 89, 96, VIII*
Westermann, James 69
Westermann, Mariët 14
Wilkinson, Toby 137
writing system 124, 138–9, 143–7; *78*

Yale University 9–10, 12–13, 20, 63–4, 92